Also by John Roberts

The Grayling Angler (Witherby, 1982)
The New Illustrated Dictionary of Trout Flies (Allen & Unwin, 1986; Unwin Hyman, 1988)
To Rise a Trout (The Crowood Press, 1988)

A Guide to River Trout Flies

John Roberts

The Crowood Press

First published in 1989 by
The Crowood Press
Ramsbury, Marlborough,
Wiltshire SN8 2HE

British Library Cataloguing in Publication Data

Roberts, John, *1953–*
A guide to river trout flies.
1. Trout. Fly fishing. Flies
I. Title
799.1'755

ISBN 1 85223 167 X

Typeset by Avonset, Midsomer Norton, Bath
Printed and bound in Spain by Graficas Estella, S.A. (Navarra)

To Nick Bradley for his enthusiasm, and to all those with whom I fish, whose company is as pleasurable as the fishing.

Contents

Acknowledgements

Producing a book of this size and scope almost inevitably puts the whole of its subject beyond the experience of any individual. I doubt whether few could honestly claim to have given a fair trial to all the patterns I have mentioned and fished all the major trout rivers and streams. Therefore I have consulted trout fishers wiser than I and more experienced in certain areas of the country, and those of considerably more dexterity at the fly-tying vice. Where I have included modern patterns I tried to contact their creators to request a sample of the dressing for illustration and for comment on the origin, use or tying of the fly. I am pleased to acknowledge the help of the following, all of whom have supplied superbly tied flies for illustration and many of whom commented in detail on the patterns; the reader can regard these dressings as being totally accurate and tied in a style exactly as their creator intended.

Geoff Bucknall
Bob Carnill
John Davison
Larry Duckwall
Peter Duinmeyer
Oliver Edwards
Roger Fogg
Jerry Garner
John Goddard
John Harwood
Alan Hudson
Preben Torp Jacobsen
Frans Jansen
Charles Jardine
Chris Kendall
Kees Ketting
Hans van Klinken
Gary LaFontaine
Michael Leighton
Gordon Mackie
Lance Nicholson
Ted Painter
Neil Patterson
Tony Pepper
Freddie Rice
Reg Righyni
Terry Ruane
Pat Russell
Randy Swanberg
Patrick Veale
Tony Waites
Ian Warrilow
Lee Wulff
Harry Whitmore

I doubt whether I could have completed the book without the fly-tying skills of Nick Bradley, who tied the majority of the patterns that were not sent by their creators. Flies tied by my own hand catch almost all my trout and grayling; however, no trout fisher would give them a second glance and few are of a standard to copy from. I am indebted to Nick for his fly-dressing skills and for his advice as we reasoned and debated about some of the alternative materials and tying styles.

Additionally I must thank Larry Duckwall, who tied many of the American patterns. He has been described correctly as one of the best American fly dressers and specialises in the historical accuracy of his dressings. Thanks are also due for help in an assortment of ways to Gary LaFontaine, Dutch friends, Rolf Pasteuning and Hans van Klinken, and also to D. J. 'Dev' Deverell.

I am grateful to Farlow's of Pall Mall, London; Flycraft, Worcester, Mass., USA; and to Ultimate Fisherman for generously supplying some of the synthetic materials, and to Alan Bramley of Partridge of Redditch.

Finally I extend my thanks to Tony Pugh, the photographer responsible for the superb colour plates.

Introduction

For a whole generation of British fly fishers Courtney Williams' *Dictionary of Trout Flies* was rightly regarded as the reference book that surpassed all others. At this point I hesitate before continuing, lest I upset those who might misunderstand my purpose in writing. Detracting from Williams's book will appear to some as taking issue with holy writ. I'm not and it isn't. The dictionary did its job exceedingly well for about thirty years but it has failed to keep up with new trends or take into account the influence of new fly design and tying methods and the use of modern materials. Much has happened in trout fly design and materials that has not been offered in a specific way for the river trout fisher and the continuing evolution in river trout patterns has not been interpreted in a single volume since Courtney Williams. The need is there to be fulfilled.

Al McClane wrote that 'the age of synthetics has greatly expanded the art of fly fishing from top to bottom'. So far as British river fishing is concerned, McClane's comments are grossly beyond their mark. I don't doubt that fly selection on rivers is still fairly traditional, with patterns over a century old still in very effective use on both chalk streams and freestone rivers. In river fly fishing there has been great inertia in the face of new ideas, patterns and materials. In the stillwater scene new patterns are born overnight and within a few weeks they are being used (albeit often ephemerally) across the country. This almost never happens to river patterns. But what has been happening is that in addition to some genuinely new patterns worthy of national appreciation there has been some worldwide progression in trout fly design and materials. One of the aims of the book is to highlight what has been done in fly design and what can be done with new materials, particularly where some of the natural materials are now very scarce or expensive. To this end I have dressed some of the older patterns with new materials, making use of lighter, finer, more translucent, more natural-looking synthetics. The purist might raise an eyebrow but the new flies will rise more trout.

Parts of the book will appeal to the exact imitationists, others to the impressionists or caricaturists amongst fly dressers and trout fishers. There has been a trend away from detailed imitation of the natural upwinged fly but dressing such an imitation offers a challenge to the fly tyer and an interesting diversion for those who attribute at least as much importance to the means as to the end.

All the important natural aquatic flies and terrestrials are considered and I offer imitations of the relevant stages of the life cycle for each. Many of these are well proven, well established dressings. Alongside the older patterns I include modern dressings, incorporating some of the new tying styles and materials into some of the imitations to offer new variations on older themes. One only has to look at the superbly tied flies of Oliver Edwards, Terry Ruane or Ian Warrilow to see how the judicious use of modern materials brings a more natural imitation a step closer.

Nobody carries 400 different flies in their fly box. I guess that for a typical season somewhere between a half-dozen and a dozen patterns will cover most opportunities; indeed, a few anglers succeed with just one or two flies. One of the fascinating aspects of the choice of which dozen or so are used is that the selection will vary enormously between anglers and will probably encompass most of the 400 within this book.

Experimenting with different patterns and carrying the peripheral patterns for occasional use are all part of the fun of fly fishing and fly dressing. All the patterns in this book are good trout flies, but how successful they are in attracting trout largely depends on the skills of the fly fisher and to a much lesser extent on the dexterity of the fly dresser.

A note about Hooks

Hook sizes are at best approximate; one manufacturer's long-shank size 18 is another's standard length narrow-gape 12, and so on. Perhaps one of the most adventurous manufacturers in terms of hook design and in attempting some measure of standardisation is Partridge of Redditch. The quality of their wide range is excellent and I have been impressed with their reliability.

The majority of the flies in the illustrations are tied on Partridge hooks and in each description one or more recommended hook designs are given to suit the fly design and the use of each pattern. Where flies for illustration have been sent by their creators, the choice of hook manufacturer, hook design and size was at their discretion, but I have included my recommended Partridge equivalent with its code. There is a laudable trend to the use of barbless hooks and Partridge have a representative range. I very much like their Roman Moser Arrowpoint hooks (CS20) for my general dry flies and, although I haven't mentioned them each time in the dressings, they can be used for most floating flies of a standard design and some of the flies are tied on them. The Partridge hooks listed and described in detail below are the ones I recommend.

A – Albert Partridge Wide Gape Down Eye hook
For standard and soft-hackle wet flies, short-bodied nymphs and very strong dry flies. Offset bend; middleweight wire. Size 8–16

AFY
Identical to A except barbless and not offset.

B – Albert Partridge Wide Gape Up Eye hook
Identical to A except up eye.

D4A – Bucktail/Streamer hook
For lures and longer nymphs requiring a long shank and down eye. Size 2–14.

D4AY
Identical to D4A except barbless.

D5B – Mayfly hook
An up-eye long-shank dry-fly hook for larger flies like the Mayfly. Size 8–14.

E1A – Hooper L/S Dry Fly hook
A 4×fine-wire hook with 1×long shank and down eye. Suitable for slightly longer dry flies and floating nymphs. Size 10–18.

E3AY
Identical to E1A except barbless.

E6A – Hooper 1×Short Dry Fly hook
Slightly shorter than standard, 4×fine wire, down eye for standard and lightly dressed dry flies. Size 8–18.

G3A – Sproat Forged Wet Fly hook
Sproat style with forged bend for greater strength. Suitable for wet flies and heavier nymphs. Size 6–20.

H1A – Captain Hamilton Nymph hook
Wide gape and about 2¼×long on middleweight wire. Suitable for longer nymphs. Size 2–18.

H3ST – Draper Flat-Bodied Nymph hook
A unique design for use in imitating wide flat-bodied nymphs. Use a size or two smaller than normal. Size 6–16.

J1A – Partridge Limerick Wet Fly hook
Very strong hook in heavyweight wire for traditional wet flies. Size 4–18.

K1A – Vince Marinaro Midge hook
Offset bend and slightly down eye for tiny midges and caenis. Size 24–28.

K2B – Yorkshire Sedge hook
Fine curved shank with slight up eye. For sedge pupa, larva, shrimp and grub patterns. Size 8–18.

K3A – Swedish Dry Fly hook
For upside-down dry flies. A long hook, so choose a hook two sizes smaller than normal. Size 10–18.

K4A – John Veniard Grub/Shrimp hook
Offset bend with curved shank for grub and shrimp imitations. Size 2–18.

K12ST – Emerger/Nymph hooks
Fine wire and straight eye suitable for sedge larvae and pupae, and some nymphs and emerger styles. Even the smallest size 22 is very easy to tie on. Size 8–22.

L2A – Captain Hamilton Wet Fly hook
For lighter wet flies and nymphs and strong dry flies with a down eye. Size 4–18.

L3A – Captain Hamilton Dry Fly hook
4×fine lightweight wire with down eye, suitable for all kinds of dry flies. Size 8–22.

L3AY
Identical to L3A but barbless.

L3B – Captain Hamilton Dry Fly hook
Identical to L3A except with an up eye. Size 10–18.

L4A – Captain Hamilton Featherweight Dry Fly hook
6×fine wire with down eye. Excellent for lightly dressed dry flies, floating nymphs and no-hackles. Size 10–20.

CS7 – Captain Hamilton International Series
CS7SHW Superheavyweight for heavy wet flies and nymphs. Size 10–14.
CS7HW Heavyweight for standard wet flies and nymphs.
CS7MW Middleweight for lighter wet flies and nymphs.

CS20 – Roman Moser Arrowpoint Dry Fly hook
A unique barbless arrowpoint hook based on the E6A design, suitable for most dry flies and floating nymphs. Size 10–18.

Grey Shadow Series
This is a new series with a nickel grey finish which offers two advantages. First of all the nickle finish is corrosion-resistant and much better than the black or bronze finish normally applied to hooks. Also it has a PTFE content, which makes it a very slippery finish, which aids hooking and prolongs the life of the hook. The hooks have flash-pointed points (a process similar to chemical sharpening). It is planned that a number of ranges will be offered with this finish. Those of particular interest to the river fisher are the GRSA based on the Captain Hamilton Wet Fly hooks L2A, the new GRS3A based on the 4×fine lightweight dry-fly hooks L3A, and the GRS12ST based on the long-shank sedge hook K12ST.

DRY FLIES

Introduction to Dry Flies

Dry-fly selection is conservative. Orvis in the USA recently revealed that of their seven top-selling dry flies only one was devised in the last fifty years. That was Al Troth's Elk Hair Caddis. Even though the most popular trout fly patterns seem incredibly long-lived, I think that modern trout fishermen are much more open to experiment and new ideas when the popular patterns fail. We may still catch most of our trout on well established flies but we now have so many alternative patterns and designs to fall back on. It is not just a question of whether to fish a dun or nymph imitation in a hatch. Rather, when the first line of approach fails we also consider whether a hatching nymph, floating nymph, hatching dun, emerger, stillborn or no-hackle, funneldun, USD, comparadun, paradun, thorax fly, parachute, loopwing or waterwalker is what is required.

With the exception of terrestrial imitations, which are considered elsewhere, the floating artificial represents an adult aquatic fly, usually an upwinged species or sedge and occasionally a stonefly, midge or alder. Therefore the style of tying, size and colouring of the artificial to imitate the natural should be the foremost consideration of dry-fly design. Coupled with this is the overriding priority that the fly should float and, in the case of most patterns, avoid penetrating the surface film at all. There are many exceptions to this principle and some dry flies in this section may be as much as 90 per cent under the surface. Hatching patterns, emergers, stillborns and egg-laying females may require some aspect under the surface.

Certain characteristics of the natural adult fly are important features that trout are often aware of if they are able to view the fly through a clear, unrippled surface. It follows that the artificial should also take into account the size, shape, wing and body colour, translucency, light pattern and movement of the natural. The more rippled the surface, the less discerning a fish can be over the floating fly and, as a general rule, the less accurate the imitation required.

In addition to being the correct colour, the materials used to tie a dry fly need to be of the lightest weight and of minimum absorbency, and have a degree of translucency. Materials such as quill and peacock herl which don't fully conform to these guidelines are used in some of the best patterns, proving that these qualities are ideals only and that most trout are remarkably tolerant. Perhaps the most useful synthetic material to have been developed is polypropylene. It is extremely light with a specific gravity of less than 1 and is therefore lighter than water. It is translucent and available as a fine dubbing in at least 40 colours; it is also sold as a yarn or in sheets and is a superb material for bodies and wings.

The biggest hindrance to the floating fly is the metal hook acting like an anchor and penetrating the surface. It follows that the finest-wire hooks should be used. Most of the dry flies in the following plates have been tied with down-eye hooks, the exceptions being where a feature of design necessitates an up-eye or where the fly creator has sent the fly for illustration. The down-eye doesn't just look better but it marginally improves the hooking ability.

It is not the purpose of this book to describe dry-fly strategy or presentation techniques but I must emphasise that the presentation of the fly is as important, and in some instances more important, than the choice of fly. If I might be permitted to recommend my own recent book, *To Rise a Trout*, which is a thorough treatise on all aspects of fishing with dry flies, it will explain the problems and supply the answers. It looks in some detail at all aspects, including the challenge of hatch matching, reading the water, streamside strategy, and dealing with selective trout and non-risers.

Eight of the Best

Seven of these eight flies are probably the most proven and reliable dry flies for most river trout fishing in Britain. The eighth fly is worthy of this accolade and I think will, in time, enjoy much wider and more frequent use. Of course there are scores of others in this book that are used very successfully across the country but perhaps none more than these have tempted some dry-fly fishermen into becoming one-fly-only men. Forsaking all others, they have found the pill to cure all diseases. It sounds a bit boring to me; it also makes a nonsense of our high ideas of trout intelligence and selectivity. What it does show is that here are eight flies that have trout-appeal. All are highly recommended. Dress one or all of these eight and you can throw the book away.

1 Grey Duster

COMMENT

Authorities variously suggest that the Grey Duster in the appropriate sizes is useful to imitate caenis, midges, assorted olives, four or five stonefly species, the mayfly and moths. I'm not too sure how effective it is for any of these specifically, but I do know from frequent experience of the fly that it is a general utility fly that is hard to beat. It takes trout throughout the season, whether it is fished alongside a natural dun on the surface or to tempt non-rising fish. Both designs work well but I've found that the parachute-hackled version is more attractive than the standard tie.

DRESSING

Hook: 12–16 Code L3A, E6A or A.
Thread: Brown.
Tail (optional): Badger cock fibres.
Body: Blue-grey rabbit's fur.
Hackle: Badger cock.

2 Beacon Beige

COMMENT

It is no coincidence that many of the patterns which have tempted some to become one-fly men are good imitations of the olives, so important are these upwingeds all the year. The Beige was originally a West Country olive dun dressing devised during the First World War by a member of the Wills family in conjunction with Fred Tout, a well-known West Country professional fly tyer. Peter Deane amended it with great success. It is very highly regarded on its home waters, on the southern chalk streams and on freestone rivers throughout the country.

DRESSING

Hook: 14–16 Code L3A, E6A or A.
Tail: Plymouth Rock cock fibres.
Body: Well marked stripped peacock eye quill.
Hackle: Plymouth Rock with a red Indian game-cock wound through.

1 Grey Duster **2** Beacon Beige **3** John Storey **4** Coachman
5 Greenwell's Glory **6** Kite's Imperial **7** Pheasant Tail **8** Grizzle Mink

3 John Storey

COMMENT

This dry fly is found in almost every northern fly fisher's fly box and is worthy of much wider use. Everyone I know who has used it catches trout on it with unfailing regularity. The advance wing is unusual and may account to some degree for the fly's success. A trout viewing a surface fly through its window of vision sees an early view of the wing as it leaves the mirror and enters its window. If the wing is the stimulus needed then the advance wing-style works very well. A down-eye hook is essential if ease of tying on the tippet is to be considered.

DRESSING

Hook: 14–16 down-eye Code L3A or E6A.
Thread: Black.
Body: Copper peacock herl.
Wing: A small whole mallard breast feather tied in a bunch forward-sloping.
Hackle: Dark Rhode Island Red cock (natural dark-red cock).

4 Coachman

COMMENT

Despite being about 150 years old, the Coachman remains a very attractive fly in its many guises. Although originally a wet fly, the floater is probably more widely used. It bears no obvious comparison with any natural flies except that its bulk perhaps suggests a sedge and the white wings a moth. A wingless version includes an additional white hackle behind the red one or mixed with it. Despite being not much like many aquatic flies it is a very good fly; perhaps the highly visible wing is the stimulus. The excellent Hackle-Point Coachman has white cock hackle-tip wings tied semi-spent.

DRESSING

Hook: 12–16 L3A, E6A or A.
Thread: Black, brown or red spinner.
Body: Bronze peacock herl.
Wing: White duck or swan (*see* text).
Hackle: Natural red cock.

5 Greenwell's Glory

COMMENT

The winged wet fly is the original version of the joint effort between Canon Greenwell and James Wright in 1854, though it was likely based on an earlier dressing. It is an imitation of all the olives, from the large dark olive on a size 12 or 14 hook, through the medium olives to the small dark olive on a size 16 or 18. It even works when the iron blues are hatching. Because olives of one sort or another can be found hatching in good numbers during every month of the season, this floating Greenwell is an excellent standby. The wingless version has a medium blue-dun cock hackle in front of the furnace.

DRESSING

Hook: 12–16 Code E6A or L3A.
Thread: Waxed yellow.
Tail: Greenwell or furnace cock fibres.
Body: Waxed tying thread.
Rib: Fine gold wire.
Wing: Pale starling wing or moorhen (*see* text).
Hackle: Greenwell or furnace cock.

6 Kite's Imperial

COMMENT

In addition to being an effective publicist for Frank Sawyer's nymph techniques, Oliver Kite managed to leave his mark with an exceptionally good dry-fly pattern. It is very likely based on an earlier Welsh dressing. Whatever its parentage and Kite's amendments to it, what resulted is an excellent general dry fly, now with a nation-wide following as a result of Kite's regular column in the *Shooting Times*. It is particularly effective early season as an imitation of the large dark olive wherever it hatches. Kite rarely used any other dry fly.

DRESSING

Hook: 14–16 Code E6A or L3A.
Thread: Purple.
Tail: Grey or brown hackle fibres (early season); honey-dun (mid-/and late season).
Body: Natural heron herl.
Rib: Fine gold wire.
Thorax: Natural heron doubled and redoubled.
Hackle: Honey-dun cock.

7 Pheasant Tail

COMMENT

This is a marvellous fly, excelling as a general spinner imitation, particularly of the olives, iron blue and pale wateries. It also works when many duns are hatching. The hackle seems to vary amongst commercially dressed flies but Payne Collier's original of about 1901 called for a honey-dun. One of the successful variants has a blue-dun or rusty-dun hackle but don't accept any with a dull brown or natural red hackle. It is probably the best evening fly for general use when many spinner species return to the water.

DRESSING

Hook: 14–16 Code L3A, E6A or A.
Tail: Honey-dun hackle fibres.
Body: Cock pheasant centre tail fibres.
Rib: Fine oval gold twist or wire.
Hackle: Honey-dun cock.

8 Grizzle Mink

COMMENT

Neil Patterson devised this nondescript pattern commenting that 'Few flies can claim to be as downright scruffy . . . If it has nothing else going for it, a roughly tied Grizzle Mink lives. It has life! . . . I cannot stress enough that untidiness and pure scruff are the keys to successful Grizzle Mink tying'. How often it is that a well used dry fly that has caught a dozen or more trout seems to be the effective one. This style capitalises on that observation. It is very effective, particularly as an olive imitation, wherever it is fished.

DRESSING

Hook: 14–18 Code L3A, E6A or A.
Thread: Brown.
Tail: A bunch of grizzle fibres.
Body: Dun-coloured mink fur mixed with some longish hairs, some of which should stick out through the rib (do not trim).
Rib: Fine gold wire.
Hackle: Red cock wound through a grizzle cock (early season); ginger through a grizzle (summer).

Chalkstream Classics

The English chalk streams were the nursery for dry-fly fishing where many of the imitation theories and early dry-fly tying developments took place. Today the floating fly is fished wherever trout are found. For most fly fishers the chalk streams are looked upon as the Eldorado of trout fishing, where brown trout rise freely in gin-clear waters to large hatches of duns. The trend in recent years has lessened the attraction a little; the stocked brown and rainbows do rise in often semi-opaque waters to diminishing aquatic fly hatches. Nevertheless, they are the best of British trout fishing where big trout can cast a critical eye over a surface fly or nymph.

1 Lunn's Particular

COMMENT

William Lunn devised a number of patterns for the River Test at Houghton which he keepered for fifty-five years until 1932. It is strange that William Lunn didn't take up fly tying until 1916, when aged 54, the year before the birth of this his most enduring dressing. He used medium-blue hackle-point wings in an era when solid feather-fibre wings were in vogue. They are not very durable and Ian Warrilow offers a more durable variant with an additional thorax. It is a red spinner (female olive) imitation.

DRESSING

Hook: 14–16 Code A, L3A or E6A.
Thread: Crimson.
Tail: Rhode Island Red hackle fibres.
Body: Undyed stripped Rhode Island Red hackle stalk.
Thorax: Rich brown Antron.
Wing: Cream poly yarn.

2 Terry's Terror

COMMENT

This is the work of collaboration between professional fly dresser Ernest Lock and Dr Cecil Terry, a Bath surgeon. Peter Deane recalls that Terry modestly passed on the dressing to others, telling them that trout took it for anything between a trout pellet and a dipper's dropping! The original dressing called for the lower hackle to be clipped level with the hook point to represent an emerging olive. Modern usage is apt to omit clipping the hackle. It doesn't look much like an olive but it is a reliable olive dun or spinner dressing and considered by many an excellent sedge imitation.

DRESSING

Hook: 12–16 Code A, L3A or E6A.
Thread: Black or brown.
Tail: Two bunches, together not mixed, of orange and yellow goat hair trimmed short (hackle fibres also work).
Body: Peacock herl.
Rib (optional): Fine flat copper-coloured tinsel.
Hackle: Natural red cock.

1 Lunn's Particular **2** Terry's Terror **3** Leckford Professor **4** Red Quill
5 Caperer **6** Little Marryat **7** Gold-Ribbed Hare's Ear **8** Straddlebug

3 Leckford Professor

COMMENT

The reverse-hackle has never been very popular but just a few patterns in that style survive. This is probably the best known of them. It was devised by Ernest Mott, a Test river keeper. According to those who regularly fish the Test today it is still a very useful fly. I have not been lucky enough to cast it on its home waters but I have caught many freestone trout with it. The hiding of the point within the hackle is a useful feature when fishing heavily bushed streams, where the misdirected cast into foliage is not unusual.

DRESSING

Hook: 12–14 up-eye Code B or L3B.
Body: Dark hare's ear fur.
Rib: Fine flat gold tinsel.
Hackle: Bright-red cock with a white cock, tied at the rear of the shank.

4 Red Quill

COMMENT

The original wet version was probably devised as long ago as 1803 by Thomas Rushworth. Halford popularised it with his claim that it is 'the sheet anchor of the dry-fly fisherman on an unfamiliar river'. It is not supposed to represent any one upwinged species in particular; rather, trout can see in it what they want to see. It is effective when many of the olives and iron blues are hatching. Some dressings have a wing of an upright bunch of blue cock fibres, or omit the wing and include an additional pale blue-dun cock hackle.

DRESSING

Hook: 14–16 Code A, L3A or E6A.
Thread: Black.
Tail: Natural red cock fibres.
Body: Stripped peacock eye quill.
Wing: Starling (see text).
Hackle: Natural red cock.

5 Caperer

COMMENT

This adult sedge is quite a large fly about ¾ of an inch long. They are widely distributed and fairly common, particularly on chalk streams and other alkaline rivers. The wings are mottled yellow-brown and the body orangy-brown. It is mainly an evening fly with the largest hatches occurring from August onwards. William Lunn's dressing is the national standard pattern which also doubles up as an excellent general sedge for daytime use. The wing is a later addition. An easier-to-obtain wing material than the standard is the secondary feather from a moorhen wing.

DRESSING

Hook: 12–14 Code A, L3A or E6A.
Thread: Crimson.
Body: Four or five strands of dark turkey tail herls either side of a centre section of two yellow-dyed swan fibres.
Wing (optional): Coot's wing dyed chocolate-brcwn.
Hackle: Medium Rhode Island Red cock with a black cock in front or wound together.

6 Little Marryat

COMMENT

This is a pattern from the early days of the development of chalkstream dry-fly fishing; it is as good today as when G. S. Marryat first devised it. It is mainly used as an imitation of the pale watery and spurwing duns. The original dressing called for a light-buff Cochin China cock hackle but the nearest substitute is cream-coloured dun or the closest to this to be found. I don't care for the opaque starling wing quills on floating flies and I prefer bunched feather fibres or poly yarn or simply a second lighter-coloured hackle such as a pale blue-dun or grizzle.

DRESSING

Hook: 14–16 Code A, L3A or E6A.
Thread: White.
Tail: Cream-coloured dun cock.
Body: Australian opossum flank fur or pale coffee-coloured seal's fur substitute.
Wing: Pale starling.
Hackle: Cream-coloured dun cock.

7 Gold-Ribbed Hare's Ear

COMMENT

Whether this is fished as a floating dry fly, as an emerger in the film or as a nymph it excels on chalk streams and freestone rivers. Its origins are obscured by age but its reputation was established even a century ago when Halford, who praised its trout-taking qualities, was to discard it as being too nondescript for his liking. A winged version exists with starling wings but this is rarely used. Much better is the hackleless tying, which is better than the dressing tied with a rusty-dun cock hackle. It is an excellent olive imitation and all the better for being fished damp rather than dry.

DRESSING

Hook: 14–16 L4A or E1A.
Thread: Brown or yellow.
Tail: Three long body strands or guard hairs from a hare's face.
Body: Dark hare's ear fur.
Rib: Fine flat gold tinsel or gold wire.
Legs: Long body fibres picked out.

8 Straddlebug

COMMENT

This is a popular imitation of the mayfly *(Ephemera danica, E. vulgata)* on the chalk streams but it is rarely used elsewhere. I was taken to task for omitting it in my earlier *Dictionary* and I'm pleased to rectify my mistake. A number of variations have appeared but this version has been strongly recommended as a reliable imitation, with some big catches made on it.

DRESSING

Hook: 10–12 long shank D5B or E1A.
Thread: Brown.
Tip: Very fine oval gold tinsel.
Tail: Two or three black cock fibres.
Body: Natural raffia.
Rib: Brown thread.
Hackle: Orange cock followed by a brown-speckled summer duck feather or French partridge breast feather.
Head: Peacock herl.

General Olive Imitations

Probably the majority of upwinged flies hatching on most streams are olives of various species. From the large dark or early spring olive in March through to late hatches of blue-winged, medium or large dark olives in November, olives can be expected any day of the trout season. It is not surprising that many of the nondescript floaters or some of the flies that have tempted anglers into being one-fly men are good olive imitations.

These eight flies were all devised as olive imitations and all can be adapted to match the various naturals by altering the shades of the materials. Other imitations are listed under their species name or if they represent other species as well they are listed in the index under olives.

1 Itchen Olive

COMMENT

This is a dressing devised by Gordon Mackie for the paler duns, such as the small spurwing and pale evening dun. The fly takes trout that refuse to look at the standard dressings for these naturals and in its creator's hands has accounted for hundreds of fish. Gordon Mackie comments that because many naturals are so similar in appearance this dressing is essentially a general-purpose fly. Other olives, such as the medium olive, can be represented by varying the tying thread under the semi-translucent thinly dubbed body.

DRESSING

Hook: 14 Code L3A, E6A or A.
Thread: Primrose.
Tail: Four or five stiff pale-grey spade hackle fibres.
Body: Thinly dubbed medium-grey seal's fur substitute.
Rib: Primrose thread.
Hackle: Three or four turns of a stiff and springy light-grey cock hackle.

2 Light Ollie

COMMENT

Preben Torp Jacobsen tied this medium and large dark olive imitation for his native Danish streams, where the double hackle was necessary to enable it to float well on slightly polluted water. It was named after the English fly fisher Oliver Kite, a friend of Jacobsen. The version with darker hackles is the better large dark olive imitation.

DRESSING

Hook: 14–16 Code L3A, E6A or A.
Thread: Primrose.
Tail: Buff Orpington hackle fibres.
Body: Four heron herls dyed in picric acid and twisted round the thread, and palmered with a natural blue-dun.
Rib: Fine silver wire.
Hackle: Light honey-dun cock (like Metz sandy-brown).

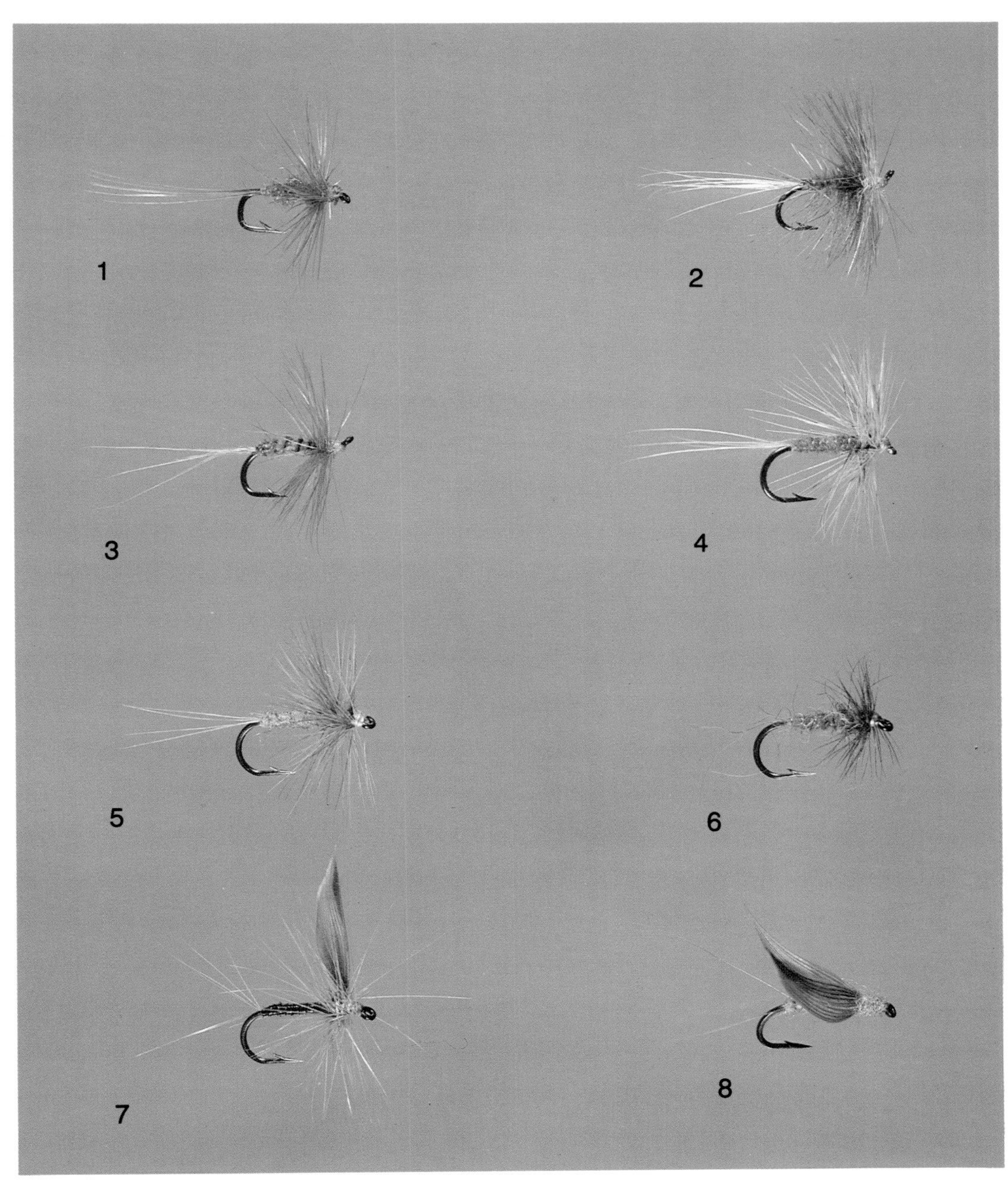

1 Itchen Olive **2** Light Ollie **3** Misty Blue Dun **4** Blue Dun
5 Rough Olive **6** Barton Bug **7** Olive Quill **8** No-Hackle Olive

3 Misty Blue Dun

COMMENT

The Driffield Beck is a glistening jewel in the East Yorkshire countryside, a rare outpost of true chalkstream fishing. The head keeper of the Driffield Anglers' Club (founded in 1833) is Tony Waites. To see him in action with a fly rod on his home stream, with his deadly accurate presentation of a nymph or dry fly, is a marvel. He devised this medium olive dun imitation, naming it after his dog.

DRESSING

Hook: 14 Code L3A.
Thread: Yellow.
Tail: Three long fibres from a light-blue cock hackle.
Body: Yellow thread with a strand of heron herl wound closely so the thread just shines through.
Hackle: Light-brown and light-blue-dun cock wound together.

4 Blue Dun

COMMENT

For over three hundred years since Charles Cotton trout fishers have used a pattern by this name. No single species was represented by it and the name came to be a synonym for any olive dun, or, more specifically, the large dark olive or iron blue. The term is slowly dying out, with more specific names being used. There are a dozen regional dressings for the wet and floating versions, most of which have passed into disuse. I suggest this modern version. Another dressing is given on page 77.

DRESSING

Hook: 14–16 Code L3A.
Thread: Yellow.
Tail: Pale blue-dun cock fibres.
Body: Dubbed blue rabbit's fur.
Rib: Yellow thread.
Hackle: Mixed grizzle and blue-dun cock hackles.

5 Rough Olive

COMMENT

The Rough Olive is a general olive imitation which, in varying shades of materials and different hook sizes, represents all the olives. One of the appealing features of this dressing is the ease of tying. Many olive dressings use starling wing quills but I've never been convinced of the importance of specific wing imitation if the hackle colour and breadth is sufficiently suggestive of the natural's wings. If wings are insisted upon it is much easier and no less effective to use a single bunch of blue or grey hackle fibres or poly yarn.

DRESSING

Hook: 12–14 Code L3A or E6A.
Thread: Primrose.
Tail: Pale blue-dun fibres.
Body: Olive seal's fur substitute or poly dubbing.
Rib: Fine gold wire.
Hackle: Olive-dyed badger cock with a blue-dun wound through.

6 Barton Bug

COMMENT

Named after the famous stretch of the Itchen at Abbotts Barton, this is a hatching medium olive dun devised by Roy Darlington for selective Itchen fish. It is fished so that the rear half of the fly is submerged and the front half floating, supported by the thorax and hackle well soaked in floatant. The tails are exaggerated to represent the nymphal shuck hanging below the surface. The extra-long tails are a simple but effective way of dressing an emerger if it is fished at the right angle on the water. There is often no need to resort to more elaborate emerger styles.

DRESSING

Hook: 14 Code L3A or E6A.
Thread: Primrose.
Tail: Long fur fibres from a rabbit's neck.
Body: Hare's ear fur dressed thinly with a slight thorax.
Rib: Fine oval gold tinsel.
Hackle: High quality short-fibred blue-dun cock.

7 Olive Quill

COMMENT

I haven't been able to trace the origins of this general olive imitation but it has survived constant use over many years and is of proven value. The peacock quill body makes no concession to translucency, with its only value being a segmented body of a realistic colour in reflected light. Trout viewing the backlit fly see a solid body with absolutely no suggestion of even the smallest amount of light passing through. However, this and other notable quill-bodied flies catch a lot of fish.

DRESSING

Hook: 14 Code L3A, A or E6A.
Thread: Pale yellow.
Tail: Medium-olive cock fibres.
Body: Peacock quill dyed olive.
Wing (optional): Medium starling wing.
Hackle: Medium-olive cock with a blue-dun cock wound through in the wingless version.

8 No-Hackle Olive

COMMENT

My own experience suggests that the smaller sizes of no-hackles work much better than the larger ones and I recommend that sizes 14 and 16 be used to represent the medium and smaller olive duns. Because of the lack of supporting hackle this style of fly should be well soaked in floatant and tied with the lightest materials on the finest-wire hooks. Polypropylene dubbing is excellent and available in a range of forty colours. The tail fibres should be widely spaced to help balance the fly on the surface.

DRESSING

Hook: 14–16 fine-wire Code L4A or L3A.
Thread: Olive or pale yellow.
Tail: Clear or olive Microfibetts (Orvis) or Magic Spinner Tails (Traun River Products).
Body: Olive poly dubbing, shade to match the natural.
Wing: Matched pair of mallard quills.

Parachute Dry Flies

When American William Avery Brush patented the parachute hackle in 1931 it was the first major departure in the style of the floating fly for fifty years. One of the principal benefits is the delicate presentation as the fly's descent is slowed down by the parachute effect. The fly is well balanced and usually floats very well. What is less satisfactory is its use to represent the fully emerged winged adult dun. The hackle holds the body on or in the surface film, quite unlike the natural, which is fully supported by its six legs; and the image in the mirrored undersurface and through the trout's window is not like that of a dun. However, it is a fair imitation of a floating nymph, stillborn, emerger or spinner, and that is why the style is very successful. Any dry fly can be adapted in this way.

1 No. 3 Para

COMMENT

Pat Russell devised this fly for those trout which rise once and never do so again and he claims great success with it for bringing reluctant risers to the surface. Apart from specific imitations for the mayfly and sedges, Pat Russell uses this dressing for almost all his dry-fly needs. He comments that it also works when trout are nymphing and the nymph-like body of the fly held in the film makes it attractive. It was created during the Falklands war and it owes its name to the parachute regiment who fought so bravely.

DRESSING

Hook: 14–16 Code L3A.
Thread: Scarlet.
Tail: Rhode Island Red hackle fibres.
Body: Rhode Island Red hackle stalk and tying thread.
Hackle: Barred ginger or light red cock, in parachute style.

2 Tup's Parachute

COMMENT

The Tup's Indispensable (*see* page 60) has been amended by Pat Russell in this parachute version. Traditionally the Tup's is useful to represent the pale watery and small spurwing female spinners. Pat is very keen on the parachute hackle for dry flies and uses them to great effect on his local stretch of the Test. He won't hesitate to fish his parachute patterns down to a size 24 for the renowned pernickety risers on some parts of the Test.

DRESSING

Hook: 14–18 Code L3A or E6A.
Thread: Yellow.
Tail: Six to eight cream cock fibres.
Body: Wind a hackle stalk halfway up the shank from the bend and cover with yellow floss.
Thorax: Mixed pink, orange and yellow fine dubbing behind and in front of the hackle.
Hackle: Four or five turns of small cream cock hackle round a hackle-stalk loop; secure by tightening the loop.

1 No. 3 Para **2** Tup's Parachute **3** Whitmore's Fancy
4 Ruane's Para Spinner **5** Black Pensioner **6** Light Pensioner
7 Thorax Parachute Nymph **8** Klinken's USD Spinner

3 Whitmore's Fancy

COMMENT

One of the pleasures in writing a book of this type is that I can introduce to a wider audience some excellent patterns that are hitherto largely unknown. For quite a few seasons I have fished this dressing on northern streams with a very satisfactory success rate. It was devised by Harry Whitmore, a York trout fisher and fly tyer of forty years experience. It is a nondescript dressing which manages to pass for whatever trout are on the look-out for.

DRESSING

Hook: 12–14 Code L3A.
Thread: Red.
Tail: Medium natural red cock fibres.
Body: Peacock herl.
Rib: Red thread.
Hackle: Medium natural red cock in parachute style.

4 Ruane's Para Spinner

COMMENT

One of the interesting features of Terry Ruane's dressing is the use of Magic Spinner Wing fibres for the upright wing. This synthetic material is available in a wide range of colours, all of which are shiny and very reflective and are an excellent representation of the natural spinner's wing. The natural spinner has its wings fully erect only at the moment it touches the water; they soon collapse to the fully spent position as she oviposits. The colours can be varied to match the natural.

DRESSING

Hook: 12–14 Code L3A.
Thread: White Danville Spider Web or very fine equivalent.
Tail: A few honey-dun hackle fibres.
Body: Muskrat's fur.
Wing: Magic Spinner Wing.
Hackle: Honey-dun cock wound round the roots of the wing.

5 Black Pensioner

COMMENT

The Pensioner series of parachute dry flies were devised by Peter Mackenzie-Philps for an elderly customer with poor eyesight who required a highly visible fly that could be seen on the surface. The black version is excellent when black gnats or hawthorn flies are being blown onto the river. It is also a useful search pattern over non-rising fish or the likely lies when there is nothing rising; trout expect a terrestrial imitation at any time but more readily as the summer progresses.

DRESSING

Hook: 12 Code L3A.
Tail: Black cock fibres.
Body: Black dyed cock pheasant centre tail fibres.
Rib: Fine gold wire.
Wing: White mink tail hair tied upright in a single bunch.
Hackle: Black cock wound round the wing roots.

6 Light Pensioner

COMMENT

This was the first of the Pensioner series to be devised in 1979. The white mink wing is extremely visible for the fly fisher, and, I've no doubt, for the watching trout too. Sometimes trout need to see a clear view of the upright wings of the adult dun before they will rise. The advance wing design often works better than most in that situation, but so too should this style, with the unobscured view of the highly visible bunch wing. It is an excellent olive imitation and because olives can be anticipated every month of the season it is a reliable standby.

DRESSING

Hook: 12 Code L3A.
Tail: Greenwell cock fibres.
Body: Hare's fur.
Rib: Fine gold wire.
Wing: White mink tail hair tied upright.
Hackle: Greenwell cock (ginger/black) in parachute style round the wing roots.

7 Thorax Parachute Nymph

COMMENT

This one has a very mixed parentage, incorporating some good ideas from well proven designs. At first glance it's a paradun or parachute fly or nymph, depending upon your viewpoint. It is a combination of all these aspects with the hackle and wing placement moved into the middle of the fly. The main width of the natural's wing is over the middle of the body and not near the shoulder, as most imitations are tied. This dressing places the upright wing where the natural wing is at its widest. The centre hackle also balances the fly well. Tie to represent the natural's colours.

DRESSING

Hook: 14–18 Code L4A, E6A or E1A.
Tail: Widely spaced cock fibres.
Body: Polypropylene dubbing or natural fur.
Wing: White or coloured poly yarn.
Hackle: Light-ginger or honey-dun cock.

8 Klinken's USD Spinner

COMMENT

Hans van Klinken has based his spinner dressing on the upside-down design of John Goddard and Brian Clarke, which makes use of the parachute hackle to support the fly body. He also uses other very light modern materials and the excellent spinner wing material from Traun River Products. This style of tying represents the newly alighted spinner before it becomes spent with its wings horizontal and the body in the film. The style is also suitable for the dun if the wings are a single upright bunch of the same fibres or poly yarn. Colour to match the natural.

DRESSING

Hook: Long-shank fine-wire 18–22 Code KS12.
Tail: Magic Spinner Tails.
Body: Fine polypropylene dubbing.
Wing: Magic Spinner Wing.
Head: Peacock herl.
Hackle: Ginger cock wound in parachute style.

Fast-Water Floaters

Fast water is often too quickly passed over by the fly fisher, yet beneath the faster flow at the surface trout will lie in the calmer, slower water nearer the riverbed or sheltering in the calm pockets around obstructions. Here trout are unable to be selective and have to decide on the basis of a blur of colour, a vague outline and the dimpled light pattern on the surface. They have to make their minds up fast or go hungry. All fast-water patterns are easily seen by both trout and angler; they float well and their light pattern or silhouette is the trigger to a hungry trout. If the straight drift doesn't work, try twitching or skittering a long-hackle fly. Sedges landing on fast water often try to work upstream and a fly can be dragged or twitched from an upstream position.

1 Renegade

COMMENT

The hackle at either end of the body allows this North American pattern to be kept well clear of the surface. Often all the hungry trout sees of the surface fly in fast, rough water is the light pattern, and in this pattern the fore-and-aft hackles are a planned exaggeration of the light pattern from any natural fly. The white hackle colour matters very little to the trout but it is much more important to the angler trying to keep track of the fly bouncing along on the current.

DRESSING

Hook: 10–18 Code A, L3A or E6A.
Thread: Black.
Tip: Flat gold tinsel.
Rear hackle: Brown or natural red cock.
Body: Peacock herl.
Rib (optional): Fine gold wire.
Front hackle: White cock.

2 Irresistibles

COMMENT

There are a number in this series devised by an American, Joe Messinger, all of which have the buoyant deer hair body which make them almost unsinkable. Most are named after differing hackle and wing colours. They are good adult sedge imitations on fast water, despite the poor sedge-wing representation. Other variants include a white version which doubles as a moth pattern and is very visible at dusk.

DRESSING

Hook: 10–14 Code A, L3A, E6A or E1A.
Thread: White or grey.
Tail: Fine stiff white deer hair or ginger or white cock fibres.
Body: White deer hair spun and clipped so that it tapers to the rear.
Wing: White bucktail or calf tail tied upright and slightly divided.
Hackle: Ginger cock.

1 Renegade **2** Irresistible **3** Black Bivisible **4** Badger Bivisible
5 Baigent's Brown Variant **6** Cream Variant **7** Dutch Panama
8 King Palmer

3 Black Bivisible

COMMENT

This is one of a series of flies which differ mainly in the colour of the hackle and tail. In theory almost any dry fly can be made into a Bivisible by palmering the hackle and adding a white hackle in front. They were originally devised by an American, Edward Hewitt, for fast water and for dusk fishing when failing light hinders a clear sight of the fly. Hewitt is quoted as saying: 'The white wisp enables the angler to see the fly readily, hence the name I gave it – Bivisible because I can see it and the trout can see it'.

DRESSING

Hook: 10–18 Code A, L3A or E6A.
Thread: Black.
Tail: Two small black hackle tips.
Body: Tying thread with one or more palmered black cock hackles.
Head hackle: White cock.

4 Badger Bivisible

COMMENT

Variations include tinsel bodies beneath the palmered hackle, though some anglers feel that the unnatural flash puts fish down. The body hackle should be tied in by the hackle tip and be wound from the rear forwards. Blue, brown and grizzle are alternative colours. A brighter coloured alternative is the Pink Lady Bivisible, which has a tail of ginger hackle tips, a flat gold tinsel body with a palmered badger hackle and a yellow or white cock at the shoulder.

DRESSING

Hook: 10–18 Code A, L3A or E6A.
Thread: Black.
Tail: Two small badger hackle tips.
Body: Tying thread with one or more palmered badger cock hackles.
Head hackle: White cock.

5 Baigent's Brown Variant

COMMENT

In the 1890s Dr William Baigent was one of the first North Country dry-fly fishers. For his rougher dales rivers he developed a series of long-hackled variants to ride the fast water. Because the hackles are longer they are less stiff than shorter-fibred hackles. This means that they spread more readily and support the fly better. The longer-hackled fly rocks in the breeze more readily on its hackle tips, giving the artificial the suggestion of life. Baigent once said of his Variant design that it 'is not tied to represent any fly, it is tied to catch trout'.

DRESSING

Hook: 12–14 Code L3A or E6A.
Body: Yellow floss.
Wing: Hen pheasant wing tied thin and forward-sloping.
Hackle: Long-fibred furnace cock.

6 Cream Variant

COMMENT

There are dozens of Variants, all of which have much longer hackles. This is Art Flick's pattern, and one which I remember with affection because with it I caught my first North American brown trout on Robinson Creek, Idaho. Arriving at the water I was faced with a 100-yard riffle without a sign of a rising fish. The guide must have seen the blank, helpless look on my face and handed me this fly, which he praised highly as a good reliable standby. I was pleased to prove him right, quite a few times over.

DRESSING

Hook: 12–14 shortshank Code E6A, L3A or A.
Thread: Yellow.
Tail: Long stiff cream cock fibres.
Body: Stripped cream hackle stalk which should be soaked well in water before use.
Hackle: Long-fibred cream cock.

7 Dutch Panama

COMMENT

The original Panama is a popular fancy French dry fly. This is a variant which differs considerably from the original. It is used successfully on a number of European rivers in the earlier part of the season. The semi-palmered body makes it a good floater and suitable for faster water. It comes from the vice of Hans van Klinken.

DRESSING

Hook: 12–14 E1A, E6A or L3A.
Thread: Grey.
Tail: Golden pheasant tippets.
Body: Peacock herl at the rear; fluorescent green wool at the front.
Hackle: Palmered natural red or brown over the wool.

8 King Palmer

COMMENT

Palmer-style flies are always a good bet on fast water. They look a good mouthful, something worthwhile for a trout to move through the current to intercept, and their many hackle fibres ensure an exaggerated light pattern in the trout's mirror. This European dressing from Peter Duinmeyer uses the well proven technique of mixing the hackle colours so that whatever the light conditions part of the fly should be noticeable.

DRESSING

Hook: 10–16 Code A, E1A or L3A.
Thread: Black.
Tail: Golden pheasant tippets.
Body: Black, natural red, and grizzle, white or badger cocks.
Rib: Fine oval or round gold tinsel.

Welsh Border Flies

The Welsh border counties have produced some notable fly dressers – Cosmo Barrett, the Revd Edward Powell, W. M. Gallichan, Harry Powell and others, all of whom have left their mark with dressings in regular and widespread use today. Michael Leighton has written and published an excellent book of trout flies of this area, *Trout Flies of Shropshire and the Welsh Borderlands*, a fascinating book which details patterns that will also find success on rivers across the whole country.

One feature of many of these flies is their extensive hackling, often requiring many turns of a single or double hackle, to carry the fly over the rough and tumble faster border streams.

1 Borderer

COMMENT

Earlier this century W. M. Gallichan was a prolific angling writer. This is one of many patterns to his name. It is probably one of the best known border patterns, and is used much farther afield. Michael Leighton comments: 'Deadly is a word used to described many patterns, but this fly is the deadliest of the lot! I can recommend it for use throughout the season; indeed, it is a fly that could easily turn you into a one-fly man'. The rusty blue-dun hackle the dressing calls for is very rare but a recommended substitute/variant is to mix a natural red-brown with a blue-dun cock.

DRESSING

Hook: 12–16 Code A, L3A or E6A.
Thread: Red.
Tail: Rusty blue-dun cock fibres.
Tip: Red thread.
Body: Blue rabbit underfur.
Hackle: Rusty blue-dun cock (*see* text).

2 Tanat Dun

COMMENT

Although the Tanat Dun is barely a decade old it is becoming much more widely known than on the border stream which it was first tried out on and named after. Ted Painter created it when the usual olive dun imitations didn't work as they should and it has now been used to great effect on freestone rivers across the country as well as on the Test and smaller chalk streams. The original dressing had a honey-dun hackle but Ted Painter advises that a brassy cream cock seems to work as effectively.

DRESSING

Hook: 14–16 Code A, L3A or E6A.
Tail: Honey-dun cock fibres.
Body: Light condor herl substitute dyed medium olive.
Rib: Very fine gold wire.
Hackle: Honey-dun cock with a cree (barred ginger) in front (*see* text).

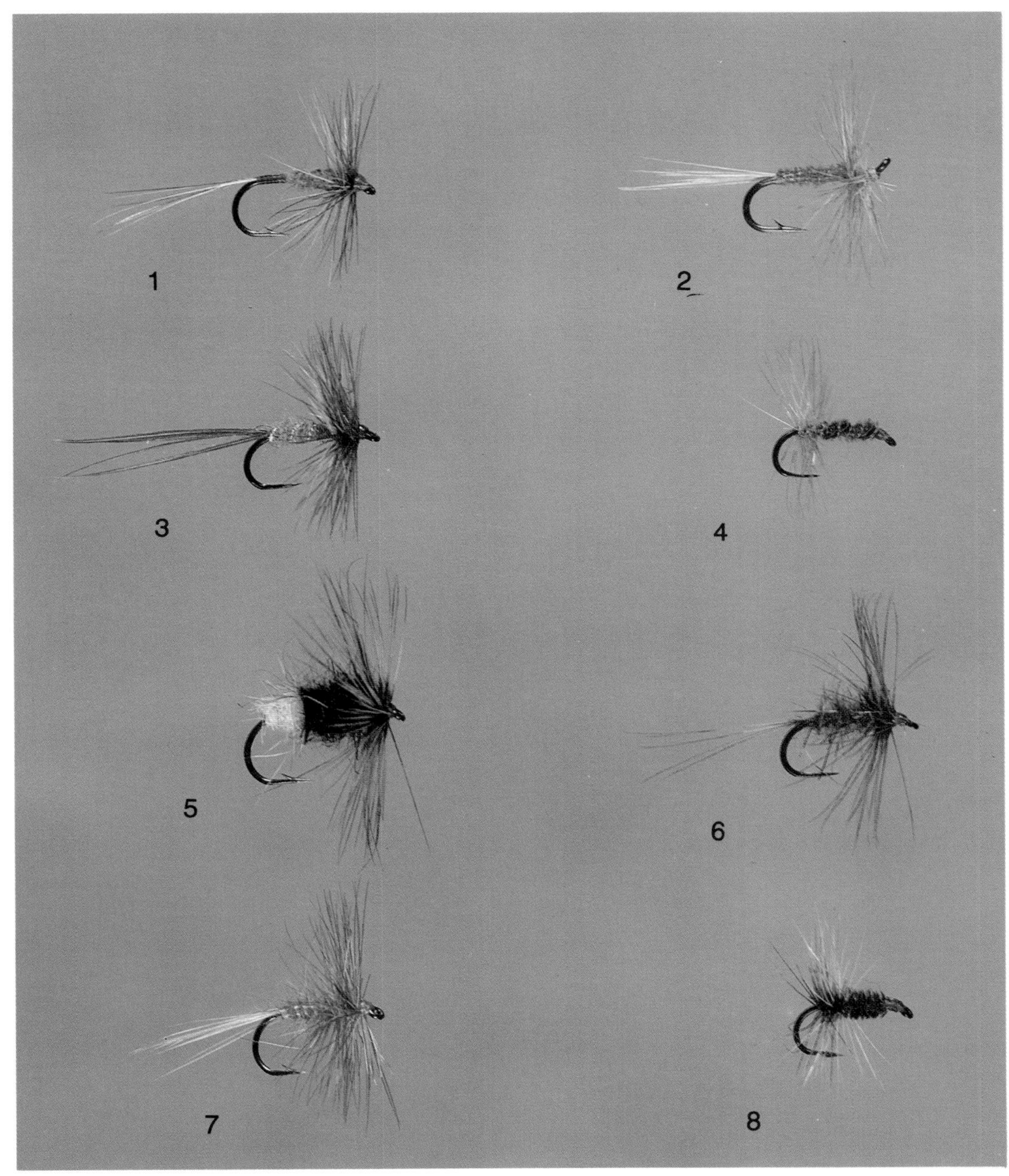

1 Borderer **2** Tanat Dun **3** Dogsbody **4** Barrett's Bane **5** Doctor
6 Baby Sun Fly **7** Grizzly Bourne **8** Coltman's Duster

3 Dogsbody

COMMENT

The story is that hairdresser and fly dresser Harry Powell created this pattern in 1924 from the camel-coloured hair from a dog of one of the customers in his barber's shop. What resulted is a fly that is very widely used as a nondescript pattern for use throughout the season. My guess is that there are many variants floating on border streams as different-coloured dogs are combed to provide the body material. Michael Leighton suggests that with this light-bodied fly and the darker Borderer the dry-fly fisherman could almost cover the season with just two patterns.

DRESSING

Hook: 14–16 Code A, L3A or E6A.
Thread: Brown.
Tail: Cock pheasant tail fibres.
Body: Camel coloured dog's hair.
Rib: Fine oval gold tinsel.
Hackle: Plymouth Rock followed by a natural red cock.

4 Barrett's Bane

COMMENT

Anyone with the name Roland Milton Cosmo Barrett has to overcome more than most of us in life. Cosmo Barrett made his name in the Welsh borders with his dry flies, of which this is the most popular. It is a Herefordshire Alder tied in reverse, that is to say with the hackle at the bend-end of the shank. It therefore succeeds in hiding the bend and point from the fish but it may make it more difficult to hook trout feeding with sip rises. I've fished it with success on Yorkshire rivers as well as streams in its home territory.

DRESSING

Hook: 14–16 up-eye Code B or L3B.
Thread: Brown.
Body: Cock pheasant tail fibres.
Rib (optional): Gold wire.
Hackle: Blue-dun cock.

5 Doctor

COMMENT

It seems likely that this dressing of the Revd Edward Powell's is a derivation of the Devonshire Doctor. It is to be tied fat and was quite likely a beetle imitation. taking some of its parentage from the famed Coch-y-bondhu. The black body with a bright yellow rear reminds me of a much later and very successful pattern. I wonder if Eric Horsfall Turner was aware of the Doctor when he created his Eric's Beetle. The Doctor is always fished dry whereas Eric's Beetle is usually fished subsurface.

DRESSING

Hook: 12–14 Code A, L3A or E6A.
Thread: Brown.
Body: Rear quarter bright yellow dyed rabbit's fur; front three-quarters black rabbit's fur, tied fat.
Hackle: Very generous turns of Coch-y-bonddhu cock.

6 Baby Sun Fly

COMMENT

Those who have tried this pattern seem to swear by it and, having once used it, fish it on a wide variety of rivers, from the Welsh borders to the classic chalk streams. It is recommended as an early-season pattern and whenever black gnats or hawthorn flies are found on the water. It came from the Revd Edward Powell, who spent much of his life fishing the Shropshire streams. The body fur is a light brown and black dubbing taken from the triangle between the eyes and nose. It should not include the blue fur nearer the skin.

DRESSING

Hook: 12–16 Code A, L3A or E6A.
Thread: Brown.
Tail: Black or Coch-y-bonddhu cock fibres.
Body: Rabbit's face fur (see text).
Rib: Brown thread.
Hackle: Generous turns of Coch-y-bonddhu or black cock.

7 Grizzly Bourne

COMMENT

Michael Leighton devised this fly, naming it after its hackle and the tiny River Bourne, on which it was so successfully used. His comments are that it is a general purpose pattern, working throughout the season, regardless of the fly on the water. He uses it almost to the exclusion of other patterns. I agree with Michael's comments that the supplementary grizzle hackle makes the natural red/brown hackle more attractive and gives it extra sparkle, which make the upper fibres more suggestive of a wing.

DRESSING

Hook: 12–18 Code A, L3A, L4A or E6A.
Thread: Orange.
Tail: Honey cock fibres.
Body: Rabbit's blue underfur.
Rib: Pearsall's Golden Yellow multi-strand floss wound very close.
Hackle: Light red/brown cock wound through a grizzle cock.

8 Coltman's Duster

COMMENT

Not until I read Michael Leighton's book was I aware of this pattern. It is a pattern he suggests all anglers should make room for in their fly box. The high praise bestowed upon it there ensured its place here. For about forty years it has been catching fish in Shropshire and farther afield and it deserves a wider airing. It shares with other border dressings the unusual feature of the reverse dressing.

DRESSING

Hook: 14–16 Code A, L3A or E6A.
Thread: Brown.
Body: Natural condor herl substitute.
Hackle: Badger cock tied at the bend.

Spinner Styles

Only when the female spinners arrive on the surface do they have their wings held erect. They soon drop to the horizontal spent position. All ovipositing females and all spent flies are touching the surface or are in the film, highly visible to the trout, but less so to the angler. Accurate imitations should be fished to rest on the surface. For this reason I believe that parachute-style flies with the hackle on top of the body are often taken for spinners (or floating nymphs or stillborns) and not for the duns they are fished as. With the exception of the Sunk Spinner, all the dressing styles below are for fishing on or in the film. All are system flies and can be adapted to match any upwinged species.

1 Sunk Spinner

COMMENT

The female spinners of the *Baetis* species – medium olive, large and small dark olives and the iron blue – all oviposit their eggs below the surface. They can be seen crawling down obstructions or items on the water's edge so they can crawl below the surface. After depositing their eggs some females are able to break back through the film and fly away. Many more die before they can make it and these spent adults drift downstream, often just below the surface. If trout are feeding just below the surface in the late evening it may not be to nymphs but to subsurface adults. This is Neil Patterson's imitation.

DRESSING

Hook: 12–16 Code A, G3A, L2A or CS7.
Thread: Crimson.
Tail: Two hare's whiskers or white horsehair separated by a dab of varnish.
Underbody: Dark red enamel copper wire with a built-up thorax.
Overbody: Flattened nylon mono (6lb BS).
Rib: Hare's whisker or white horsehair.
Wing: Two or three turns of badger cock trimmed in spent style.
Thorax: Cock pheasant tail fibres over the wing roots.

2 USD Poly-Spinners

COMMENT

John Goddard and Brian Clarke devised this tying style to produce a spinner that always has its body flush in the surface film – achieved by the parachute hackle on top of the body – and has clear translucent wings with an acceptable light pattern. They used keel hooks or the Partridge upside-down hooks, which ensure that the body is well down in the film. The polythene wings are cut and lightly pierced with a thick sharp needle before tying in. Only size 14 and smaller are suitable, otherwise the wings cause the fly to spin in casting. This is a red spinner dressing.

DRESSING

Hook: 14–16 Code K5ST.
Thread: Brown.
Tail: Three widely spaced Magic Spinner fibres.
Body: Fine rust polypropylene dubbing (Fly-Rite # 5).
Wing: Clear polythene.
Hackle: Light-red game.

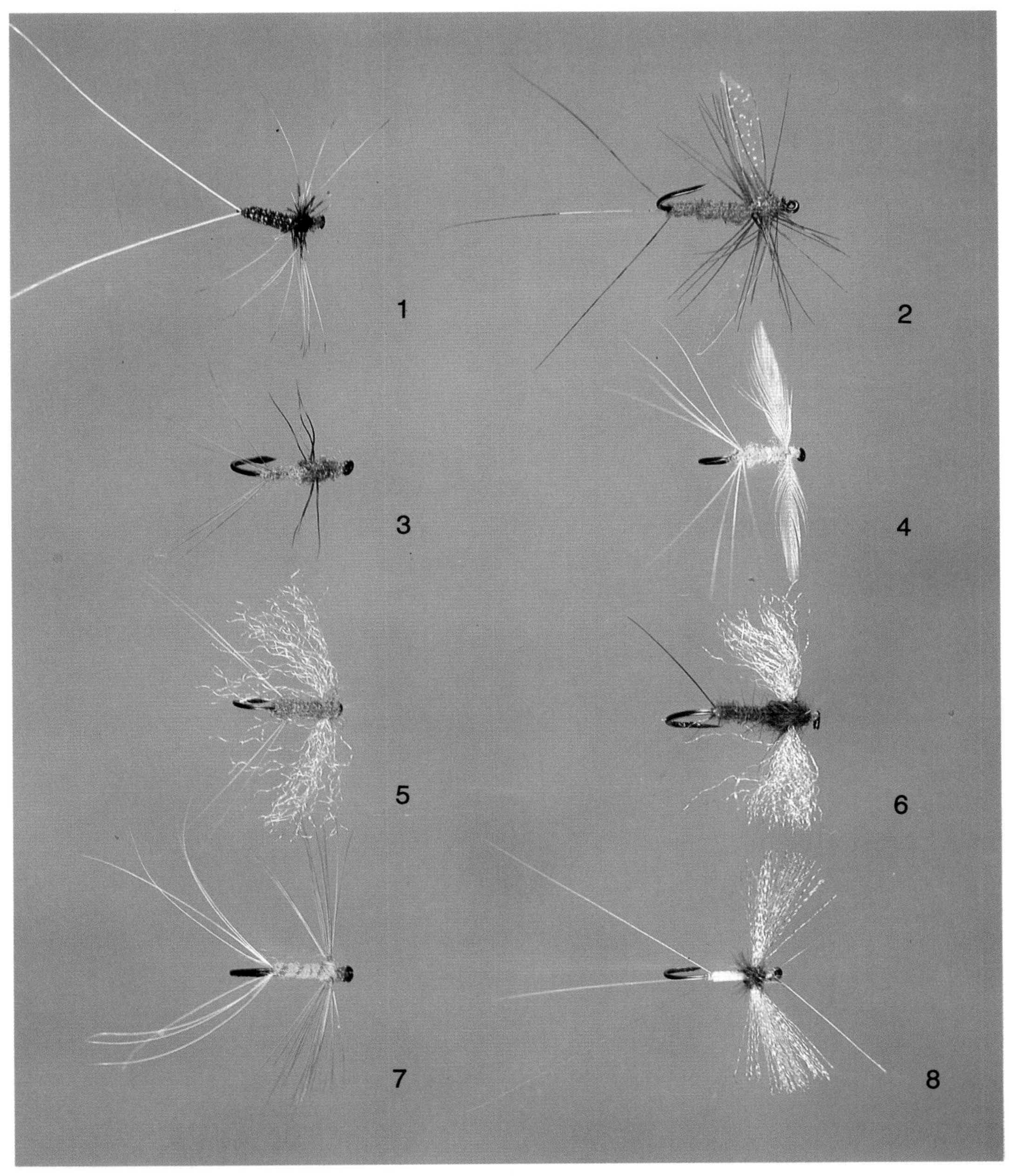

1 Sunk Spinner **2** USD Poly-Spinner **3** No-Wing Spinner
4 Hen Spinner **5** Polypropylene Spinner **6** Clear-Winged Spinner
7 Orange Spinner **8** Magic Spinner (Caenis)

3 No-Wing Spinner

COMMENT

Doug Swisher and Carl Richards devised a wingless, hackleless spinner for the times they believed trout were unable to see anything of the natural's wings. They considered that the near-transparent spent wings of spinners in the film were invisible in low light conditions against a very dull grey-blue background sky. Visible artificial wings are a deterrent. Their design consists of a body and wide-spread tail fibres, and six short-fibred legs as an aid to balance more than imitation. To aid floating, use polypropylene dubbing and fine-wire hooks, and soak well in floatant.

DRESSING

Hook: 14–16 Code L3A, L4A or E1A.
Tail: Cock hackle fibres in two widely spaced bunches.
Body: Dubbed natural fur or poly yarn with a darker shade at the thorax.
Legs: Six stripped hackle stalks, deer hair fibres or longer Microfibetts.

4 Hen Spinner

COMMENT

Wide, webby hen hackle-tip wings are used. Swisher and Richards stress that the butts should be clipped, not stripped, as this makes them stronger, with the butts bent back and bound to the shank. Other winging materials for No-Hackle spinners include light partridge breast feathers, tied concave side down, which are speckled and when wet become nearly transparent. This is a spent large spurwing or large amber spinner.

DRESSING

Hook: 12–16 Code L3A, L4A or E1A.
Thread: Orange.
Tail: Cream cock hackle fibres in two widely spaced sparse bunches.
Body: Mixed olive, white and amber seal's fur substitute or poly dubbing (2:1:1).
Wing: White webby hen hackle tips.

5 Polypropylene Spinner

COMMENT

With growing popularity polypropylene is being used in the body and wing materials of floating flies. The material has a specific gravity of less than 1 and is therefore an obvious answer to the problem of keeping a dry fly afloat. The material is available in a wide range of colours and is soft and fine, making it an excellent dubbing material. The yarn is used in winging and can be tied figure-of-eight for spent patterns. This is the dressing for a spent blue winged olive sherry spinner with its egg ball.

DRESSING

Hook: 14–16 Code L3A, L4A or E1A.
Tail: Two sparse widely spaced bunches of white Magic Spinner tails or Microfibetts.
Body: Rusty (Fly-Rite # 5) poly dubbing with a tip of green poly dubbing.
Wing: Pale grey or white poly yarn tied spent.

6 Clear-Winged Spinner

COMMENT

Gary LaFontaine, who has done much to publicise the attributes of Antron fibres in fly-tying, uses them in the winging of spent spinners. He believes that semi-opaque hackle fibres, hackle tips and polypropylene fall well short of a good imitation. Rarely are the natural's spent wings smooth and flat; they are invariably pleated. Antron fibres collect air bubbles just like the pleated natural's wings. Clear Antron is just the job for the spent wings. As an example of the tying style, Gary has supplied this dressing for the important *Tricorythodes* spinner fall. The wing is so bright that the fly is easy to see.

DRESSING

Hook: 14–20 Code L3A, L4A or E1A.
Thread: Orange.
Tail: Two widely spaced dark grey cock fibres or Microfibetts.
Abdomen and thorax: Dark grey fur.
Wing: Bunched clear Antron fibres.

7 Orange Spinner

COMMENT

Goddard and Clarke's book *The Trout and the Fly* first showed the subsurface view of the effect of a red sunset refracted round the edge of the natural spinners on the surface. This revealed a reddish glow through the clear wings. Because trout optics are much more sensitive to colours at the red end of the spectrum, this orange-bodied imitation is an effective late evening fly. Many spinner species; drained of most of their colour after shedding their eggs, are indistinguishable from each other except by careful examination – most of all at dusk, with the refracted red light shining through them.

DRESSING

Hook: 14 Code L3A.
Thread: Hot orange.
Tail: White cock hackle fibres, widely spaced in two bunches.
Body: Orange seal's fur substitute.
Rib: Fluorescent orange floss.
Hackle: Bright ginger cock wound and bunched spent.

8 Magic Spinner (Caenis)

COMMENT

Terry Ruane has never been afraid to experiment with modern materials and this spinner pattern is a fine example of their use. The Magic Spinner Wing from Traun River Products is excellent for this purpose. It is available in seven colours and is shiny and translucent like the natural spinner wings. The tails are Magic Spinner Tails from the same company or Orvis Microfibetts, both of which are produced in natural colours. If these nylon tail fibres seem expensive then the fibres from artists' nylon paintbrushes balance the fly just as well and are just as effective. Use materials to match the naturals.

DRESSING

Hook: 12–18 Code E6A.
Tails and antennae: Widely spaced Magic Spinner Tails or Microfibetts.
Abdomen: Tying thread or fine dubbing.
Thorax: Furry foam wound over the wing roots.
Wing: Spent bunches of Magic Spinner Wing fibres.

General Dry Flies 1

I have little doubt that every fly-tying trout fisher experiments with patterns and variations of his own. No doubt many of these achieve a measure of success for there are times when trout will rise to anything vaguely food-like that passes above them. When trout are so co-operative it is tempting to offer them the weird creation we concocted in a moment's aberration at the tying vice. Success under these circumstances is no measure at all of a pattern's attraction or imitation; if trout are stupid enough to rise at the tuft of wool I use as bite indicator when nymph fishing then they'll rise to *anything* that has been tied to look like a fly. The flies in these sections, indeed in this book, are all well proven and not based on a moment of fleeting success.

1 Enigma

COMMENT

Pat Russell devised this fly as a pale watery dun imitation for both trout and grayling. It is also a useful caenis imitation if a few turns of brown thread are wound as a thorax each side of the hackle. Originally devised for the rippled water of the Devonshire River Creedy, it is equally at home on the chalk streams. Pat describes it as an excellent fly for bringing to the surface fish lying uninterested. After five or six drifts over a fish it will often bring about a response. The Mark II has a palmer-hackled body. Even better is the parachute version.

DRESSING

Hook: 14–18 Code L3A or E6A.
Thread: Brown.
Tail: Pale cream cock fibres.
Body: Cream cock hackle stalk.
Hackle: Top quality glassy pale-cream cock wound at the shoulder, or palmered, or in parachute style.

2 Olive Parachute

COMMENT

This is an olive-green parachute fly that represents many natural olives and is also a good representation of an emerger. The parachute hackle ensures that the floss body stays in the film and, depending on how long and thick it is tied, the floss-fibred tail can represent the nymphal shuck. Even though the hackle is on top of the body, the hackle style offers a good copy of the silhouette of the spread legs of the natural supporting itself on the surface.

DRESSING

Hook: 14–16 Code L3A, E1A or E6A.
Tail: Olive-green floss fibres.
Body: Olive-green floss.
Rib: Finest gold or copper-coloured wire.
Hackle: Green cock in parachute style.

1 Enigma **2** Olive Parachute **3** Coch-y-bonddhu **4** Driffield Dun
5 Blanchard's Abortion **6** Sanctuary **7** Treacle Parkin
8 Red Butt Brownie

3 Coch-y-bonddhu

COMMENT

This is an old Welsh beetle dressing. It is open to debate which beetle it is meant to imitate, and so is its spelling. Moc Morgan, an authority on Welsh trout flies, insists upon Coch-a-bon-ddu but most fishing books use this spelling so I'll stick with it. A rough translation of the Welsh is 'red with black trunk'. The beetle imitated is probably *Phyllopertha horticola*, a common summer species with a reddish-brown body and legs and a dark peacock-green thorax. It is a good reliable fly on many rough streams fished either wet (on the top dropper) or dry.

DRESSING

Hook: 12–16 Code A, G3A or E6A.
Thread: Black or brown.
Tip (optional): Flat gold tinsel.
Body: Peacock herl.
Hackle: Coch-y-bonddhu (natural red with black centre and tips).

4 Driffield Dun

COMMENT

The history of this pattern is obscured by time but it was no doubt named after the Driffield chalk stream. Driffield born angling historian Donald Overfield suggests that the fly is of most use on its home waters when pale wateries are hatching. The wing and hackle would help to imitate these but the mole's fur body is dark. But who can say what trout make of flies? We make too much of trout intelligence and I'm sure most trout are not so selective of the fly pattern as we like to believe.

DRESSING

Hook: 14–16 Code L3A or E6A.
Thread: Yellow.
Tail: Ginger cock fibres.
Body: Mole's fur.
Rib: Yellow thread.
Wing: Pale starling wing (alternative is upright bunched grey hackle fibres, or light-grey poly yarn, as illustrated).
Hackle: Ginger cock.

5 Blanchard's Abortion

COMMENT

This is a popular fly originating in the north-west. It was named after its creator, who managed a Manchester tackle shop. The story is that some thirty or more years ago, whilst fishing the River Dane, Blanchard hurriedly tied on a fly using a turle knot and accidentally caught some of the hackle fibres in a knot loop, forcing them forwards like a forward wing. It caught fish when others were failing. Blanchard's friends named this fluke dressing for him. It is an excellent general pattern. The original had a rabbit's fur body ribbed with gold but now pheasant tail is more common.

DRESSING

Hook: 10–14 Code A, L3A or E6A.
Thread: Olive or claret.
Tail: Natural medium-red cock fibres.
Body: Pheasant tail herls.
Wing: A single forward-sloping bunch of light-brown or ginger cock fibres.
Hackle: Natural medium-red cock.

6 Sanctuary

COMMENT

I'm almost tempted into suggesting that it is difficult to tie a dry fly with a hare's ear body that won't take fish. Dr Thomas Sanctuary's pattern, now a century old, is a very good general pattern. I have found it an excellent September and October fly. Sanctuary was closely associated with Marryat, Halford and Hall, all three important figures in the history of dry-fly fishing. In later life he lived at Scarborough and fished the streams that run off the North Yorkshire Moors. I can vouch for its effectiveness on these waters.

DRESSING

Hook: 14 Code L3A or E6A.
Thread: Primrose.
Body: Dark hare's ear fur.
Rib: Fine flat gold tinsel.
Hackle: Coch-y-bonddhu.

7 Treacle Parkin

COMMENT

This is clearly a Red Tag variant with an orange, or more usually a yellow, wool tag. The uninitiated may scorn the need for such a simple variation but it can make a very big difference. The Red Tag is a very modest trout fly; the Treacle Parkin can be a killer on its day, for both trout and grayling, fished either wet or dry. As a youngster embarking on my first season's fly fishing I was informed by a fly fisher of forty years' experience of northern streams that a Treacle Parkin, Sturdy's Fancy and John Storey would kill trout and grayling from April until November and that I needed no others.

DRESSING

Hook: 14–18 Code L3A or E6A.
Thread: Black.
Tag: Yellow or orange wool (or poly yarn on the floater).
Body: Peacock herl.
Hackle: Natural red cock.

8 Red Butt Brownie

COMMENT

This is primarily a grayling fly inspired by the Red Tag. In this variant the red butt is smaller than that on the Tag and therefore less of a distraction to trout. As a trout fly it is more useful than the Red Tag and more likely to catch trout if it is fished where both species are surface-feeding. Also, the tail fibres ensure that the red butt does not touch the surface and offers a more accurate impression of a dun. I have used it with success for brown and rainbow trout and grayling. It was devised by Peter Duinmeyer.

DRESSING

Hook: 14–16 Code L3A or E6A.
Thread: Black.
Tail: Natural light-red cock fibres.
Butt: Bright red or scarlet-dyed feather fibres.
Body: Peacock herl.
Hackle: Medium-red game or furnace cock.

General Dry Flies 2

To argue that fly tying is an art is emotive, and to my mind questionable. Tying to dupe trout is a craft; dressing to please the human eye is, an art. It becomes inevitable that flies are tied for reasons other than fishing. The mixing, blending and interweaving of fur and feather to imitate a natural insect calls for some dexterity and a little knowledge of entomology. It may seem to some that hair, fur and feather are fast fading from the scene and the fly tyer's materials are now, to use a borrowed phrase, vinyl, nylon and polypropylene. There is no doubt that the modern fly dresser should make use of suitable synthetic materials but for many dressings there is no substitute for the properties of animal fur and bird plumage. May I suggest that it is the judicious and selective use of synthetics to supplement the natural materials that will create the most effective flies. When we build rigid models of nymphs and adult flies as is done in some vices it is time to backtrack and consider what fly tying is all about.

1 Wickham's Fancy

COMMENT

For over a hundred years the different versions of this pattern have been used as a wet fly and a floater. As a river fly it is best used as a floater in its smaller sizes and has always been regarded as a useful pattern when trout and grayling are smutting. The main variant is the Olive Wickham, which uses olive cock hackle for the tail fibres and head and body hackle.

DRESSING

Hook: 14–18 Code L3A or E6A.
Thread: Brown.
Tail: Ginger cock fibres or guinea-fowl dyed reddish-brown.
Body: Flat gold tinsel.
Body hackle: Palmered ginger-red cock.
Rib: Fine gold wire.
Wing: Medium starling set upright.
Hackle: Ginger-red cock.

2 Ginger Quill

COMMENT

For over a century the Ginger Quill has been a reliable dressing whenever any of the paler flies are hatching. The spurwings, pale wateries and pale evening duns can all be represented with this pattern. Its age is betrayed by its quill body, which offers no translucency and allows no transmitted light, but in reflected light accurately imitates the natural's segmented abdomen. Most dressings call for wings of light starling primaries but a more lifelike solution than opaque starling is pale blue-dun hackle tips or bunched fibres tied upright.

DRESSING

Hook: 14–16 Code L3A or E6A.
Thread: Brown.
Tail: Ginger cock fibres.
Body: Natural peacock eye quill.
Wing (optional): Starling or pale blue-dun hackle tips or fibres (*see* text).
Hackle: Ginger cock (optionally a blue-dun cock may be wound through the ginger on the wingless dressing).

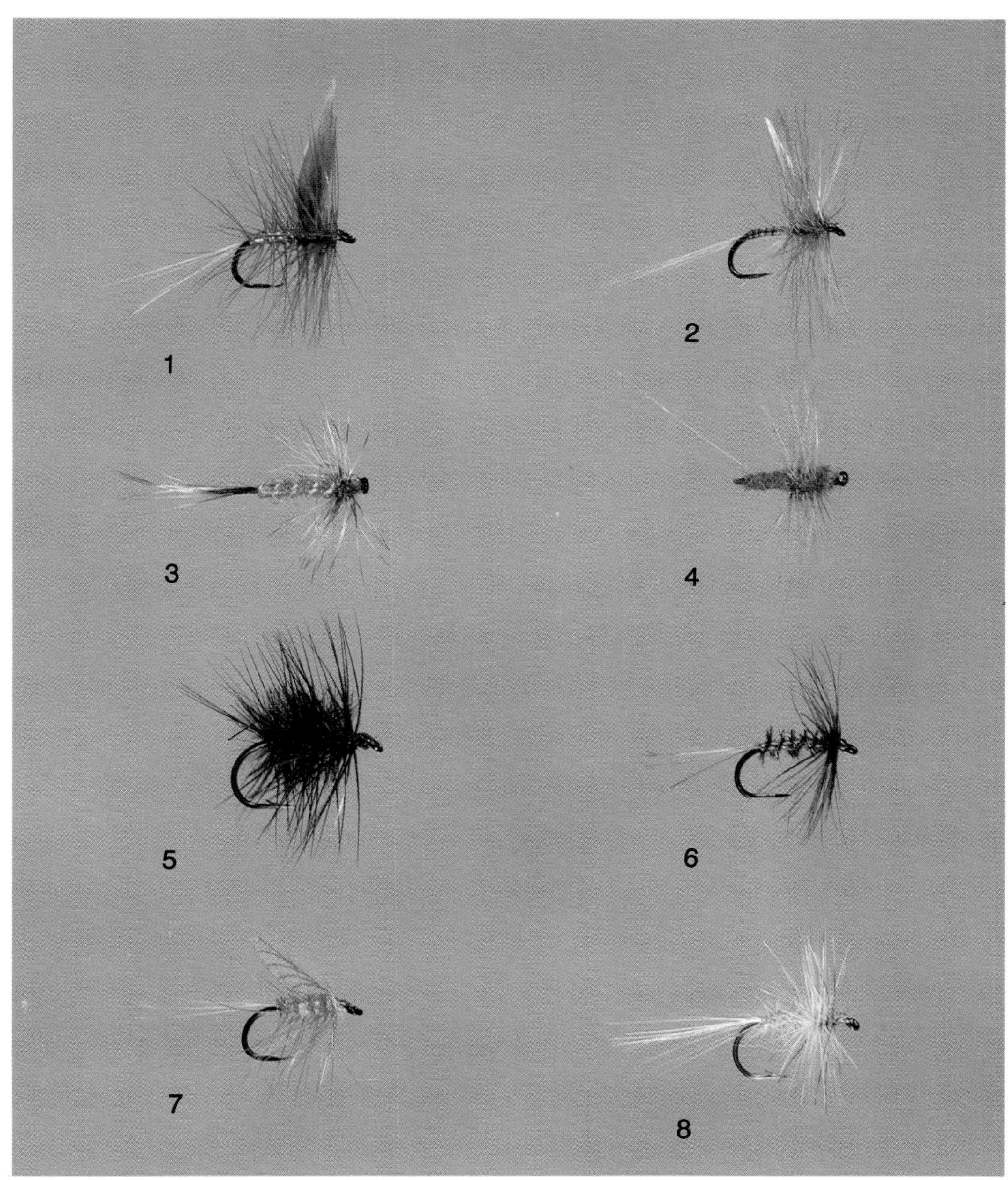

1 Wickham's Fancy **2** Ginger Quill **3** Amber Spinner
4 Sunset Spinner **5** Black Palmer **6** Furnace
7 Roman Moser Dun (Olive) **8** White Grizzly

3 Amber Spinner

COMMENT

The spent female pale watery and spurwing spinners are well represented by Roger Fogg's dressing. Because it is a spent dressing it is most appropriately fished in the early morning or late evening and best between late April and July on the smooth glides. Like all spent dressings it should be fished low in the film and in a straight drift. Trout rising to spent spinners on the glides often remain just below the surface and quietly pick off flies that come into their window. Because that window is relatively small, they rarely move far to intercept food. The artificial must be accurately presented.

DRESSING

Hook: 12–16 Code L3A.
Thread: Amber or orange.
Tail: Cree cock fibres.
Body: Amber seal's fur substitute.
Rib: Amber thread or marabou floss.
Hackle: Generous turns of cree cock with the upper and lower fibres cut away.

4 Sunset Spinner

COMMENT

A red sunset can pose problems for the fly fisher. Any surface fly that is even slightly translucent takes on a reddish glow when viewed from below the surface. Charles Jardine has devised this spinner dressing to represent a wide range of species. With their abdomens drained of much of their colour, the differences between female spinners of various species are insignificant; it is size and the reddish tinge that are the triggers to the rise.

DRESSING

Hook: 14–18 Code L3A, L4A or E1A.
Thread: Maroon.
Tail: Two white nylon paintbrush bristles (Artist's Daler Oil #8 or 10) widely spaced.
Body: Well mixed and blended rust/orange Poly II, red–brown Poly II and red Burgess body gloss or Antron in the proportions 5:4:1.
Rib (optional): Lurex, Lureflash or Flashabou.
Wings: Two good quality blue-dun cock hackles wound together through the thorax an clipped in a V top and bottom, with the option of two strands of Pearl Twinkle, tied spent.

5 Palmer Series (Black Palmer)

COMMENT

Palmering a hackle down the length of the body is one of the earliest styles of tying a trout fly and one which we still have good reason to use today. Whether it is used in a subsurface fly, awash in the film, or as a floating pattern, the hackle fibres give the fly an impression of movement – and, with movement, of life, the attribute most difficult to imitate in an artificial fly. As floaters they best represent sedges; as wet flies, nymphs; in the film, emerging upwingeds or sedges. Tie in a wide range of colours and sizes to match the naturals.

DRESSING

Hook: 12–18 Code A, E1A, L2A, L3A, E6A as appropriate.
Thread: Black.
Body: Black ostrich herl.
Hackle: Palmered black cock.
Rib: Fine gold wire.

6 Furnace

COMMENT

Halford rated this highly for the chalk streams, describing it as 'a very favourite hot weather pattern'. I've not fished it under those circumstances but it may well be worth a try because success with a dry fly in the heat of a summer's day can be hard to achieve. Contemporary writers have also praised it and others rate it highly for chalkstream winter grayling. I don't know why the tail fibres should be optional; a fly of this style is much better balanced and a better floater if tails are included.

DRESSING

Hook: 14–16 Code L3A or E6A.
Thread: Light-brown.
Tail (optional): Furnance cock fibres.
Body: Orange floss.
Rib: Peacock sword feather herl.
Hackle: Furnance cock.

7 Roman Moser Dun

COMMENT

The Austrian fly fisher and excellent fly dresser Roman Moser has devised a series of pre-made translucent wings for upwinged duns, sedges and stoneflies. Each is shaped to be tied upright, roof-shaped or flat across the back in the manner of each natural. They are available in a range of sizes and in different natural shades and any dressing can be adapted to include the appropriate wing. They are marketed by Traun River Products. This is a general olive dun dressing.

DRESSING

Hook: 12–14 Code L3A, E6A or CS20.
Thread: Yellow.
Tail: Light-ginger cock fibres.
Body: Natural or synthetic olive dubbing.
Rib: Finest gold wire through the hackle.
Wing: Preformed dun wing.
Hackle: Palmered light-ginger cock with the upper fibres trimmed away.

8 White Grizzly

COMMENT

This is a fly of Michael Leighton's, designed with the Welsh border waters in mind, though it has been used more widely on freestone and chalk streams. It is regarded as an effective pale watery imitation, particularly for the often dour days after the mayfly hatch has died away. Like many border patterns it carries two hackles: first, to float well on the riffles and, second to produce the impression of a wing by the variegated effect of the grizzle hackle.

DRESSING

Hook: 14–16 Code L4A.
Thread: Orange.
Tail: Honey cock fibres.
Body: White rabbit's fur dyed a very pale honey shade.
Rib: One strand of golden yellow multi-strand floss closely wound.
Hackles: Grizzle cock with a pale badger cock wound behind, through and in front.

General Dry Flies 3

In the search for the successful fly at a particular moment it is tempting to hurry through the fly box and offer everything that looks suitable. I try to control this naive urge; I should know better. Having satisfied myself that my presentation of the fly is acceptable and my choice of fly pattern has a reasonable chance of success, I prefer to persevere. More often than not it is the size of the fly that is the critical factor. Even a hook size difference can represent a huge disparity to fish able to make a close scrutiny. If the pattern ought to work but doesn't, try a size or two smaller. It is often the answer. Most autopsies reveal many more small flies than big ones. On fast water where fish need a good view of the fly, move up a size; make it worth their while rising.

1 Parody

COMMENT

I've enjoyed a dozen seasons with this general dry fly and it has served me well in the late season for trout and into November as a grayling fly. It isn't very suggestive of any natural duns other than by its overall shape and size but it has done well as a search fly or cast to fish that are only intermittent risers.

DRESSING

Hook: 14–16 Code L3A or E6A.
Thread: Orange.
Tag: Yellow wool, poly yarn or floss.
Body: Mixed orange and claret seal's fur substitute (2:1).
Rib: Fine gold tinsel.
Hackle: Grizzle cock.

2 Pepper's Own

COMMENT

Pepper's Own first received a national airing when Richard Walker praised it highly in *Trout and Salmon* and later in a book. It has gone on to become a firm favourite with many northern trout and grayling fishers. It was originally devised in 1971 by Tony Pepper for fast water but it has proved to be equally effective on the slower chalk streams of Hampshire and Wiltshire. Richard Walker's first trial of it produced a dozen fish and a fine two pound grayling. The second honey grizzle hackle gives a useful variegated effect.

DRESSING

Hook: 14–16 Code L3A or E6A.
Thread: Purple.
Tail: Three strands of cock pheasant tail, about twice the body length.
Body: Cock pheasant tail herls.
Rib: Red silk.
Hackle: Natural red cock with a honey grizzle nearest the eye.

1 Parody **2** Pepper's Own **3** Ginger Dun **4** Grey Spinner **5** Eureka
6 Silver Sedge **7** Cree Duster **8** Orange Quill

3 Ginger Dun

COMMENT

This is a useful fly when the paler olives and other small pale flies are hatching. The example illustrated is tied on a size 22 hook and looks rather overdressed for the size. Tied in this way with the tail fibres pointing downwards and with an oversized hackle, the small body is held well clear of the surface. Thus it gives a very good impression of the delicately balanced dun. Dressed in this way flies can fool trout that are proving reluctant to take an artificial. The only drawback is that hooking them can be a problem.

DRESSING

Hook: 14–22 Code L3A or E6A.
Thread: Orange.
Tail: Pale blue-dun cock fibres.
Body: Ginger polypropylene dubbing.
Wing: Two pale blue-dun cock hackle tips slightly split and tilting back slightly.
Hackle: Ginger cock.

4 Grey Spinner

COMMENT

It is quite feasable to represent the female spinner at the moment of landing on the surface with a fly with a fully wound hackle. Patterns like the Pheasant Tail have been doing it successfully for generations. The ovipositing fly needs the rear of the body in the film and the fully spent female needs to be flush on the surface without a fully wound hackle to support it. This is a general pattern to represent the lighter coloured spinners when they are returning. A quick solution to copying the spent female is to clip away the lower hackle fibres flat in line with the body.

DRESSING

Hook: 14–18 L3A.
Thread: Light-brown or black.
Tail: Light-brown cock fibres or widely spaced Microfibetts.
Body: Grey Australian opossum or grubby cream seal's fur substitute.
Rib: Black thread.
Hackle: Sandy-dun cock or light-honey-dun.

5 Eureka

COMMENT

'I've found it!' How often must that have been muttered when at long last after an evening of frustration, when rising trout have refused each artificial, the successful pattern is found. Pat Russell experienced some very difficult Test trout on late summer evenings. What finally cracked the problem was this spinner pattern, which offers a good view of the green egg ball of some species. The wings are in the correct upright position; they are only spent after the egg ball is released. Pat's first choice spinner imitation is a parachute fly but if those fail then this does the trick.

DRESSING

Hook: 18 Code E1A.
Egg ball: Green thread.
Tail: Rhode Island Red cock fibres.
Body: Olive-dyed stripped peacock eye stalk.
Wing: Starling.
Hackle: Blackish hen.

6 Silver Sedge (Duinmeyer)

COMMENT

In addition to the many sedge patterns I've included elsewhere I felt I ought to find space to include this one from Peter Duinmeyer. It is a good pattern to represent the paler sedges and is an excellent floater because of its body of wound polypropylene yarn. Because of the body buoyancy, the lower hackle fibres can be cut away so that the fly lies in the film to represent one of the species that oviposits in this way. Other species can be represented by varying the body and wing colours.

DRESSING

Hook: 10–16 Code L2A.
Thread: Black.
Body: White polypropylene yarn.
Tip: Oval or round gold tinsel.
Wing: A bunch of mallard breast fibres.
Hackle: Generous turns of golden badger.

7 Cree Duster

COMMENT

I've always regarded this fly as a cross between a Grey Duster and an Adams, two of the very best dry flies and no mean parentage. Roger Fogg developed it for stillwater use but it is also a very good river pattern under a range of circumstances. Like its two forebears, this offspring is readily accepted by surface feeding fish and they seem to see in it whatever they are looking for.

DRESSING

Hook: 14 Code L3A or E6A.
Thread: Brown.
Tail: Cree cock fibres.
Body: Mixed pale-blue rabbit's underfur and hare's ear fur, tied fairly short.
Hackle: Three turns of two cree cock hackles, tied back to back, dull sides facing each other.

8 Orange Quill

COMMENT

At first glance this orange-bodied fly would not pass for a blue-winged olive, but as a late evening fly it is sometimes exceptional and rated by some fly fishers as the best imitation of that fly. The dressing is sometimes attributed to G. E. M. Skues but it wasn't devised by him, though he was responsible for its popularity. Some dressings are hot orange, others darker. Part of its success may be due to the orange hue surrounding all natural flies on the surface when there is a red sunset. This in part explains its success in the late evening. Others have suggested that it is taken as the female spinner.

DRESSING

Hook: 12–16 Code A, L3A or E6A.
Thread: Orange.
Tail: Natural red cock fibres.
Body: Stripped quill dyed hot orange or dark orange.
Wing: Pale starling set upright.
Hackle: Natural dark-red cock.

West Country and General Dry Flies

The design of some patterns clearly indicates their regional origin. The stiff, bright, steely hackles on many West Country patterns were once a feature of the locality. Whether the flies were fished wet or dry, they included the same stiff hackles for the rough and tumble streams. The wet flies were in complete contrast to the soft-hackled northern flies; they seem less subtle than the delicate northern counterparts. The West Country fish wanted something meaty. Few specialist West Country flies are still widely used except the Beacon Beige and those below. The local trout are obliging enough with the nationally acclaimed patterns.

1 Blue Upright

COMMENT

R. S. Austin was a well known fly tyer of his day and contributed a number of regional patterns, some of which received a wider following, often through the writings of Skues. This dressing is usually fished as a large dark olive or iron blue dun imitation but is also sometimes fished wet. Skues suggested that the lighter olives could also be represented by replacing the tail and hackle with pale honey-dun materials, but that would rather detract from the name and the modified fly really ought to be called something else. In addition to the Blue Upright below, black, olive and red variations are tied.

DRESSING

Hook: 12–18 Code L3A, E6A or A.
Tail: Medium-blue-dun hackle fibres.
Body: Well marked peacock eye quill.
Hackle: Medium-blue-dun cock.

2 Half Stone

COMMENT

This started off as a wet fly, probably best fished as an emerging dun just below the surface or as a sedge pupa swimming to the surface. It is now more widely used as a general floater. In the same manner as the Blue Upright, a lighter-coloured version is tied with a honey-dun hackle and tail fibres. This is known as the Honey Half Stone.

DRESSING

Hook: 12–16 Code L3A, E6A or A.
Thread: Cream.
Tail: Blue-dun cock fibres.
Body: Rear two-thirds, yellow floss; front third, mole's fur.
Hackle: Blue-dun cock wound at the shoulder or palmered over the mole's fur.

1 Blue Upright **2** Half Stone **3** Tup's Indispensable **4** Infallible
5 Burnt-Wing BWO **6** Wonderwing Stonefly **7** Everybody's Caddis
8 Rolf's Fly

3 Tup's Indispensable

COMMENT

There is probably no more famous West Country fly than R. S. Austin's unusual dressing dating back to 1900. The thorax dubbing originally included the fur from around a ram's testicles but this is replaced today by any fine white fur or a ready-made 'Tup's' mixture. Skues was responsible for the crimson seal's fur addition. The extremely rare yellow-spangled lightish-blue cock hackle called for is now replaced with a somewhat commoner hackle. Austin suggested that it was a female olive spinner imitation. It also sometimes works well for the paler upwingeds.

DRESSING

Hook: 14–16 Code L3A or E6A.
Thread: Yellow.
Tail: Honey-dun cock.
Body: Rear half, yellow floss silk; front half, a mixture of white, cream, yellow and crimson seal's fur substitute.
Hackle: Honey-dun cock.

4 Infallible

COMMENT

Alas, no fly could live up to this name. However, I am reliably informed that when the iron blues are hatching this is a suitable pattern and is a useful general fly even when no iron blues are about. It is another of the West Country patterns that can be fished both above and below the surface.

DRESSING

Hook: 14–16 Code L3A or A.
Thread: Claret or crimson.
Tail: Dark-blue-dun fibres.
Body: Mole's fur with a tip of tying thread exposed at the rear.
Hackle: Dark-blue-dun cock (dry) or hen (wet).

5 Burnt-Wing Blue-Winged Olive

COMMENT

The burnt-wing method of winging a dry fly originated in North America but has never really caught on in the UK, probably because of the longer than normal tying process. Ian Warrilow, a professional fly dresser from Birmingham, rates the style very highly and ties this blue-winged olive version. The wing feathers are a Metz colour and taken from the top of a saddle cape, with each having a good webby triangular base. These are burned in a wing burner and the two matched wings are tied in so that they curve outwards.

DRESSING

Hook: 14 Code L3A.
Thread: Olive.
Tail: Olive cock fibres.
Body: Brown-olive goose or swan herl.
Rib (optional): Olive thread.
Wing: Dark dun spade feathers burnt to shape (*see* text), tied in before the body and hackle.
Hackle: Olive cock, optionally clipped level with the hook point.

6 Wonderwing Stonefly

COMMENT

The adult stoneflies are an important surface fly on many Welsh border and northern freestone rivers when the females return to lay their eggs. This winging style comes from an American, Chauncy Lively, and imitates some of their smaller species. The wing is made from part of a single hackle. By one of a number of ways the hackle fibres are pulled back and the wing feather tied in flat. It is strengthened by a fine coat of clear varnish. Different-coloured materials can be used to match various stoneflies and flat-winged terrestrials. This is a small stonefly or needle fly dressing.

DRESSING

Hook: 12–18 Code L3A, E1A or 22 Code K12ST.
Thread: Hot orange.
Body: Dubbed fur or polypropylene (Fly-Rite rust #5)
Wing: Dark-red game cock spade hackle.
Rear hackle: Dark-red game cock with the upper fibres trimmed.
Front hackle: Dark-red game cock fully wound.

7 Everybody's Caddis

COMMENT

Larry Duckwall is probably America's finest tyer of classical trout flies. He doesn't just tie the classics but has a few of his own patterns to his credit. He calls this the Everybody's Caddis because he acknowledges that he has taken some of the best ideas from everybody else – from Leiser, LaFontaine, Goddard and others – and combined them in one dressing. Do all these experts know they've co-operated to jointly devise a supersedge? The dun cock used in the darker version is a Metz colour but the higher grade hackles are not necessary as the lower fibres are cut away.

DRESSING

Hook: 12–20 Code L3A.
Body: Dubbed natural or synthetic fur.
Wing: Elk mane fibres.
Hackle: Dun cock for the dark-bodied fly; ginger or cream on the lighter version, with the lower fibres trimmed in line with the body.
Antennae: Hackle stalks.

8 Rolf's Fly

COMMENT

I've done quite well with this little fly in the single season that I've tried it on the Yorkshire rivers. Rolf Pasteuning tied it for late summer trout and grayling on the Continent and it has caught its fair share of grayling for me on warm sunny October days. I think its size is critical and I've not caught any fish when I've used hooks larger than size 18. I have also varied the body colours slightly, using different natural colours, and each has met with some success.

DRESSING

Hook: 16–18 Code L3A or E6A.
Thread: Grey.
Tail: Light ginger or grey cock fibres.
Body: Dampened natural or coloured raffia.
Hackle: Badger or grizzle cock.

American Classics 1

Initially the trade in trout fly patterns across the Atlantic was a one-way affair: America took English designs, copied them and used the wide range of indigenous furs and feathers to match their naturals. Beyond our introduction to the dry fly they haven't taken much more from us; they haven't had to, such has been their ingenuity over the last century. The direction of ideas and patterns is now largely reversed: we take more of their patterns than they do of ours. Some of those below are old by American standards but they are used to great effect on British rivers. The Humpy design and the Elk Hair Caddis (page 204) are two of the more recent innovations and are really catching on foı British rivers.

1 Dark Hendrickson

COMMENT

Roy Steenrod devised this and the lighter version in about 1915. Hendrickson was one of Steenrod's customers. Although British rivers have very few duns with wings the colour of these two flies, they are nevertheless effective, the dark version as a useful iron blue imitation.

DRESSING

Hook: 12–16 Code A, L3A or E6A.
Thread: Grey.
Tail: Dark-blue-dun hackle fibres.
Body: Dark-blue-grey fur (original muskrat).
Wing: Barred wood duck fibres set upright and divided (brownish-olive mallard as a substitute).
Hackle: Dark-blue-dun cock.

2 Grey Fox Variant

COMMENT

Preston Jennings, author of the American standard work *A Book of Trout Flies*, devised the original pattern which was later to be amended by Art Flick to this dressing. Flick has so much faith in the fly that he wrote that, if he had to be limited to just one pattern all season, this was it. Because of the longer than normal hackles it is an excellent rough-water fly with good visibility. Whether fished in a straight drift or with imparted drag over the likely fast water lies, it is a very good fly for British rivers and streams.

DRESSING

Hook: 10–14 Code A, L3A or E6A.
Thread: Yellow.
Tail: Honey-dun or ginger cock fibres.
Body: Light-ginger quill (previously well soaked in water).
Hackle: Dark ginger, grizzle, light-ginger cock, mixed and wound in that order, all much longer-fibred than usual.

1 Dark Hendrickson **2** Grey Fox Variant **3** Quill Gordon **4** Adams
5 Light Hendrickson **6** Light Cahill **7** Humpy **8** Royal Humpy

3 Quill Gordon

COMMENT

Theodore Gordon was greatly influenced by Halford, who sent some of his dry flies across the Atlantic to inspire Gordon into dressing floaters for the Eastern streams. This pattern of Gordon's has survived almost ninety years. Various dressings have appeared in print, largely because Gordon regarded it as a pivotal pattern which, with slight modifications in the materials, could be tied to represent a number of naturals. To quote Gordon 'I can vary them to suit'.

DRESSING

Hook: 12–16 Code A, L3A or E6A.
Thread: Cream or light-brown.
Tail: Barred summer duck feather fibres (brownish-olive mallard as a substitute.
Body: Dark stripped well marked peacock quill for spring; lighter-coloured quill for summer.
Wing: Barred summer duck (also known as wood duck) fibres set upright (brownish-olive mallard as a substitute).
Hackle: Smoke-grey cock or dark-blue-dun (spring); or a pale honey-dun (summer).

4 Adams

COMMENT

The Adams is probably North America's most popular fly pattern. It has spawned a score of variants since its creation by Leonard Halliday in 1922. It is reckoned by some to imitate sedges, upwingeds, stoneflies and midges. It has become quite popular on English rivers because of its nondescript dressing and excellent dun silhouette and is a useful olive imitation on our streams. The standard dressing is given opposite but probably the commonest variation is to have spent wings.

DRESSING

Hook: 14–16 Code A, L3A or E6A.
Thread: Grey.
Tail: Mixed grizzle and brown hackle fibres.
Body: Muskrat fur or poly equivalent (blue-grey).
Wing: Two grizzle hackle tips tied upright and slightly divided.
Hackle: Mixed grizzle and brown cock.

5 Light Hendrickson

COMMENT

This, the original of Steenrod's two dressings, was tied to represent the female dun *Ephemerella subvaria*, unknown in the UK. Such was the success of the artificial that its name was adopted as the common name for the natural. Despite the upright slightly split wings, it is a useful general spinner imitation. It won't represent the spent spinners but the newly alighted females with their wings still near vertical can be represented.

DRESSING

Hook: 12–16 Code A, L3A or E6A.
Thread: Brown or grey.
Tail: Light- or medium-blue-dun fibres.
Body: Cream fox fur (lower belly) or tan, olive, and yellow rabbit fur mixture.
Wing: Barred wood duck set upright and slightly divided (brownish-olive mallard as a substitute).
Hackle: Light- or medium-blue-dun cock.

6 Light Cahill

COMMENT

The original Cahill produced two better and more widely used variants, the Light and Dark Cahills, of which this is probably the most popular on American rivers. All were devised by New York railroad worker Daniel Cahill in the 1880s. On British rivers it is effective for the lighter upwingeds such as the pale wateries, spurwings and pale evening dun.

DRESSING

Hook: 14–16 Code A, L3A or E6A.
Thread: Yellow or tan.
Tail: Cream or light-ginger cock fibres.
Body: Creamy fox fur or seal's fur substitute.
Wing: Barred wood duck flank or breast fibres tied upright and slightly divided.
Hackle: Light-ginger, cream or buff cock.

7 Humpy or Goofus Bug

COMMENT

The Humpy is a variant of the Horner's Deer Hair, devised by Jack Horner of San Francisco. I had read about the Humpy in American fly books but it wasn't until I visited some of the USA's best trout fishing in Montana, Idaho and Wyoming and saw the Humpy in action for myself that I decided it was well worth a test on British waters. It has done exceedingly well. It is probably taken for an adult or emerging sedge or, in its smaller sizes, an emerging upwinged. The usual body colour is yellow.

DRESSING

Hook: 10–18 Code A, L2A or E1A.
Thread: Black, brown, red or yellow to match the body colour.
Tail: Tan elk or moose hair, or tips of the deer hair body fibres.
Body: Floss, or tying thread overlaid with an overbody of tan deer body hair, which is tied in overlong for the wing fibres.
Wing: A bunch of the back fibres set upright and slightly divided.
Hackle: Mixed grizzle and natural red cocks.

8 Royal Humpy

COMMENT

This Humpy variant was created in 1972 by Jack Dennis of Jackson Hole, Wyoming, and Charlie Ridenhauer. It is mainly a fast-water attractor with very good floatability and visibility. Jack Dennis is an excellent fly tyer and his two books, *Western Trout Fly Tying Manual, I and II*, have sold over 300,000 copies. His tackle store is the best I have ever been in. It is a vast superb display of everything to interest the game fisher, from fly-tying materials to beautiful angling paintings and prints. I doubt if we have a shop in Britain that approaches half his stock.

DRESSING

Hook: 10–16 Code A, L2A or E1A.
Thread: Red monocord.
Tail: Dark moose hair.
Body: Red monocord (yellow or green variants) with light-grey or black deer hair as an overbody.
Wing: White calf tail, upright and divided.
Hackle: Blue-dun, brown, badger, grizzle or cree cock.

American Classics 2

It is probably inevitable that a nation that has a population of more than a million committed fly fishers and scores of thousands of miles of trout waters will produce some of the best patterns and tying innovations. Lee Wulff's dressing is one major theme that has been taken up the world over. Individuals such as Hewitt, Troth, Schweibert, LaFontaine, Swisher, Richards, Lively, Darbee, Betts, and others have devised flies or techniques or made use of new materials which have later been adopted in Europe. Perhaps Europe has benefited most from the use of synthetic materials, which are included in patterns in other sections.

1 Grey Wulff

COMMENT

One of the world's best known trout and salmon anglers, Lee Wulff devised this series in the spring of 1930. Sixty years later they are widely used across the world wherever trout rise to the dry fly. Most of the series are also used where dry-fly fishing for Atlantic salmon is popular. The mark of any really successful fly is that it produces variants of one sort or another or its style or use of materials is incorporated in other patterns. The Wulff style has been copied more than any other. This is an excellent mayfly spinner imitation.

DRESSING

Hook: 10–18 Code A, L2A, E6A or E1A.
Thread: Black.
Tail: Brown calf tail.
Body: Grey rabbit fur, or muskrat or synthetic substitute.
Wing: Natural brown calf tail or deer hair tips tied upright and divided.
Hackle: Blue-dun cock.

2 White Wulff

COMMENT

Just as an all-black fly is what trout sometimes need before they'll rise, occasionally it is the all-white floater that does the trick. Perhaps it is a question of shock tactics for the non-riser, in which case the White Wulff might be the required stimulus. As well as being a useful dusk pattern as a moth imitation that both trout and fly fisher can see, it can also represent the mayfly spinner. Except in the smaller sizes all the Wulff series may need more than one hackle.

DRESSING

Hook: 10–18 Code A, E1A, E6A or L2A.
Thread: White.
Tail: White bucktail or calf tail.
Body: Creamy-white wool or fur.
Wing: White calf tail or bucktail, upright and divided.
Hackle: Badger cock.

1 Grey Wulff **2** White Wulff **3** Royal Wulff **4** Blonde Wulff
5 Grizzly Wulff **6** Golden Double Wing **7** Royal Coachman
8 Rat-Faced MacDougall

3 Royal Wulff

COMMENT

This fly very much falls into the attractor class and is most frequently used on fast water. In the flat calm water that poses the most difficult problems for the dry-fly fisher, trout have a clear and leisurely view of the surface fly and their reluctance to take an artificial is well known. Sometimes their shyness can be overcome if they are offered a small attractor pattern such as a size 16 or 18 Royal Wulff or Royal Coachman. For the smaller size white goat hair wings are more suitable.

DRESSING

Hook: 10–18 Code A, E1A, E6A or L2A.
Thread: Brown or black.
Tail: Brown deer body hair, or bucktail or calf tail.
Body: Peacock herl with a band of red floss silk in the centre.
Wing: White calf tail or bucktail, upright and divided.
Hackle: Dark-brown cock.

4 Blonde Wulff

COMMENT

Lee Wulff devised the series because he was dissatisfied with the delicate dry flies of the time. He writes: 'Those dry flies had only the barest wrappings of silk or quill around the hook-shank. I didn't think they offered much meat to a hungry trout and wanted something that had as much body as a good greendrake or a terrestrial, so I beefed up the bodies, and needing a better floating material for a heavier body than the feathered tails of the time, used bucktail for durability and strength on both tails and wings'.

DRESSING

Hook: 10–18 Code A, E1A, E6A or L2A.
Thread: Tan or black.
Tail: Tan elk hair or bleached ginger mink guard hair.
Body: Light-tan fur.
Wing: Tan elk hair or bleached ginger mink guard hair, tied upright and divided.
Hackle: Light-ginger cock.

5 Grizzly Wulff

COMMENT

Lee Wulff comments: 'Essentially the Wulff series is a category of flies rather than a particular pattern or patterns'. The style can be copied to colour match the natural flies or whatever the local trout find attractive. Others in the series include brown and black versions. Sometimes the wings are tied forward-slanting and they work very well. However, Lee Wulff emphasised to me that for the true Wulffs the wings must be vertical. This too is a passable mayfly dressing.

DRESSING

Hook: 10–18 Code A, E1A, E6A or L2A.
Thread: Brown or black.
Tail: Brown calf tail or bucktail.
Body: Pale-yellow floss.
Wing: Brown calf tail or bucktail, tied upright and divided.
Hackle: Mixed brown and grizzle cock.

6 Golden Double Wing

COMMENT

The Double Wings are a new series of attractors from Gary LaFontaine and not surprisingly they have the hint of a caddis about them. Gary comments that they are a series of flies to be tied in a range of colours and that they have a number of attributes. The body hackle gives it some stability on the water and the impression of legs. The trout viewing it from below sees through the hackle fibres to the translucent body and beyond through the dyed or natural deer or elk hair and white overwing to a prismatic blend of colour.

DRESSING

Hook: 10–14 Code A, L2A or L3A.
Thread: Orange.
Body: Mixed brown dubbing of golden Sparkle Yarn and brown fur.
Body hackle: Dyed red cock, clipped top and bottom.
Underwing: Pale yellowy-orange deer or elk hair.
Overwing: White calf tail, slightly longer than the underwing.

7 Royal Coachman

COMMENT

When the wet Coachman crossed the Atlantic Theodore Gordon adapted it to a dry fly and in the 1870s John Haily added the red silk band to create the distinctive feature on all Royal patterns. Since then a dozen or more variations have followed. The usual wing is upright and divided white duck quill sections but white hackle-tip wings are also used. The Royal Trude Coachman has a white calf-tail wing over the body extending to the middle of the tail.

DRESSING

Hook: 12–16 Code A, E1A, E6A or L2A.
Thread: Brown.
Tail: Golden pheasant tippet fibres.
Body: Peacock herl with a red floss centre band.
Wing: White duck quill sections, upright and divided, or white calf-tail.
Hackle: Brown.

8 Rat-Faced MacDougall

COMMENT

This is very similar to the Irresistible series and is a variant of them from Harry Darbee of New York. The buoyant deer hair body makes it almost unsinkable and a good fast-water pattern, when its meaty silhouette brings trout to the surface.

DRESSING

Hook: 10–14 Code A, E1A, E6A or L2A.
Tail: Deer hair or ginger cock fibres.
Body: Light-tan-grey deer hair spun and clipped so that it tapers to the tail.
Wing: Light-grizzle hackle tips tied upright and slightly divided.
Hackle: Ginger cock.

Alternative Dry-Fly Styles 1

Over the years some thoughtful fly fishers and fly tyers have tried to improve upon the design of the 'standard' floating fly. Many of the new designs were created with selective trout in mind – the 1 per cent in the stream which have become wise to the usual flies and view with suspicion each floating dun and imitation. Some theories have disappeared in the same manner as the resulting flies sank beneath the surface; some designs are rediscovered again with each new generation of anglers; relatively few are truly innovative. Some of the few genuinely new designs have risen high on a wave of publicity and have enjoyed a certain amount of success. My skill at the vice ensures that in practice, if not theory, my own bias is towards those easiest to tie.

1 Fore and Aft

COMMENT

Horace Brown, a Kennet fly fisher, created this style with a second hackle at the rear of the body. The style has never found great favour over the standard shoulder-hackled patterns. It does have a number of benefits because the body is held away from the surface like a natural dun. One should beware of excessive hackling: too many fibres on the surface create an unnatural light pattern. It is a useful design and has been surprisingly neglected except for mating midge and gnat patterns and a few fast-water flies. The dressing given is a general nondescript fly.

DRESSING

Hook: 12–18 Code A, L3A or E6A.
Rear hackle: Ginger cock.
Body: Natural raffia.
Front hackle: White cock.

2 Reverse Hackle

COMMENT

A few dressings are in regular use with the hackle wound at the rear end of the shank. The purpose is to prevent the point penetrating the film and being visible (doubly so in the trout's mirror), and to minimise the chances of fouling up on foliage on an errant cast. Those dressings that have tail fibres have them tied on top of the shank but I think this can be improved by tying the fibres under the shank. This improves the chances of keeping the body clear of the surface.

DRESSING

Hook: 14–16 up-eye Code L3B or B.
Thread: Brown or pale yellow.
Tail (optional): Blue-dun cock fibres.
Body: Hare's ear fur.
Rib: Fine gold wire.
Hackle: Mixed grizzle and blue-dun cocks.

1 Fore and Aft **2** Reverse Hackle **3** Thorax Dun 1 **4** Thorax Dun 2
5 USD Paradun 1 **6** USD Paradun 2 **7** Loop-Wing Dun
8 Swedish Dry Fly

3 Thorax Dun 1

COMMENT

This design is the work of Vincent Marinaro in the 1940s. He created a fly that holds the body well clear of the surface and offers a realistic light pattern from the two crossed hackles and a clear view of an accurately positioned wing. The resulting fly is very well balanced, with the tail fibres rarely touching the water. Marinaro believed the thorax was a visible feature on the natural dun and emphasised this in his original design. A larger hackle can be used for the one for the rear lower fibres so the fly tilts forward slightly. This is a pale watery dressing.

DRESSING

Hook: 14–18 Code L3A or E6A.
Tail: Four cream cock fibres in two widely spaced groups.
Body: Cream seal's fur substitute or poly dubbing either side of the hackles.
Wing: Cut from the broad webby middle part of two pale-grey neck hackles, tied upright together.
Hackle: Two ginger or honey-dun cocks in a cross shape in the centre of the body.

4 Thorax Dun 2

COMMENT

Marinaro could claim credit for being the first to tie split tails on a dry fly. In later life he modified the thorax style and considerably reduced the thorax and abdomen, replacing them with a single layer of tying thread. At the wing roots a dubbed ball of fur is wound in round the base of the wings. Care should be taken with the choice of wing and the way it is tied in. If they are too stiff and slightly split the fly will spin in casting; they must be close together. An alternative is to cut the wings from the tips of duck breast or small duck covert feathers. This is a general olive imitation.

DRESSING

Hook: 14–18 Code L3A or E6A.
Thread: Dark-olive.
Tail: Two long dark-olive spade fibres or fibres from the hackle used.
Body: Dark-olive thread either side of the hackle and wing.
Wing: Cut from the broad webby middle part of two duck breast feathers.
Thorax: Hare's ear fur wound round the wing roots.
Hackle: Two furnace or Greenwell cocks tied in a cross shape.

5 USD Paradun 1

COMMENT

With this design I think Goddard and Clarke have devised the most accurate imitation of the natural dun. It certainly isn't the easiest fly to tie but for the really pernickety trout it can be just the answer. The parachute hackle supports the body and tails clear from the surface, giving an accurate light pattern without the problem of the hook bend being visible. The wings are cut from cock or hen wing or neck feathers with wing cutters and the tails are widely spaced for balance. A single upright bunch of poly yarn is also a suitable alternative. This is an iron blue imitation.

DRESSING

Hook: 14–18 Code L3A or K5ST Upside-Down hooks.
Thread: Black.
Tails: Iron-blue cock fibres *tied first*.
Body: Iron-blue seal's fur substitute *tied third*.
Wing: Moorhen wing feather from the leading edge or dark grey poly yard *tied second*.
Hackle: Iron-blue cock wound in parachute style *tied fourth*.

6 USD Paradun 2

COMMENT

In larger sizes two or three muskrat or mink whiskers are used for the tails, and in the smaller sizes bunches of hackle fibres are better. In both cases they should be tied so that they stick up in the air in the manner of a natural. John Goddard and Brian Clarke suggest that the wings should be tied with a pronounced outward curve, which has a stabilising effect. In my experience it also makes them spin in the process of casting and I favour fully upright wings. This is a good olive imitation and utilises the ever effective hare's ear body.

DRESSING

Hook: 14–18 Code L3A or K5ST Upside Down hooks.
Thread: Black.
Tail: Fibres of a honey or light-ginger hackle with black tips.
Body: Hare's ear fur.
Wing: Grey goose.
Hackle: Light-ginger or light-Greenwell cock with black tips wound parachute style.

7 Loop-Wing Dun

COMMENT

The loop-wing method was devised by Andre Puyans of San Francisco and offers an attractive and easy-to-tie winging style. Fibres of natural grey or brown or dyed mallard flank or shoulder feather are used. The tips can be used as the tail fibres. The wing fibres are bound onto the top of the shank, are doubled over into a loop the size and approximate shape of the wing, and bound in upright. Then the wing is divided in half and bound in slightly parted. The wing is remarkably durable. This is Nick Bradley's olive dressing.

DRESSING

Hook: 12–16 Code L3A or E6A.
Thread: Brown.
Tail: Olive-dyed mallard flank fibre tips.
Body: Olive-dyed mallard flank fibres.
Rib: Brown thread in opposite turns to the wound body.
Wing: Body fibres looped and slightly parted into two wings.
Hackle: Greenwell cock.

8 Swedish Dry Fly

COMMENT

The Swedish Dry Fly hook is a design of hook that enables the fly tyer to produce an upside-down pattern with the choice of a parachute or shoulder hackle. The shank includes a short vertical length round which a parachute hackle can be wound. The extra shank in front of the hackle base enables a prominent thorax to be tied. Because the shank length is disproportionate to the gape, if you need a 14 normal size shank length then a size 18 Swedish Dry Fly hook is appropriate. This is a large dark olive dressing.

DRESSING

Hook: 14–18 Code K3A.
Thread: Olive or brown.
Tail: Greenwell cock fibres.
Abdomen: Light hare's ear fur from the ear base.
Rib: Fine gold wire.
Thorax: Dark hare's ear fur from the ear tip.
Wing: White poly yarn.
Hackle: Greenwell cock in parachute style.

Alternative Dry-Fly Styles 2

The styles illustrated in these two plates are all system flies and should be adapted with the appropriate materials and hook sizes to match the naturals on the water. Additionally, standard patterns can be tied in these styles, so it is quite possible to have an Adams Funneldun, Loop-wing Coachman or Greenwell Waterwalker.

Take a poll amongst dry-fly fishers and a range of opinions about the best flies for selective fish would result; everyone has his own favourite for difficult trout, with the reasons soundly based on experience. Some styles will work for you and others won't, but those same flies on someone else's leader will have the opposite effect. Don't be afraid to experiment.

1 No-Hackle Dun 1

COMMENT

Carl Richards and Doug Swisher's excellent book *Selective Trout* (1971) launched a new series of dry flies that floated without the aid of a hackle. The authors maintain that the wings and body of the natural fly are the essential triggers to the rise and that the light pattern created by the legs is irrelevant. Their patterns float with the fly body on the surface and offer a clear view of the wings and body to the trout. The best known version is the Sidewinder, with matched duck wing quill slips. This is a dark olive imitation.

DRESSING

Hook: 12–18 fine-wire Code E6A, L3A or L4A.
Thread: Brown.
Tail: Two widely spaced bunches of cream cock fibres tied either side of the shank, separated by a ball of dubbing.
Body: Olive polypropylene dubbing (Fly-Rite #10), dark tan (#20) at the thorax over the wing roots.
Wing: Two grey duck wing quill slips.

2 No-Hackle Dun 2

COMMENT

Alternative winging materials are small duck shoulder feathers, hen hackle tips, shoulder or body feathers. It is important that the feathers offer some width and cock hackle tips are unsuitable. Fly-Rite Poly II is useful for winging as it offers translucency and lightness and is available in a wide range of colours. The Roman Moser Dun wings also offer similar advantages. Over a number of seasons of experimenting with No-Hackles, I am inclined to believe that only the small sizes – 16 and below – offer any advantage. In these sizes the clear view of the wing and body is probably more of a stimulus.

DRESSING

Hook: 14–18 fine-wire Code E6A, L3A or L4A.
Thread: Olive.
Tail: Olive or pale-yellow hackle fibres (see previous dressing).
Body: Olive polypropylene dubbing (Fly-Rite #3).
Wing: Grey or blue-grey Fly-Rite Poly II.

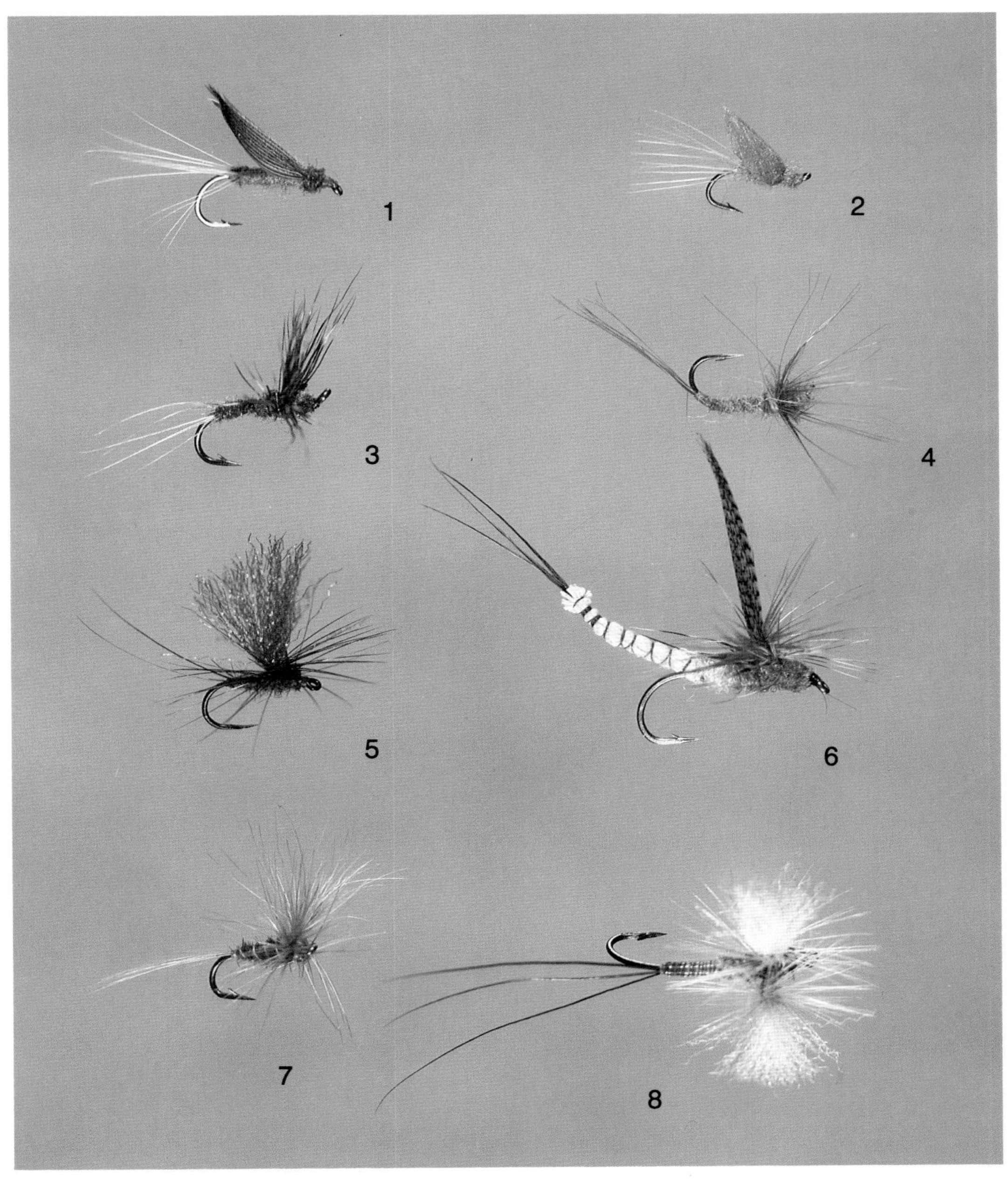

1 No-Hackle Dun 1 **2** No-Hackle Dun 2 **3** Comparadun
4 Funneldun **5** Paradun **6** Paradrake **7** Waterwalker **8** Twiny

3 Comparadun

COMMENT

I am uncertain who devised this style but Al Caucci and Bob Nastasi named the style and offered it as their answer to the closest imitation of the natural dun. The principal feature is the 180-degree wing of deer's face hair, which they felt offered a distinctive silhouette while its breadth simulated the flapping of the natural's wings preceding take-off. I've found that Comparaduns sometimes work very well but at other times fail badly. I suggest that a good wing impression is offered but the light pattern produced by the body in the film is inaccurate. This is an olive imitation.

DRESSING

Hook: 12–18 Code L3A or E6A.
Thread: Olive.
Tail: Widely spaced stiff lemon-dyed cock fibres.
Body: Olive seal's fur substitute or poly dubbing.
Wing: Deer's face hair tied in before the body; bind in the butts and pull tightly on the thread so that the fibres flare, and bind in a semi-circle.

4 Funnelduns

COMMENT

Neil Patterson devised this style. He was impressed with the USD series of Goddard and Clarke but wanted something a little easier to tie. He produced this, I think, quite unique design, utilising the benefits of the upside-down hook. The hackle need not be a high-quality stiff feather as it is 'funnelled' forwards at about 45 degrees with a V cut out on the leg side. A dubbed thorax is wound on between the eye and the hackle before funnelling. Because the resultant fly is longer than normal, tie it on a hook size smaller than usual. A bunch of feather-fibre wings can be added.

DRESSING

Hook: 14–18 Code L3A or E6A.
Thread: Olive.
Tail: Cock fibres tied slightly round the bend.
Body: Seal's fur substitute or poly dubbing with a darker thorax round the hackle roots.
Wing (optional): Bunched hackle or feather fibres.
Hackle: Cock hackle 'funnelled' forwards over the eye with a V cut out on the side that will become the underside.

5 Paradun

COMMENT

The wide-spread tail of two bunches of hackle fibres and the parachute hackle balance the fly very well, but as is often the case with Swisher and Richards' flies there is no concession to the need to keep the body of the fly off the surface in the manner of a natural dun. My own opinion is that the Paraduns are not an outstanding imitation of the fully adult dun. They catch very many fish, but for the wrong reasons! The body in the film makes it an excellent spinner or emerger. The wing material is either hen hackle tips, polypropylene yarn, or a spread clump of hen hackle fibres. This is an iron blue pattern.

DRESSING

Hook: 14–18 Code A, L3A or E6A.
Thread: Crimson.
Tail: Three iron-blue cock hackle fibres divided by turns of thread.
Body: Dubbed mole's fur.
Wing: Dark-grey poly yarn.
Hackle: Iron-blue cock wound round the wing roots.

6 Paradrake

COMMENT

A design popularised, if not created, by Swisher and Richards. Initially the hackle was placed on top of the shank and wound round the wing roots. Later they suggested the option of the parachute hackle wound under the shank as a means of support for the body. Some of the bigger duns like the mayfly are represented by the Paradrake style of having an extended body of elk or deer hair with a wing of elk hair or feather fibres, round the base of which the parachute hackle is wound. This is a Chauncy Lively Mayfly pattern adapted by Charles Jardine.

DRESSING

Hook: 10 fine-wire down-eye Code L2A or L3A.
Thread: Green.
Tail: Three pheasant tail fibres.
Extended body: Light deer hair (10–15 fibres) or moose mane ribbed with green thread.
Abdomen and thorax: Creamy-yellow polypropylene dubbing or Orvis Antron-Hare blend.
Wing: Wood duck tied upright, slanting back, with 10–15 turns of thread around the base for support.
Hackle: Golden olive and grizzle cocks wound together in parachute style round the wing base.

7 Waterwalker

COMMENT

Frank Johnson of Montana came up with this novel and highly effective style of dun imitation. The basic design is one of a split V wing of elk hair or bunched hackle fibres with a cock hackle wound round the base of each wing. The resulting fly is supported by two hackles and the lower fibres of each are quite widely spaced from the other, giving an accurate light pattern. The body is twice as well supported as in the standard style. Although it is quite a difficult and time consuming style to tie, the design does have its advantages and is very successful. This is a blue dun (olive) dressing.

DRESSING

Hook: 14 Code A, E6A or L3A.
Thread: Primrose.
Tail: Light-ginger cock fibres *tied second*.
Body: Mole's fur dubbed in *fourth*.
Rib: Primrose thread wound *fifth*.
Wings: Bunched blue-dun cock fibres tied in *first*.
Hackle: Two light-ginger cock hackles tied in *third* and wound round wing bases *sixth* – one wound clockwise, the other counter-clockwise (3–5 turns).

8 Twiny

COMMENT

The Twiny is based on the same design as the Waterwalkers and again it is a design of fly rather than full pattern. Materials of appropriate colours should be used to match the naturals. It is an excellent fast-water fly because of its double hackle support and the light materials used. The white polypropylene yarn wings are also highly visible. The fly's creator, Hans van Klinken, has two designs: the first with a normal dubbed body and hackle fibre tails; the second with a moose mane tail and an emphasised thorax, with a very slim abdomen.

DRESSING

Hook: 10–18 fine-wire long-shank Code E1A or L3A.
Thread: To match the body colour.
Tail: Cock hackle fibres or three moose mane fibres.
Body: In three sections: wound elk at the rear; fine Fly-Rite poly dubbing, tapering (colour to match the natural); and a peacock herl thorax.
Wings: White poly yarn tied flat or at about 45 degrees.
Hackle: Suitably coloured cock hackles wound round the wing base, as for the Waterwalker.

SUBSURFACE FLIES

An Introduction to Subsurface Flies

Most trout take a substantial proportion of their diet from below the surface. It's quite logical that any fish should feed on the most readily available food without having to wait for a fly hatch on the surface or a fall of spinners or terrestrials. Anything edible below the surface has a chance of being eaten, but the wet-fly or nymph fisher usually restricts himself to imitating the nymphs, larvae and pupae of aquatic flies and shrimps.

Just how one goes about imitating the natural nymphs in terms of fly design, fishing style and presentation varies between the extremes of river types – from the clear chalk stream with its large population of agile-darting and weed-inhabiting nymphs and shrimps to the rough, rocky freestone stream with a nymph menu comprising stonefly nymphs and stone-clinging nymphs of upwinged species. Sedges are common on both river types. In between the two extremes are the majority of trout rivers which enjoy a mixed population of a wide range of flies. The northern wet-fly fisherman uses fairly small, often wingless, sparse spider patterns; West Country practice makes use of a stiff hackle; the Clyde area has thin, sparse flies; Derbyshire, the well palmered imitation; and the chalk stream a more specific imitation, more easily recognisable as a nymph. The nymph fisher of Western America uses Woolly Buggers and Girdle Bugs. The use of these regional and national patterns is now by no means so confined and fly fishers across the country acknowledge the worth of another area's patterns, tying style and fishing methods. Perhaps now more than ever, once highly localised patterns are achieving a much wider following. For example, chalk stream nymphs (many inspired by earlier hackled North Country flies) are used on freestone waters and some of the northern spider patterns are used in almost every region. This liberation from restricted regional use also extends internationally, and now more than ever the same patterns are appearing in fly boxes across the world wherever trout are fished for.

The natural ephemeropteran nymph (upwinged adult) has three tails, a partly translucent body that tapers in width and depth to the rear with darkening wingpads on the thorax as it nears maturity, six legs, and prominent gills along the back or side of the abdomen. When swimming the nymph is streamlined, holding its legs fairly close to the body. The agile-darters, common to slower weedy streams, are able to move at speed. The flatter stone-clingers seem less at ease swimming as they wobble from side to side, their wide bodies being jostled by the current as they head to the surface. The important burrowing and moss-clinging species are inefficient swimmers and, like the stone-clingers, will be found in mid-water only just before and during a hatch.

When we consider nymph design, as opposed to a wet-fly, bug and spider patterns, there is no general agreement about what makes the ideal imitation. Frank Sawyer and Oliver Kite stressed a solid, well defined silhouette and gave us flies with little translucency and no legs. An American expert, Charles Brooks, claimed that a clear view of the legs is important. G. E. M. Skues aimed at some translucency with his dubbed fur bodies, often with hen hackle fibres for legs. Polly Rosborough's nymphs, which have been widely acclaimed and successful (not the same thing!) in the USA, have a very fuzzy dressing and that fuzziness, according to Rosborough, is the successful trigger. My own experience suggests that there are times when trout in a particular river will take solid opaque legless nymphs and on other occasions they'll demand a very scruffy Gold-Ribbed Hare's Ear or a semi-palmered hackled fly. One particular feature is the trigger at that specific time. On other occasions they'll be pleased to take all three types because, after all the conflicting theories are dispensed with, they are all designed to represent a nymph and to catch trout. I am sure a large part of the answer to successful subsurface fishing lies not in the style of dressing but in where, when and – more important – how the imitation is fished.

What is a wet fly (as opposed to a nymph)? It has a body, with or without a rib, possibly a tail, a hackle and sometimes a wing. That leaves quite a lot of scope for variation on the basic design. Most winged wet flies are successful because they look generally food-like without being a specific imitation of any natural creature. Many do not closely resemble any subsurface food in the way an artificial nymph does, but they catch fish in fast and moderately paced water where a critical examination by trout is not possible. More accurate in their imitation are the wingless hackled flies and palmer-style dressings which in the flowing current take on a nymphal shape, or, when fished upstream or across, with their hackle fibres enlivened by the current, are taken as emerging nymphs, pupae or drowned duns and spinners.

Stonefly nymphs, caddis larvae and pupae are considered elsewhere in the book. Subsurface imitations of specific upwinged species are listed under their common name.

In the following sections I have given some advice on what each fly is intended to represent and how and where it should be fished. For a closer description of the fishing methods I highly recommend Roger Fogg's books *The Art of the Wet Fly* and *A Handbook of North Country Trout Flies* for traditional wet-fly techniques, and for nymph fishing *Nymphs and the Trout* by Frank Sawyer, *Nymph Fishing in Practice* by Oliver Kite and two American books, *Nymph Fishing for Larger Trout* by Charles Brooks and *The Masters on the Nymph* edited by J. Michael Migel and Leonard Wright.

Nymphs

The next three sections include nymphs, grubs and bugs which have been tied to represent a range of aquatic species. I considered including a number of highly elaborate nymph patterns. All were very accurately tied, right down to markings on the wing pads and legs, and including the exact number of abdomen segments. They were beautifully constructed, but built rather than tied, without a hint of any aspect of mobility in the tying materials. I discounted them as being irrelevant to fly-fishing practice; they were models to be admired and not to be used. Besides being a divergence from true fly dressing, fly-fishing evolution has proved that patterns which are difficult and time-consuming to tie are destined never to become universally popular.

1 Sawyer's Pheasant Tail Nymph

COMMENT

Frank Sawyer used relatively few patterns for all his trout fishing; he relied on a general impressionist style of fly dressing and placed great emphasis on the presentation and behaviour of the artificial. This, his most famous and widely used nymph, is representative of all the olives, the iron blue and the sepia and claret duns. Sawyer devised it on his home waters of the upper Wiltshire Avon but its use is definitely not confined to chalk streams. I've caught scores of trout and grayling on it in freestone rivers.

DRESSING

Hook: 12–16 Code A, G3A or CS7.
Thread: None.
Tail: Three cock pheasant tail fibres.
Underbody: Copper wire with a hump for the thorax.
Overbody: Pheasant tail fibres wound on with the copper wire and tied fatter at the thorax.
Wingcase: Pheasant tail fibres doubled and redoubled.

2 Bare Hook Nymph

COMMENT

It's not quite a bare hook but there's precious little dressing left. Oliver Kite fished this after he discovered that Sawyer's Pheasant Tail nymphs still caught trout when they had been well chewed and lost their body herls. It is the complete antithesis of exact imitation. What is required, though, is exact imitation in the way the nymph is fished. Kite firmly believed that the key to successful nymph fishing was that the artificial should behave like the natural nymph. If the dead drift fails, making the nymph rise in the water in front of a trout is a sure stimulus.

DRESSING

Hook: 14–16 Code A, G3A or CS7.
Thread: None.
Thorax: Copper wire built up to shape.

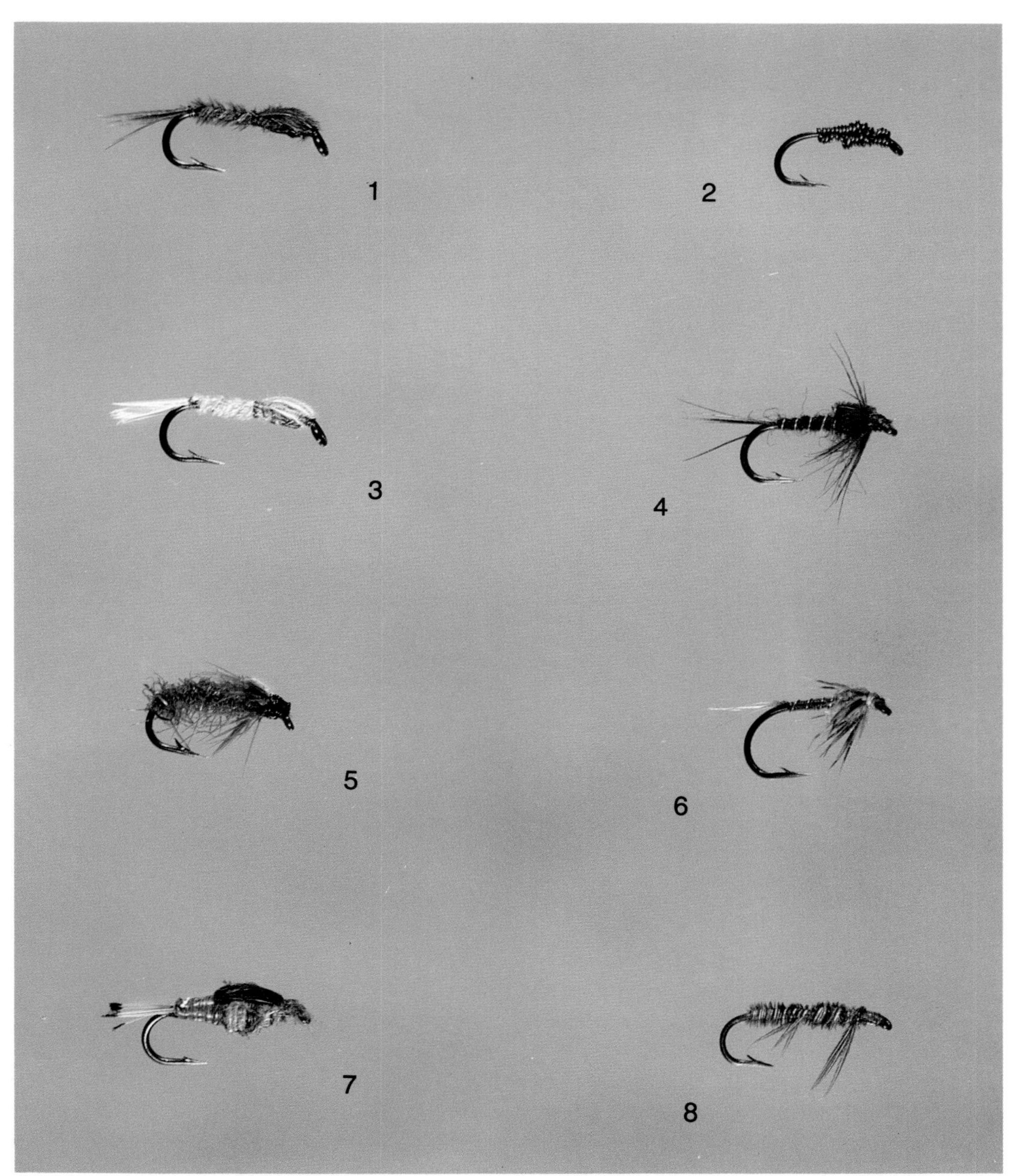

1 Sawyer's Pheasant Tail Nymph **2** Bare Hook Nymph
3 Grey Goose Nymph **4** Black Nymph **5** Brown Fuzzy Nymph
6 Greenwell Nymph **7** PVC Nymph **8** Teeny Nymph

3 Grey Goose Nymph

COMMENT

As with Frank Sawyer's other nymphs, there is no attempt to represent the legs of the natural. He believed that the flow of the current compressed the naturals' legs against their bodies and that a slim outline was a key feature. The size and shape of the nymph of a broadly acceptable colour are sufficient if the artificial is given some movement in the water so that it rises as a nymph would on its way to the surface to emerge. This is a fair imitation of the nymphs of the spurwings, blue-winged olive and pale wateries.

DRESSING

Hook: 12–16 Code A, G3A or CS7.
Thread: None.
Tail: Grey goose fibres bound in by the copper wire.
Underbody: Copper wire built up at the thorax.
Overbody: Grey goose fibres and gold-coloured copper wire wound together.
Thorax: Body fibres doubled and redoubled, tied off with the copper wire.

4 Black Nymph

COMMENT

The nymphs of some stone-clinging species are almost black and other species darken considerably as they near maturity. This nondescript black nymph represents no specific upwinged species, nor is it very accurate as a stonefly nymph imitation. Despite this the fly catches trout. No doubt this is because the general nymphal shape and the outline, silhouette and behaviour of the artificial are sufficient imitation.

DRESSING

Hook: 12–14 Code A, G3A or CS7.
Thread: Black.
Tail: Black cock hackle fibres.
Abdomen: Black seal's fur substitute with the fibres picked out.
Rib: Fine silver wire.
Thorax: Brown or black seal's fur substitute.
Wingcase: Dark-grey goose fibres.
Hackle: Black or dark-red hen.

5 Brown Fuzzy Nymph

COMMENT

This is one dressing where scruffiness is a positive advantage. Roger Fogg devised it as a nondescript pattern that could represent a range of nymphs or pupae. He says that it is 'an alternative sedge-pupa imitation which works best on rivers or stillwaters in the summer evenings when sedges are about'. There are times when fuzziness is required and seems to be the necessary stimulus. The Gold-Ribbed Hare's Ear nymph is the best example – the antithesis of Sawyer's Pheasant Tail nymph.

DRESSING

Hook: 10–14 Code A, G3A or CS7.
Thread: Brown.
Body: Brown seal's fur taken near the bend.
Rib: Stripped peacock quill or herl dyed pale watery-olive.
Hackle: Two turns of brown hen clipped short.
Wing: Any grey feather tied as normal but clipped short to a stub.

6 Greenwell Nymph

COMMENT

All the best flies have spawned variants in the hope that a successful combination of materials and colours will work well in a slightly different form or in a different style of tying. The original winged wet Greenwell's Glory has been adapted to give this general olive nymph imitation. The style of this dressing is in contrast to other, meatier, designs. It is very light and will not sink to a great depth but it is very lifelike. Most natural olive nymphs are fairly small and slim and this is a very good imitation.

DRESSING

Hook: 12–18 Code A, G3A or CS7.
Thread: Waxed primrose or yellow.
Tail: Greenwell (ginger/black) hackle fibres.
Abdomen: Yellow thread or floss.
Rib: Very fine gold wire.
Thorax: Grey or blue-grey fur.
Wingcase: Grouse hackle fibres with the ends turned down as legs.

7 PVC Nymph

COMMENT

This is a John Goddard dressing for any of the olive nymphs. One unusual feature of the dressing is the clear PVC wrapping round the abdomen to give an aspect of translucency to the imitation. Its creator also suggests that the addition of a narrow silver lurex rib beneath the PVC simulates the air bubbles beneath the skin.

DRESSING

Hook: 12–16 Code A, G3A or CS7.
Thread: Brown.
Tail: Golden pheasant tail tips dyed olive-green.
Underbody and thorax: Copper wire.
Overbody and thorax: Three strands of olive or olive-brown condor herl (heron is a substitute). The abdomen is wound with overlapping turns of 3mm wide clear PVC
Wingpads: Two or three strands of dark pheasant tail herls.

8 Teeny Nymph

COMMENT

This is an unusual dressing from Jim Teeny of Portland, Oregon, where, according to Taff Price, it has developed almost into a cult fly. I was fascinated by the look of it when I was browsing through patterns in an Idaho tackle shop. I have tried it out on a few occasions back home and it has been most effective when cast upstream into fairly slack water and fished in the top foot of water in a sink-and-draw style to give the legs some movement. Its inventor has three patents on the design, a trend in fly tying I deplore.

DRESSING

Hook: 12 CS7 or 14–16 long-shank H1A.
Thread: Black or brown.
Body: Cock pheasant tail fibres.
Legs: Two bunches of cock pheasant fibre points; one at the head, the other halfway along the body.

Nymphs and Bugs 1

Unless a hatch is in progress or about to happen, natural nymph activity is minimal. There will always be the agile-darters staying close in to the weed but for most of the time there will be little happening in open water. Joe Humphreys, professor of trout fishing at Pennsylvania University, suggests that when nymph fishing 90 per cent of the time the fly must be presented on the stream bottom, where the naturals and the trout are. To do so means special techniques and, in particular, leaded patterns with a presentation method that keeps them there. I don't think it matters too much whether a fly is fished head up or down, but when using patterns for searching the bottom I weight a hook so that it fishes point uppermost to avoid the snags – my temper frays as easily as the leader point.

1 Something and Nothing

COMMENT

Roger Fogg devised this nondescript nymph with no species in mind but simply as a food-like pattern that would represent anything the trout was hoping to see. He was inspired to dress it after a well worn Coachman seemed to catch more fish the scruffier it got. It can be fished leaded along the bottom or unleaded nearer the surface. A second version differs by its body of fine dark copper wire. This one sinks well and I've found it a useful grayling fly for deep-lying chalkstream fish. It can be tied in a wide range of sizes but its creator recommends size 12.

DRESSING

Hook: 12 Code A or G3A.
Thread: Brown.
Body: Optional lead underbody covered with peacock herl with much of the flue trimmed away.
Hackle: Brownish hackle clipped short as a rough collar.
Wing: Any white feather clipped short to a stub.

2 Fledermaus Nymph

COMMENT

This is an American nymph pattern, first devised in 1949 by Jack Schneider for big lake trout. In a wide range of sizes it has gone on to catch very many varieties of fish in America and Europe, on stillwaters and on big rivers and small streams. Because it is most effective as an evening fly it was named after the operetta *Die Fledermaus* (German for 'the bat'). It doesn't fit into the normal concept of a river trout nymph or bug but it does catch fish. It should be fished in a straight drift.

DRESSING

Hook: 12–16 long-shank Code H1A or D4A.
Thread: Brown.
Body: Muskrat body fur (mixed length fibres), tied quite bulky to look shaggy.
Wing: Grey squirrel tail.

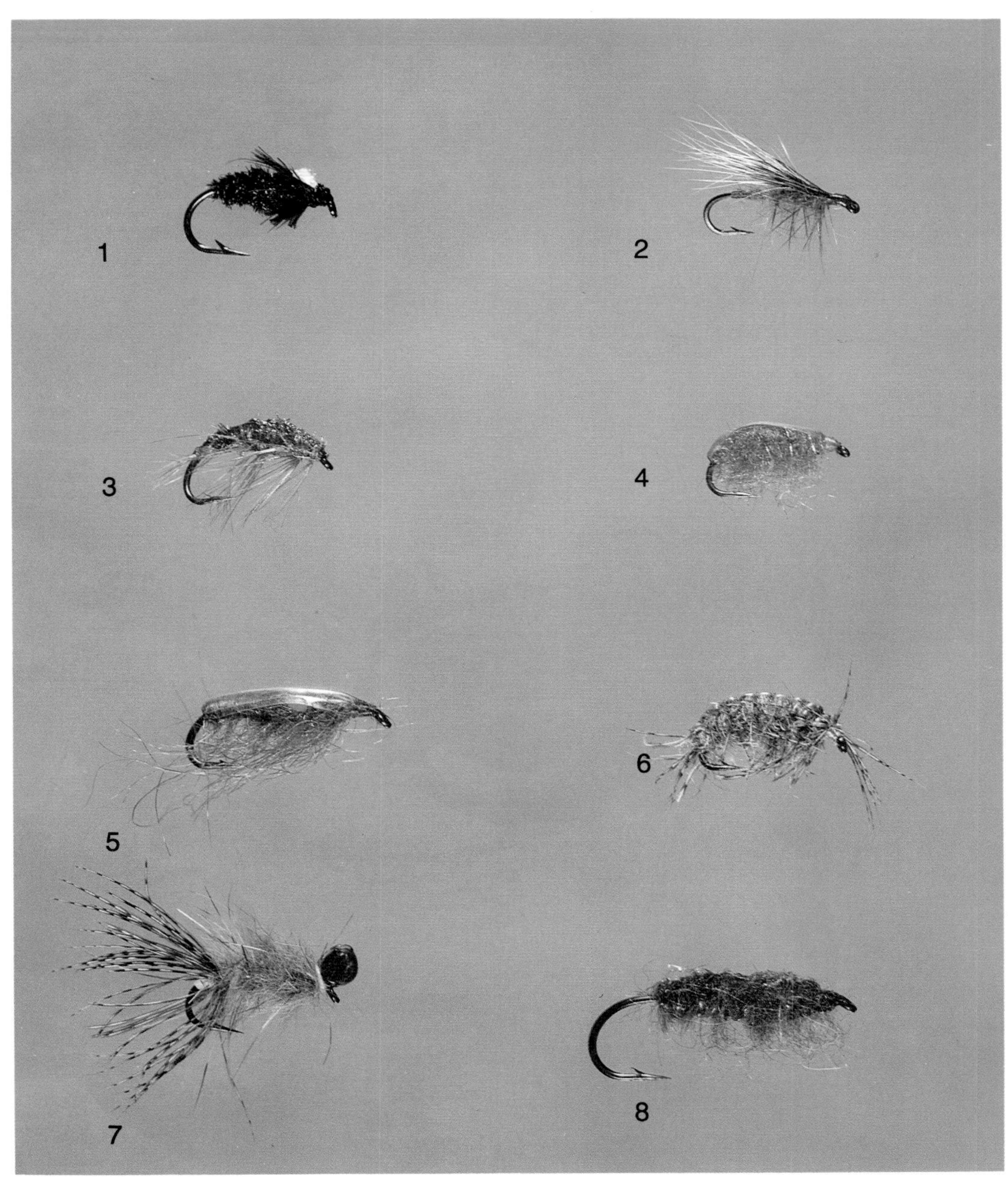

1 Something and Nothing **2** Fledermaus Nymph **3** Shrimp
4 Mating Shrimp **5** Red Spot Shrimp **6** Edwards Shrimp
7 Leadhead Nymph **8** Angora Grub

3 Shrimp

COMMENT

Shrimps are of great value to the river fisherman, especially on the chalk streams, where they abound in vast quantities. I doubt whether it is possible to overemphasise their importance on some chalk streams, where they figure as the major food source. If, as seems true in some instances, the aquatic fly life on some chalk streams has deteriorated in recent years through abstraction and pollution, then the other fauna and particularly shrimps take on a much more important role. This is a Richard Walker dressing weighted so that it fishes upside down to avoid snags.

DRESSING

Hook: 10–12 Code A, G3A, K2B or K4A.
Thread: Olive.
Underbody: Fine lead strips built into a hump.
Body: Wound olive wool.
Hackle: Palmered ginger with the top and side fibres cut away to leave the underside ones only.
Back: Clear varnish.

4 Mating Shrimp

COMMENT

The natural shrimp is easily recognisable with its arched translucent-grey body which turns orangy-brown during the midsummer mating season. They move in a peculiar stop-start motion. The natural can be fished in a straight drift but additional movement by lifting the rod tip makes the imitation more lifelike. As well as being important on the chalk streams they are abundant on many freestone rivers and I've always regarded a well weighted pattern as a good standby on any water that has even a small shrimp population. This is John Goddard's dressing.

DRESSING

Hook: Wide-gape 10–12 Code A or K4A.
Thread: Olive.
Underbody: Fine lead strips built into a hump on top of the shank.
Body: Mixed seal's fur substitute: olive, dark brown and fluorescent pink (6:3:1).
Rib: Oval silver wire.
Back: Clear PVC or polythene.

5 Red Spot Shrimp

COMMENT

Where shrimp abound they figure very highly in the diet of grayling. Shrimp live in weedbeds and on the river bottom, where grayling do much of their feeding. During the late autumn and winter months when aquatic fly life is minimal, grayling are still feeding strongly and shrimp become the major food source on many rivers. This pattern is Neil Patterson's and includes a fluorescent red spot to imitate the orangy-red mark that is seen on some naturals. It is possibly the early stages of the egg sac.

DRESSING

Hook: 10–14 Code A or K2B.
Thread: Waxed olive.
Underbody: Fine lead wire.
Body: Mixed olive seal's fur substitute and olive mohair, dubbed either side of and round a tuft of fluorescent red wool which is trimmed to leave a red blob on either side.
Rib: Gold wire.
Back: Double layer of clear plastic.
Legs: Body fibres picked out.

6 Edwards Shrimp

COMMENT

The best fly tyer I've seen at work is fellow Yorkshireman Oliver Edwards. He is also a superb fisherman. Six of his patterns grace this book's plates. Oliver ties some wonderfully realistic and highly effective flies. Most of them require some careful tying but the effort is well worth while. This is his shrimp pattern. It copies well the natural's translucent grey body and includes head and tail appendages, which most patterns omit. The body dubbing is an unusual mixture of fur and feather fibres, which when dubbed allow the feather fibres to stick out a short distance in an accurate leg imitation.

DRESSING

Hook: 10–14 Code G3A or CS7SHW.
Thread: Grey.
Underbody: Lead wire or foil bound onto the top of the shank in a hump.
Tail and head appendages: Pale olive dyed or natural grey partridge fibres.
Back: Clear polythene.
Body: Dubbed mixture of very pale olive-dyed fine fur and grey partridge hackles.
Rib: Nylon mono in a neutral colour, about 4lb BS.

7 Leadhead Nymph

COMMENT

This has a specific use for special circumstances. Hans van Klinken tied it originally for Scandinavian grayling in very fast water, where the nymph had to be weighted to get down through the fast flow to the bottom. Hans amazed some local grayling fishers on the Welsh Dee, where it took some big grayling from water normally considered too fast to fish. The lead-substitute shot at the head is bound in on the upper side of the shank so the nymph fishes point up. A number of variants are tied; all are very suggestive of food. With this one I caught 26 fish in a couple of hours from fast water and by picking the pockets.

DRESSING

Hook: 10–14 Code CS7SHW, G3A or H1A.
Thread: Brown.
Tail: Brown partridge hackle fibres wound as a collar between the butt and the body.
Butt (optional): Fluorescent green Flexibody or fluorescent lime-green wool.
Body: Brown rabbit fur well picked out.
Head: Lead substitute shot, bound in on a piece of mono (the split towards the eye).

8 Angora Grub

COMMENT

This was designed by Richard Walker as a stillwater fly but I have no hesitation in fishing it upstream on rivers for deep-lying fish, particularly grayling. It is a general grub imitation and also a good representation of those species of free-swimming caddis larvae. The leaded version can be bumped along the bottom of deep pools to unseen fish or through a shoal of grayling. I've seen grayling shoals part to allow a path for this monster to pass through and then suddenly, whether through hunger, curiosity or anger, a fish has hit it very hard. Other times they've very shyly mouthed it.

DRESSING

Hook: 10–14 long-shank Code H1A.
Thread: Dark brown.
Underbody (optional): Lead strips or wire.
Body: Wound or dubbed angora knitting wool (olive-green, amber or any brown shade) over a varnished shank or lead; ease out the underside fibres.
Rib: Clear nylon monofilament (about 20lb BS) (flattened mono is ideal but not essential).
Back: Trim the hair and clear varnish.

Nymphs and Bugs 2

If a nymph or bug is to be weighted it should be done with the natural nymph's shape and behaviour in mind. Joe Humphreys donned scuba gear and studied their behaviour underwater. He concluded that a flat nymph drifts more naturally than a round one. With the interplay of the currents it is rocked from side to side like the natural swimming nymph. Round nymphs are fine for representing the slim agile-darters but the stone-clingers are better imitated by a flat-bodied nymph in the manner of the first two dressings below.

1 Flat-Body Nymph

COMMENT

All the agile-darting nymphs, like those of most olive species, are well represented with slim imitations, but many nymphs are broad, flat stone-clingers, and are quite a different shape. From the side view they are much thinner; from above or below they are very much wider. For the imitation to be most effective this overall shape must be copied. These species will be found free-swimming to the surface only during a hatch. The nymphs should be fished deep before a hatch is expected and between the riverbed and the surface during a hatch. This is my own general pattern.

DRESSING

Hook: 14–16 long-shank Code H3ST (packed with lead wire) or H1A wound with lead.
Thread: Olive.
Tail: Three brown partridge hackle fibres.
Abdomen: Dark-olive or brown ostrich herl.
Rib: Fine gold wire.
Thorax: Dark-olive rabbit's fur with fibres picked out and upper and lower dubbing clipped flat.
Wingcase: Mottled brown quill.
Legs: Bunched brown partridge fibres.

2 Ecdyonurus Nymph

COMMENT

Stony rivers all over the country are well populated with flat stone-clinging nymphs of the *Ecdyonurus, Heptagena* or *Rithrogena* species. The differences between many of them are so small that the pattern above or this one from Oliver Edwards will represent them all. This is the tying sequence: tie in Raffene at eye; wire at head; tails; dub abdomen; tie in pheasant tail with partridge hackle on top, both with butts to rear; dub thorax; pull forward partridge feather and tie in; pull forward pheasant tail and tie in; dub head; pull back Raffene, tie in and flatten. Coat with nail varnish.

DRESSING

Hook: 16 long-shank Code H1A.
Tail: Three moose mane hairs.
Underbody: Fine lead or copper wire tied in a short broad head and flattened.
Body: Yellowish-olive fur with brown flecks (grey squirrel dyed in picric acid) picked out through the rib.
Thorax back: Cock pheasant tail fibres.
Legs: Speckled partridge (clipped).
Head: Fine yellowish-dive dubbing coated with nail varnish before winding.
Head cover: Light-brown Raffene.

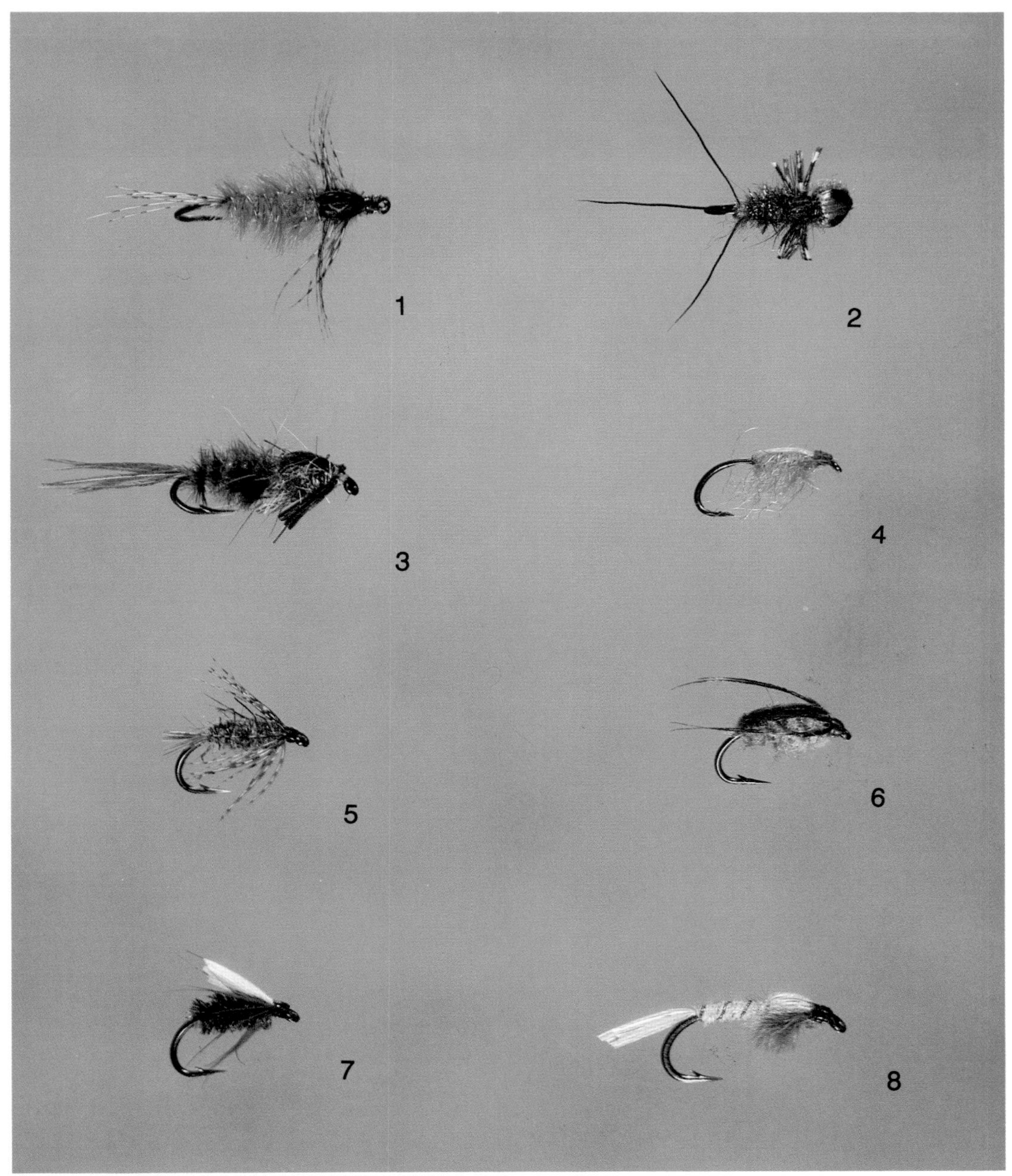

1 Flat-Body Nymph **2** Ecdyonurus Nymph **3** Klinken Nymph
4 Gerroff **5** Green Rabbit **6** Mead Mill Special **7** Clipped Coachman
8 Collyer Nymph

3 Klinken Nymph

COMMENT

On a balcony overlooking the German River Kyll, Hans van Klinken and I compared fly boxes after a successful day's fishing. This dull but appetising nymph caught my attention. 'No name', said Hans, 'just a nymph I tied up that catches trout'. I've used it to good effect on small and larger freestone rivers and chalk streams in England. I find it necessary to weight the underbody to enable the fly to be fished deeper. It is very nondescript but passes for a large upwinged or stonefly nymph, or an alder larva.

DRESSING

Hook: 14 long-shank Code H1A.
Thread: Grey.
Tail: Pheasant tail fibres.
Abdomen: Olive-brown ostrich herl.
Rib: Clear or translucent olive Swannundaze.
Thorax: Grey squirrel tail fibres.
Wingcase and legs: Pheasant tail fibres.

4 Gerroff

COMMENT

Don't ask me what trout take this one for – I don't know, although John Goddard devised it with a shrimp-type dressing in mind. It is used on small clear stillwaters and clear slow-moving streams. Its creator suggests that its success is due to the large hook and smallish buoyant body, which allows the fly to sink slowly and attractively. The 'plop' of the fly entering the water often attracts attention and in clear water trout can be seen coming from some distance to take it. It earned its name through Brian Clarke shouting at the smaller fish to 'gerroff'.

DRESSING

Hook: 10–14 slightly long-shank Code E1A or G3A.
Thread: Brown.
Body: Mixed olive-brown and pink seal's fur substitute (3:1) tied on the front half of the shank.
Back: A strip of clear PVC or latex over the back of the body.

5 Green Rabbit

COMMENT

This is a general food-like imitation, possibly being taken for a swimming sedge pupa. It should be fished like a nymph. According to its creator, Richard Walker, when leaded it is also good for grayling.

DRESSING

Hook: 10–14 Code A or G3A.
Thread: Black.
Tail: Any buff or brown feather fibres tied short.
Underbody (optional): Lead foil or wire.
Body: Wild black rabbit's fur mixed with lime-green fluorescent wool (2:1) with the fibres well picked out.
Rib: Fine gold thread.
Hackle: Short-fibred brown partridge.

6 Mead Mill Special

COMMENT

This is another bug devised by Richard Walker for grayling (they are equally effective for trout) and named after the Mead Mill stretch of the River Test, where it was first tried out. It is fished leaded to ensure that it gets well down near the bottom. The strips of lead foil are built up on the top of the shank in a slight hump to enable it to fish hook point uppermost to avoid snags. It is probably taken for a cased or free-swimming caddis.

DRESSING

Hook: 10–12 Code A or G3A.
Thread: Olive.
Body: Grass-green wool mixed with lime-green fluorescent wool (3:1).
Rib: Fine gold thread.
Back: Speckled turkey tail feather.
Legs: Two fibres of the back feather tied low over the back.

7 Clipped Coachman

COMMENT

In *Fly Patterns; an International Guide*, Taff Price describes this Coachman variant as 'an excellent fish seeker' and useful on first approaching a stream with no surface activity to attract a trout or two. He also says it is one of his most consistently successful flies for trout and grayling from rough streams. If you have never tried it, it must be worth a go. When fished near the surface I guess it's taken for an emerger with the first signs of the wing.

DRESSING

Hook: 12–14 Code A or G3A.
Thread: Black.
Underbody (optional): Copper wire.
Body: Peacock herl.
Hackle: Sparse brown hen.
Wing: A short tuft of white feather fibres.

8 Collyer Nymphs

COMMENT

These are a series of nymphs devised by Dave Collyer mainly for stillwater use, but I have had very satisfactory results from their use in freestone rivers and chalk streams. In addition to the green and brown versions, which in my opinion are best for river use, there is the grey version using natural heron herl ribbed with oval silver tinsel, and a black version of dyed black turkey herl ribbed with fine silver lurex. The brown nymph uses cock pheasant tail fibres for the body and wingcase, ribbed with oval gold tinsel, and a brown-dyed ostrich herl thorax. This is the green version.

DRESSING

Hook: 10–14 Code G3A or CS7.
Tail: Tips of the olive-dyed swan herls.
Body: Olive-dyed swan herl.
Rib: Fine oval gold tinsel.
Thorax: Ostrich herl dyed olive.
Wingcase: Body fibres taken over the thorax.

General Wet Flies

Somehow the exact imitation theories have never really penetrated below the water surface; they have been largely confined to the dry fly. Perhaps this is because so many of the subsurface nymphs and pupae of different species are so similar that often only generally impressionist patterns are ever required. The eight patterns below fall into this category.

A few nymphs, wet and dry flies have been just too successful in the eyes of some writers. The Hare's Ear, of which there is a variant below, was condemned by Oliver Kite who likened its use to fishing with 'worms, maggots or minnows'!

1 Mallard and Claret

COMMENT

The flies in the Mallard series are widely used on stillwaters and on many rivers. Some are attractors, others are suggestive of a number of food items, from nymphs, pupae and shrimps to fish fry. Most of these differ only in their body colour and the matching hackle. All are winged with the small speckled brown shoulder feather. The best of the series, and the one most useful for rivers, whether a moorland brook or a wide Scottish salmon river, is the claret version. Other colours in the series are listed under the Woodcock and Hare's Ear.

DRESSING

Hook: 12–14 Code CS7 or G3A.
Thread: Black.
Tail: Golden pheasant tippets.
Body: Dark-claret seal's fur substitute.
Rib: Fine oval gold tinsel or gold wire.
Wing: Brown mallard.
Hackle: Natural red cock.

2 Grouse and Yellow

COMMENT

The Grouse series is broadly similar to the Mallard series, the principal difference being the wing fibres, which in this series are taken from the speckled tail feathers. With different body colours the series represents a broad range of aquatic fauna. Probably the most useful river flies are the green and the yellow versions, which when fished just below the surface, are very likely taken as sedge pupae or emerging adults.

DRESSING

Hook: 12–14 Code CS7 or G3A.
Tail: Golden pheasant tippets.
Body: Yellow seal's fur substitute.
Rib: Fine oval gold tinsel or gold wire.
Wing: Grouse tail feather.
Hackle: Yellow cock.

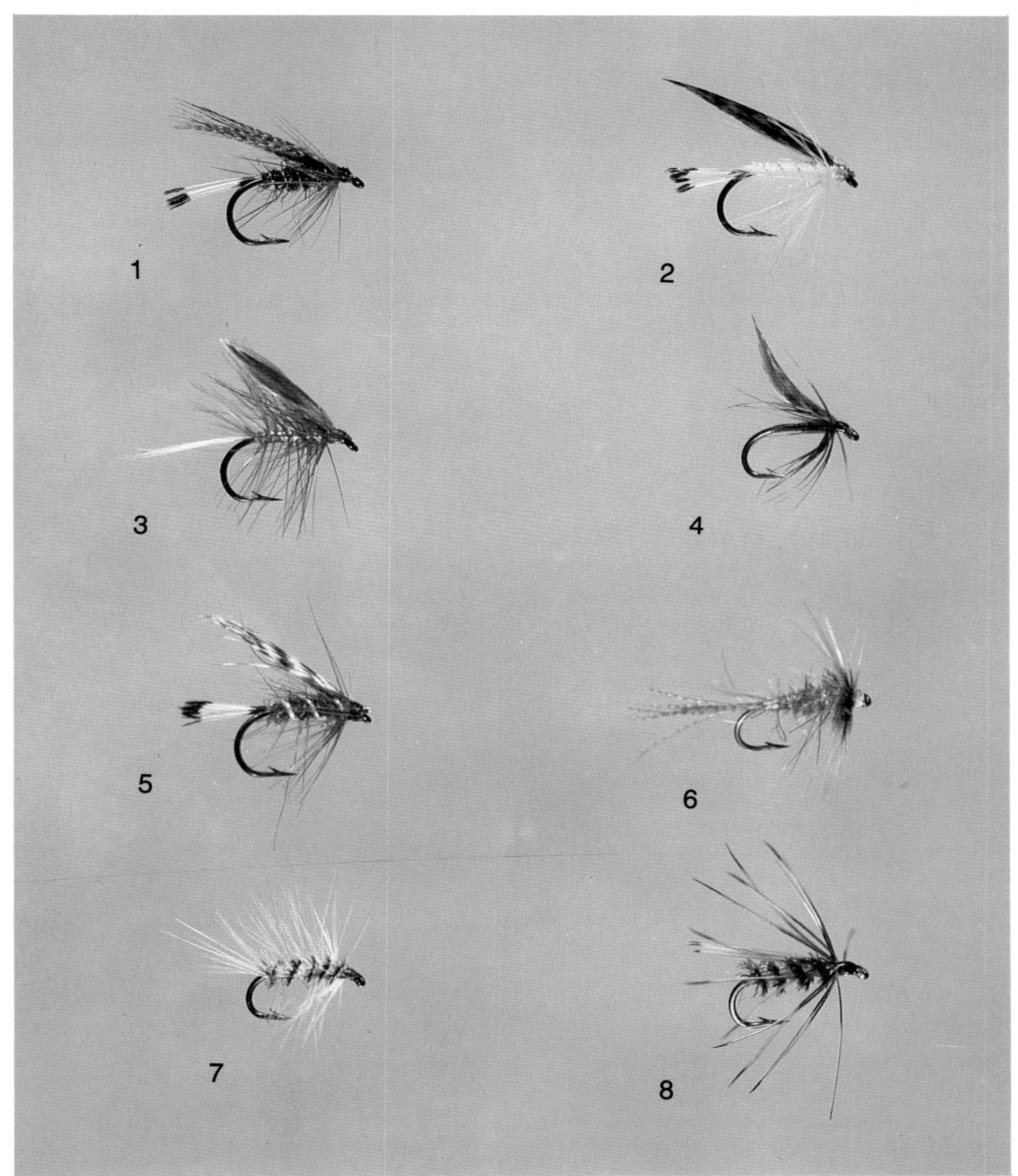

1 Mallard and Claret **2** Grouse and Yellow **3** Wickham's Fancy
4 Partridge and Black **5** Teal and Green **6** Hare's Ear Greenwell
7 Bumble **8** Bracken Clock

3 Wickham's Fancy

COMMENT

At just over a hundred years old, this so-called fancy pattern named after its creator Dr T. C. Wickham is fished both as a floater and subsurface. It is tied here as a wet fly. Sometimes the wing is omitted for the wet version. Used wet, it is most successful during a sedge hatch, when it should be fished just below the surface to represent the pupa on the point of emerging. It is also highly rated when trout are smutting.

DRESSING

Hook: 14–16 Code CS7 or G3A.
Thread: Brown.
Tail: Guinea-fowl dyed reddish-brown, or ginger hackle fibres.
Body: Flat gold tinsel with a palmered ginger-red cock hackle.
Rib: Gold wire.
Wing: Medium starling.
Hackle: Ginger-red cock.

4 Partridge and Black

COMMENT

This is a Scottish fly, originating on the Clyde and its tributaries, and has been popular for generations. There are red or yellow-bodied variations with brown or cinnamon hackles to match. Each should be tied quite sparse. Every region in the country has its own nondescript black flies for the streams and rivers of the area; each pattern passing for a wide range of black or dark-coloured aquatic and terrestrial insects. All are sufficiently generally imitative to be a reliable standby fly to include on a three-fly cast.

DRESSING

Hook: 14–18 Code A, E6A or CS7.
Thread: Black.
Body: Black thread or floss.
Wing: Marbled partridge tail feather tied slim.
Hackle: Black hen.

5 Teal and Green

COMMENT

This is one of the Teal series, which is broadly similar to the Woodcock, Mallard and Grouse series. The lighter-coloured barred wing of the teal makes the fly a useful alternative when darker-winged patterns fail. The Peter Ross is the most widely used variant. The green, claret and black versions are the most likely for rivers, with the green being useful when the green-bodied sedges are hatching.

DRESSING

Hook: 12–14 Code E6A or CS7.
Thread: Black.
Tail: Golden pheasant tippets.
Body: Green seal's fur substitute.
Rib: Fine oval silver tinsel.
Wing: Teal breast feather.
Hackle: Light-red hen.

6 Hare's Ear Greenwell

COMMENT

I have no experience of this fly (the original Hare's Ear works so well) but I know it meets with wide success. It is no coincidence that some of the variants of standard patterns combine the best aspects of other well proven flies. This one maximises the benefits of the hare's ear body and the greenwell hackle. Like its two parent flies it is a useful standby throughout the season. A further variation is to semi-palmer a greenwell hen hackle feather.

DRESSING

Hook: 12–16 Code A, L2A or CS7.
Thread: Primrose.
Tail: Speckled brown mallard.
Body: Hare's ear fur mixed with a little golden-olive seal's fur substitute.
Rib: Fine gold wire.
Hackle: Greenwell hen.

7 Bumbles

COMMENT

The series of Bumbles which developed in Derbyshire are palmer-style flies with a hint in some of their dressings that errs towards the fancy rather than the imitative. Halford used them as floaters and today they are used in both ways, but I suspect mainly wet, when they look very attractive with their soft palmered hackles. They are highly rated for grayling. This is the Honey-Dun Bumble.

DRESSING

Hook: 14–16 Code L2A or A.
Thread: Olive.
Body: Salmon-pink floss.
Rib: Peacock sword herl over the hackle.
Hackle: Palmered honey-dun cock or hen.

8 Bracken Clock

COMMENT

The origins of this pattern are obscure. It is at least 150 years old and is widely regarded as a terrestrial beetle imitation and quite likely was once another name for the Coch-y-bonddhu. On rougher streams or at the head of a pool the terrestrials that fall on the water will be soon swept below the surface and here imitations of beetles and black gnats are best fished wet.

DRESSING

Hook: 14 Code A or L2A.
Thread: Black.
Body: Bronze peacock herl tied not too fat.
Rib: Red floss closely ribbed.
Hackle: Cock pheasant neck feather, brown with black tips.

Winged Wet Flies

The winged wet fly has long been a popular style for fishing across and downstream. With the wing sloping over the back, what do trout make of them? No nymphs or pupae below the surface have wings. The only upwingeds or sedges with wings found below the surface are drowned adults or the few spinners and sedge species that oviposit by swimming or crawling below the water. Few of these patterns could be mistaken for those. There is no one answer. My guess is that some patterns when fished close to the surface offer an outline or silhouette similar to the surface fly; others pass for drowned adults or terrestrials; the rest are just generally suggestive of something edible. If trout are hungry or are already feeding but not being selective then something food-like is quite acceptable.

1 Hen Blackie

COMMENT

This is one of a number of Clyde-style wet flies which can be profitably used on rivers much further afield. It is believed to be a small stonefly imitation, probably a needle fly, but whatever it is taken for it catches trout throughout the season and also grayling into November. Traditionally, flies from this area are fished upstream and fished in this way just an inch or so below the surface this one is most effective. The finished fly should be slim and sparsely dressed. One variation is to include a single turn of gold tinsel as a tip.

DRESSING

Hook: 14–16 Code CS7 or G3A.
Body: Yellow thread waxed with brown wax.
Wing: One wing section from secondary wing feather of a hen blackbird, folded light side out and tied flat (dyed starling is a substitute).
Hackle: Very short-fibred jet-black hen or starling neck feather.

2 Blae and Black

COMMENT

This very old Scottish fly is a killer on river and stillwater. Like all small black flies it passes for a wide range of natural insects, from the hatching midge pupa to an assortment of small black terrestrial flies. The Blae and Silver and Blae and Gold are in the same series, differing only in their coloured tinsel bodies.

DRESSING

Hook: 14–16 Code CS7 or G3A.
Tail: Golden pheasant tippets.
Body: Black thread or thinly dubbed seal's fur substitute.
Rib: Fine oval silver tinsel.
Wing: Grey duck or small starling feather.
Hackle. Black hen.

1 Hen Blackie **2** Blae and Black **3** Greenwell's Glory
4 Woodcock and Hare's Ear **5** Broughton's Point **6** Coachman
7 Invicta **8** Silver Invicta

3 Greenwell's Glory

COMMENT

This most famous of trout flies has been killing trout for more than 130 years. Originating on the River Tweed, it is now widely used across the country as a general olive imitation. In different size and shades of materials all the olive nymphs can be represented. Because olives of one sort or another are hatching from March to October, the Greenwell's Glory is a good standby pattern from the opening day to the last day of the season. The original fly was the winged wet version but a nymph and dry fly have also been developed. A variant, the Woodcock Greenwell, uses a woodcock wing.

DRESSING

Hook: 12–16 Code CS7 or G3A.
Body: Waxed yellow tying thread.
Rib (optional): Gold wire.
Wing: Inside of a hen blackbird's wing (starling is a suitable substitute).
Hackle: Greenwell hen (ginger/black).

4 Woodcock and Hare's Ear

COMMENT

The Woodcock series is very like the Mallard, Teal and Grouse series of lake flies, some of which are useful river patterns. This dressing is the most useful river fly of the Woodcock series. Its origins are lost but it was established well before the middle of the nineteenth century. I don't know what this dressing represents but I would suggest that it comes closest to a sedge imitation. It works well all season. Others in the series have body colours of green, orange, red, claret, black and yellow seal's fur substitute with gold or silver tinsel. The hackle in each case should match the body or be natural red.

DRESSING

Hook: 12–14 Code CS7 or G3A.
Tip: Flat gold tinsel.
Tail: Brown mallard fibres.
Body: Dark hare's ear fur often mixed with a little olive wool.
Rib: Fine oval gold tinsel.
Wing: Woodcock wing quill.
Hackle: Body fibres picked out or natural red hackle.

5 Broughton's Point

COMMENT

The dressing given here is known as this or as the Dark Bloa. It is widely fished in the North of England as an imitation of the nymph of the claret dun. The original dressing was devised for Ullswater by Jack Broughton in about 1830. Although it is usually fished on the point of a leader it was not named because of this but after the small peninsular on Ullswater that Broughton favoured. Over a century ago it made the transition to being a river pattern, particularly as a spring fly on the Eden and its tributaries, and now on many northern streams.

DRESSING

Hook: 12–14 Code CS7 or G3A.
Body: Dark claret or purple thread (originally light-blue).
Wing: Medium-blae starling wing feather.
Hackle: Black hen.

6 Coachman

COMMENT

The original Coachman was a winged wet fly but other variations have developed. It is one of those nondescript flies which could pass for a number of insects – a moth, sedge or terrestrial – though to the human eye is barely passable as an imitation of any of them. Who knows what trout make of it? Sometimes the stark contrast between the body and the white wing is a deterrent. On such an occasion the Leadwing Coachman often works. It differs only by its wing of grey duck or starling wing.

DRESSING

Hook: 12–16 Code CS7 or G3A.
Thread: Black or brown.
Body: Bronze peacock herl.
Wing: White duck or swan fibres.
Hackle: Natural light-red hen.

7 Invicta

COMMENT

Although it is now primarily a stillwater fly, the Invicta is a very good river fly for high summer. During hot summer days when there has been a low water level and no trout moving I've picked up trout on a few occasions by fishing a small Invicta presented just below the surface on the end of a long leader. It is probably taken for an emerging sedge and usually does well whenever there is a sedge hatch in progress, whether during daylight or dusk.

DRESSING

Hook: 12–16 Code CS7 or G3A.
Tail: Golden pheasant crest feather.
Body: Yellow seal's fur substitute with a palmered natural light-red cock.
Rib: Gold wire or fine oval tinsel.
Wing: Hen pheasant centre-tail or wing.
Hackle: Blue jay.

8 Silver Invicta

COMMENT

With its bright silver body this could almost come into the attractor category and it is sometimes used in that role. The Gold Invicta, in which the silver materials of this pattern are replaced by gold-coloured ones, is also a fair sedge imitation.

DRESSING

Hook: 12–16 Code CS7 or G3A.
Tail: Golden pheasant crest feather.
Body: Silver tinsel with a palmered light-red cock.
Rib: Gold wire or fine oval gold tinsel.
Wing: Hen pheasant centre-tail or wing.
Hackle: Blue jay.

Attractor Wet Flies

A useful early-season tactic when fishing with a team of flies in the across and downstream manner on a freestone stream is to include an attractor pattern. The fly life in the earliest months is relatively sparse except during the sometimes short hatch periods, and including a flashy pattern on the team sometimes works well. If there are no natural nymphs moving upwards to hatch, trout may just view with suspicion the angler's imitations. But the attractor makes no pretence of imitating a nymph; it is there to stimulate interest or aggression. Most attractors are passable small fish imitations. All trout are carnivorous and may take fry or minnows at any time.

1 Alexandra

COMMENT

This very old fry-imitating pattern is useful in the early season when an attractor pattern on the point of a three-fly team is a useful tactic. Its use is usually confined to stillwaters but the flash of silver in a pattern often catches the eye of river trout in April.

DRESSING

Hook: 10–12 Code CS7 or E6A.
Thread: Black.
Tail: Swan fibres dyed red as red ibis substitute.
Body: Flat silver tinsel.
Rib: Oval silver tinsel.
Hackle: Black hen.
Wing: Peacock sword herls, flanked either side with swan fibres dyed red.

2 Butcher

COMMENT

This is one of the most popular attractors on river and stillwater and a number of variants have developed over its 150-year history. The two variants most useful on rivers are the Bloody Butcher, which has a scarlet red hackle, and the Gold Butcher, which is like the dressing given here with the silver tinsel body and rib replaced by gold-coloured materials.

DRESSING

Hook: 10–14 Code E6A or CS7.
Thread: Black.
Tail: Swan fibres dyed red as a red ibis substitute.
Body: Flat silver tinsel.
Rib: Oval silver tinsel.
Wing: Blue mallard, crow wing or magpie tail feather.
Hackle: Black cock or hen.

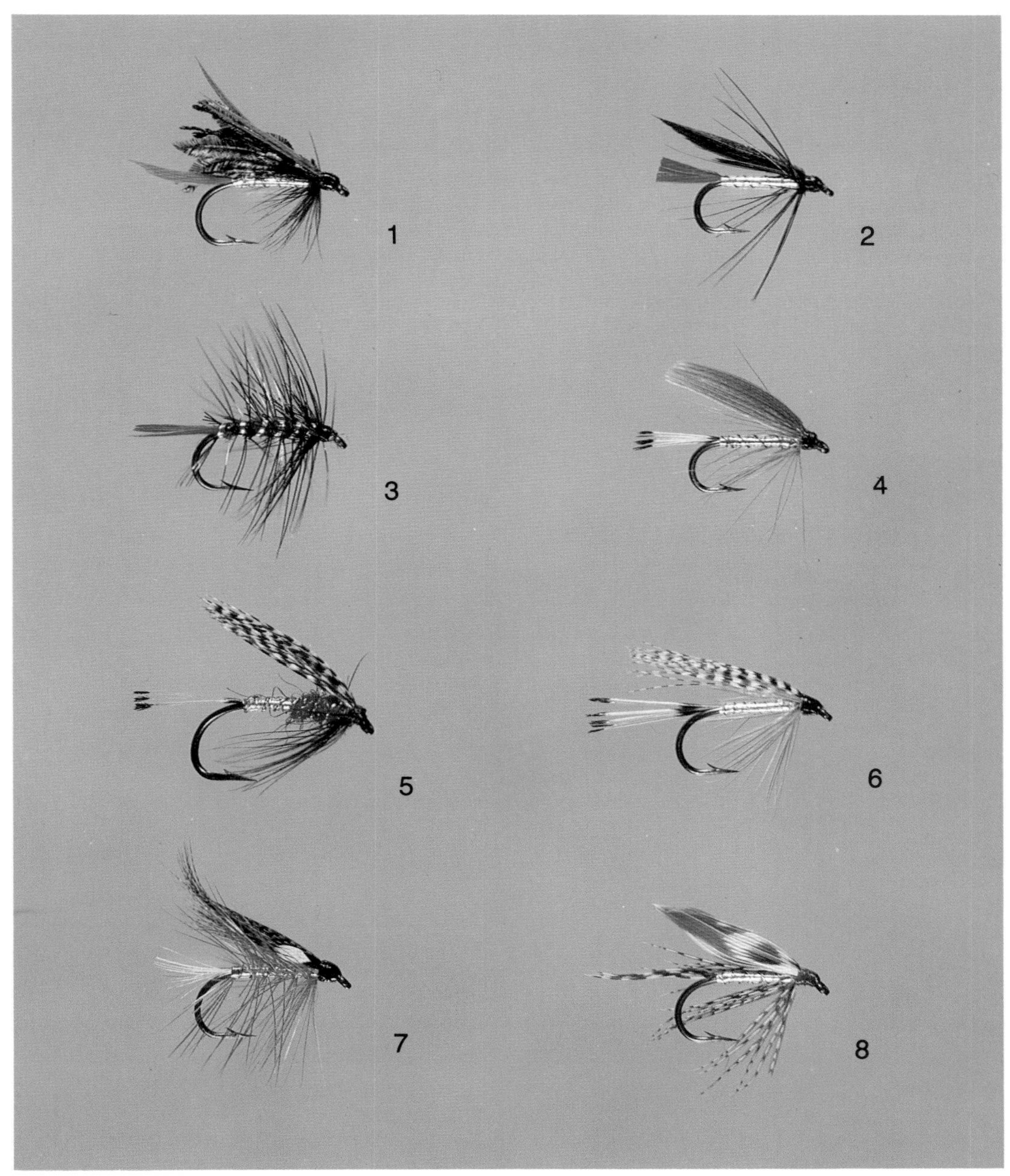

1 Alexandra **2** Butcher **3** Zulu **4** Cinnamon and Gold
5 Peter Ross **6** Teal, Blue and Silver **7** Dunkeld **8** Silver March Brown

3 Zulu

COMMENT

I can only recall ever catching two river trout on this fly and then I'm sure it was being taken for a terrestrial or aquatic beetle. The palmered black body certainly suggests something meaty and the silver rib gives the illusion of some air trapped round the body. It is best fished in its smaller sizes, when it might be mistaken for a midge pupa or reed smut. A brighter attractor variant is the Silver Zulu, which has a silver tinsel body.

DRESSING

Hook: 12–16 Code E6A or CS7.
Thread: Black.
Tail: Red wool or swan fibres dyed red.
Body: Black wool or seal's fur substitute with a palmered black cock.
Rib: Fine flat silver tinsel.
Hackle: Black cock or hen.

4 Cinnamon and Gold

COMMENT

The gold tinsel body inclines this fly towards the attractor category and I'm sure it is sometimes taken because it has been mistaken for a brown trout fry. It is probably more effective as an emerging sedge just below the surface. The cinnamon sedge, which it best imitates, appears between June and October. One variation in the dressing is to have a dull-yellow wool body.

DRESSING

Hook: 12–14 Code E6A or CS7.
Thread: Black.
Tail: Golden pheasant tippets.
Body: Flat gold tinsel.
Rib: Oval gold tinsel.
Wing: Cinnamon-dyed or natural hen wing quills.
Hackle: Cinnamon cock or hen.

5 Peter Ross

COMMENT

This is principally a sea-trout and stillwater pattern but it does also catch its share of non-migratory river trout. It is a good small-fry imitation but also it has the useful silver and red combination. The silver is a known attractor and the red a proven stimulus generally in the animal kingdom.

DRESSING

Hook: 10–14 Code E6A or CS7.
Thread: Black.
Tail: Golden pheasant tippets.
Body: Rear half, silver tinsel; front half, red seal's fur substitute.
Rib: Oval silver tinsel.
Wing: Barred teal breast or flank feather fibres.
Hackle: Black cock or hen.

6 Teal, Blue and Silver

COMMENT

This is one in the Teal Series of flies, which are mainly sea-trout and lake flies. This one is a fry-imitating pattern and general attractor. The silver and the contrasting barred feather colours make it more visible and useful in slightly coloured water.

DRESSING

Hook: 12–14 Code E6A or CS7.
Thread: Black.
Tail: Golden pheasant tippets.
Body: Flat silver tinsel.
Rib: Oval silver tinsel or silver wire.
Wing: Barred black and white flank feather.
Hackle: Bright-blue cock or hen.

7 Dunkeld

COMMENT

This is a Scottish pattern originating as a salmon fly but it is also a useful stillwater and river trout fly. Gold, orange and brown is a useful combination for wild Scottish trout. Although it is principally an attractor, the palmer-hackled non-eyed version is a passable emerging sedge when fished close to the surface.

DRESSING

Hook: 12–14 Code E6A or CS7.
Thread: Black.
Tail: Small golden pheasant crest.
Body: Flat gold tinsel, optionally palmered with a small ginger or orange cock.
Rib: Oval gold tinsel.
Wing: Brown mallard shoulder feather with jungle cock cheeks.
Hackle: Orange cock or hen.

8 Silver March Brown

COMMENT

No doubt this started out as a variant of the wet March brown to represent the nymphs of that species. This silver version bears only a passing resemblance to the natural nymph but is generally suggestive of a number of food items. It has been a very reliable early-season fly for me when fished as one of a team on the North Country rivers.

DRESSING

Hook: 12–14 Code E6A or CS7.
Thread: Brown.
Tail: Partridge tail fibres.
Body: Flat silver tinsel.
Rib: Oval silver tinsel or silver wire.
Wing: Partridge tail or hen pheasant wing.
Hackle: Brown partridge.

North Country Wet Flies 1

All the northern wingless wet flies or spider patterns are tied with soft feathers to give the impression of life to the lifeless artificial. The shoulder hackle should be sparsely tied – either rear-sloping to give a nymphal profile or bound in to produce vertical fibres, which gives a better impression of an emerging fly or a drowned adult insect.

Many of the bodies are simply a couple of layers of tying thread. The translucency of the natural fly is represented by the body being seen through the hackle fibres swept back over the body. When fished downstream a nymphal shape is achieved. If the flies are to be fished upstream the shoulder hackle is less likely to cover the body. In this situation a very thin dubbing of fur gives the necessary additional bulk to the body and offers some translucency.

1 Hare's Lug and Plover

COMMENT

What makes a great trout fly? What gives it those fish-catching qualities? If only we knew! This fly falls into the 'great' category for me. If I had to choose only one wet fly for northern rivers this would be it. It mainly represents the olives and when used in appropriate sizes it kills whenever any of the olives are about. When tied with a Stewart-style semi-palmered hackle it is an excellent emerging olive imitation. It is even better when fished upstream with the current enlivening the hackle fibres, and more so when dibbled back at the surface in the manner of the dun at the point of emergence.

DRESSING

Hook: 12–16 Code A, G3A, L2A or CS7.
Thread: Well waxed primrose or brown.
Tip (optional): A small tip of flat gold tinsel.
Body: Hare's ear fur tapering to the rear.
Rib: Gold wire.
Hackle: Golden plover (pale-brown or dark-ash feather with yellow tips).

2 Gravel Bed

COMMENT

It is not too common for a wet fly to represent a terrestrial species but when land-based insects fall on the rougher faster water they are soon drowned and swept below the surface. This is a flat-winged species very like a small crane-fly. On warm days they are often found swarming over the surface as in their pupal stage they live in damp sand and gravel along the river's edge. They appear from the end of April until early June.

DRESSING

Hook: 12–14 Code A, G3A, L2A or CS7.
Thread: Purple.
Body: Stripped peacock sword feather quill with the thread exposed at the shoulder.
Wing: Hen pheasant tail laid almost flat.
Hackle: Long-fibred black cock.

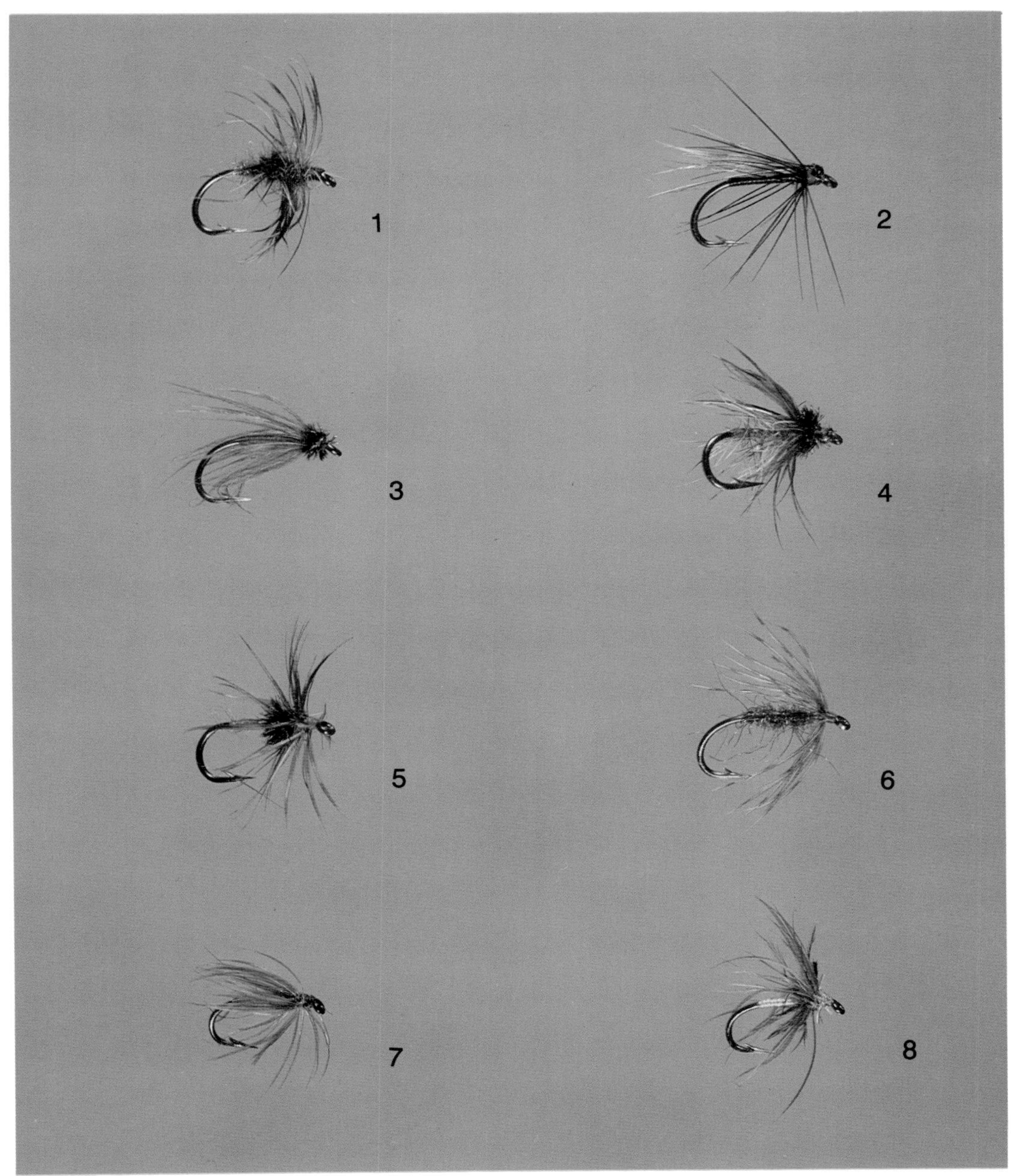

1 Hare's Lug and Plover **2** Gravel Bed **3** Brown Owl **4** Light Woodcock **5** Winter Brown **6** Woodcock and Green **7** Snipe and Purple **8** Snipe and Yellow

3 Brown Owl

COMMENT

It is usually suggested that this is a stonefly imitation, more particularly for the willow fly, a widely distributed species which appears between August and November. It is a very good general pattern and I know of anglers who fish it successfully as a small emerging sedge at dusk. The dressing is like many other sparsely hackled patterns which catch fish simply because they are suggestive of a number of aquatic flies. Flies like these can be profitably fished when sedges and upwingeds of similar colours are hatching.

DRESSING

Hook: 14 Code A, G3A, L2A or CS7.
Body: Orange thread.
Hackle: A reddish feather from the outside of a brown owl's wing.
Head (optional): Peacock herl.

4 Light Woodcock

COMMENT

This old dressing, like many of the others of the last century, is still equally effective today. It is mainly an imitation of the needle flies which appear from February until April and from August to October. For this reason it is an excellent early-season fly and a good grayling fly when their season really begins in October. The body should be only lightly dubbed with fur to allow the orange thread to be visible. I fish this with great confidence.

DRESSING

Hook: 14 Code A, G3A, L2A or CS7.
Thread: Well waxed orange thread sparsely dubbed with hare's ear fur.
Hackle: Woodcock marginal covert feather.
Head: Peacock herl.

5 Winter Brown (Orange Woodcock)

COMMENT

The name suggests a winter fly for grayling. It is primarily an early- and late-season trout fly, a needle-fly imitation. These small, very thin, brown flies appear as early as February and as late as October. There is also a dry fly to imitate the needle flies but most trout fishers would only think it profitable to use a subsurface fly. Note how similar the fly is to the Brown Owl and Light Woodcock, both stonefly imitations. This is also known as the Orange Woodcock (as illustrated), when the peacock herl is wound as a small thorax and not as a head.

DRESSING

Hook: 14 Code A, G3A, L2A or CS7.
Body: Orange thread.
Thorax: Peacock herl.
Hackle: Woodcock marginal covert feather.

6 Woodcock and Green

COMMENT

This is one of a series of spider-hackled flies, each with a well-marked woodcock hackle. The principal body colours are green, orange, brown and yellow. It seems likely that the Light Woodcock and Winter Brown are variants or developed alongside, making use of the soft brown wing feathers for hackling. They are taken for an assortment of nymphs, emerging duns and sedges. Roger Fogg regards the orange version (see Winter Brown, above) as the best of the series.

DRESSING

Hook: 12–14 Code A, G3A, L2A or CS7.
Thread: Green.
Body: Green thread or floss or green seal's fur substitute thinly dubbed.
Hackle: Woodcock marginal covert feather.

7 Snipe and Purple

COMMENT

This is an exceptional trout and grayling fly and when it is fished close to the surface a very fair imitation of the iron blue nymph or emerger. The late Reg Righyni rated this fly very highly but he was apt to include a fine copper rib on his dressing. This was solely a personal addition and no other authorities include it. Few flies can be so simply tied with just a few turns of thread and a hackle feather; indeed, some of the best trout flies are those that are the easiest to tie, and this is no exception.

DRESSING

Hook: 14–16 Code A, G3A, L2A or CS7.
Body: Purple thread.
Hackle: Dark snipe marginal covert feather, preferably spoon-shaped, sparsely tied.

8 Snipe and Yellow

COMMENT

A useful fly when some of the paler upwingeds are emerging. When these are hatching it is best fished upstream almost awash in the film. For such times the hackle should be tied Stewart-style. The very soft snipe feather is very mobile in the water and responds to the current movement. The body can be very lightly dubbed with mole's fur or a similarly-coloured seal's fur substitute. One dressing aids an optional thorax of peacock herl. Roger Fogg suggests that yellow floss silk and a lighter hackle should be used to maximise the translucent appearance.

DRESSING

Hook: 14–16 Code A, G3A, L2A or CS7.
Body: Waxed yellow thread (*see* text).
Hackle: Dark snipe sparsely tied (*see* text).

North Country Wet Flies 2

Many North Country flies are known simply by their hackle and the body colour – for example, Snipe and Purple, Red Dotterel, and so on. The name of the fly in a series changes with its body colour, so there may be half a dozen or more in the Partridge and Dotterel series, each in the same series having the same hackle but a different body colour. Just the change of body colour means that different upwinged, stonefly or sedge species are represented. Thus in a very simple but nonetheless effective way the trout fisher can represent a wide range of species for the minimum of effort. Those fly dressers of old didn't go in for over-elaborate patterns and the simplicity and success of their styles has yet to be bettered.

1 Partridge and Orange

COMMENT

This is the best-known and most widely used of the Partridge series. It is thought to be a stonefly imitation but it takes trout even if there are no stoneflies about. I think the addition of the optional gold wire rib improves the look of the fly and does represent the segmented body of stonefly and ephemeropteran nymphs. It catches thousands of trout each season and is one of the first-choice flies for many northern trout and grayling anglers.

DRESSING

Hook: 12–16 Code A, G3A, L2A or CS7.
Body: Orange thread, floss or standard.
Rib (optional): Gold wire or fine oval gold tinsel.
Hackle: Brown partridge.

2 Partridge and Orange (fluorescent)

COMMENT

Thomas Clegg, author of an interesting little book, *The Truth About Fluorescents* (1967), devised this fluorescent variation of the standard dressing. I confess I haven't used the fly, mainly because the original has been so successful, but it should give some added attraction in low light or be more visible in slightly coloured water.

DRESSING

Hook: 12–16 Code A, G3A, L2A or CS7.
Thread: Yellow.
Body: Fluorescent orange floss.
Rib: Brown silk.
Hackle: Grey partridge.

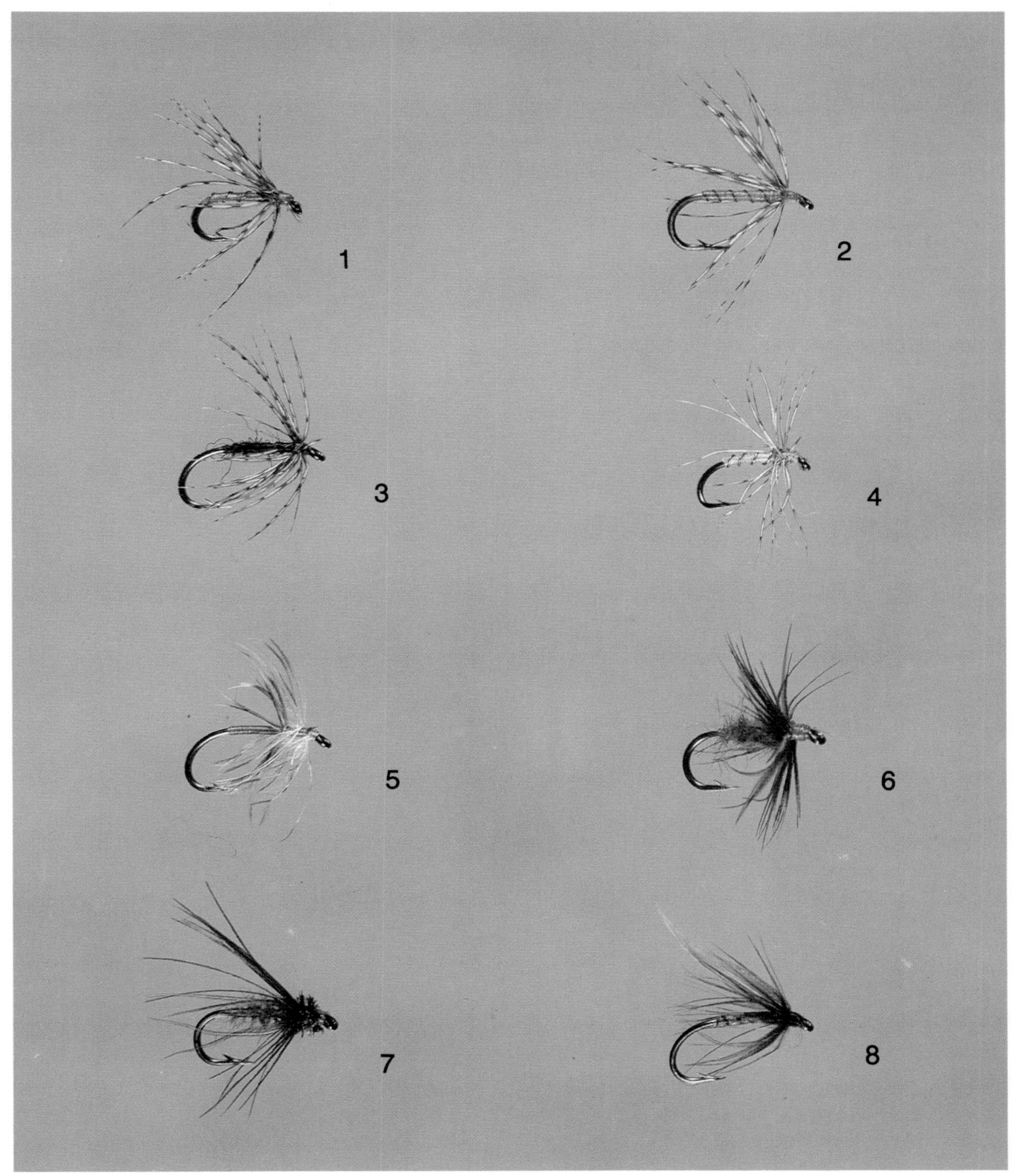

1 Partridge and Orange **2** Partridge and Orange (fluorescent)
3 Partridge and Blue **4** Partridge and Yellow **5** Orange Dotterel
6 Little Dark Watchet **7** Dark Watchet **8** Fog Black

3 Partridge and Blue

COMMENT

Although this is not one of the commonest of the series it has done well for me on a few occasions when the fishing was hard going. I don't know what it imitates but one authority suggests a gravel bed and Pritt recommended it as a 'first-rate killer in a biggish water any time after the middle of May'. I referred to its success when I wrote *A New Illustrated Dictionary of Trout Flies* and one reader, impressed with its performance, tried the fly out for himself. So pleased was he with its results that he sent me a dozen beautifully tied examples.

DRESSING

Hook: 12–16 Code A, G3A, L2A or CS7.
Body: Blue thread, optionally lightly dubbed with lead-coloured lamb's wool.
Hackle: Brown partridge.

4 Partridge and Yellow

COMMENT

A Yorkshire fly for trout and grayling. Generally most useful between April and June in the late afternoon and early evening. It is probably taken for a nymph or emerger of one of the paler upwinged species. Of the three others in the Partridge series, the Partridge and Silver has a silver tinsel body, the Partridge and Red has a wine-red tying-thread body, and the Partridge and Brown has a brown tying thread body with a gold wire rib. Roger Fogg uses a Partridge and Green with an insect-green wool body ribbed with gold wire. These variants all use the brown hackle feather.

DRESSING

Hook: 14–16 Code A, G3A, L2A or CS7.
Body: Yellow thread.
Rib: Fine gold wire.
Hackle: Light-grey partridge back feather.

5 Orange Dotterel

COMMENT

Olive, brown, green, red, yellow, slate, purple and claret versions are all variations on this theme. All are taken for upwinged or stonefly nymphs, or emerging duns if fished upstream with Stewart-style hackles. The dotterel is a rare migratory bird but the soft golden plover marginal covert feather is a suitable replacement.

DRESSING

Hook: 12–16 Code A, G3A, L2A or CS7.
Body: Orange thread.
Hackle: Small marginal covert feather of the golden plover, pale-brown or dark ash with yellow tips.

6 Little Dark Watchet

COMMENT

I am tempted to say that this is just a variation on the next pattern but it does incorporate an interesting feature rarely used in modern dressings: the twisting together of two different-coloured threads. The importance of the colour of the thread beneath a dubbed fur body should not be underestimated. A measure of translucency is achieved as light shines off the tying thread through the fur. The colour of the underlying body plays an important part. Only a very lightly dubbed body of mole's fur should be tied as this is opaque if too much is used.

DRESSING

Hook: 14–16 Code A, G3A, L2A or CS7.
Body: Orange and purple threads twisted together and dubbed with mole or water-rat's fur.
Hackle: Feather from the outside of a coot's wing.
Head: Orange thread.

7 Dark Watchet

COMMENT

Watchet means pale blue or blue-grey but it is in some parts of the north used as a synonym for the natural iron blue and patterns bearing this name imitate the nymphs and emergers of those species well. The Dark Watchet is a classic northern trout fly which has a number of different dressings, since many of the early authorities such as Pritt, Jackson, Edmonds and Lee had their own favourite ties. I suspect that the actual hackle does not matter too much so long as it is a small, soft, dark-slate-coloured feather.

DRESSING

Hook: 14–16 Code A, G3A, L2A or CS7.
Body: Orange thread lightly dubbed with mole's fur.
Hackle: Waterhen breast feather.
Head: Peacock herl.

8 Fog Black

COMMENT

A very good trout and grayling fly tied originally in the last century to copy the small black terrestrial flies that blew off the new grass after haymaking in upper Wharfedale. There are times when any small black patterns will work but this fly is highly praised by many very experienced northern anglers. T. E. Pritt's Little Black is very similar except that it omits the wing. Roger Fogg suggests that the magpie or ostrich herl should not be ribbed along the body but twisted with the tying thread when the body is being made.

DRESSING

Hook: 14–18 Code A, G3A, L2A or CS7.
Body: Dark purple thread.
Rib: Magpie or ostrich herl.
Wing: Starling wing quill.
Hackle: Starling neck feather.

Spiders

Most of these wet flies of the spider type are tied with soft mobile hackles. When the fly is fished downstream the current sweeps over the fly, drawing the hackle fibres back over its body in a general nymph shape. The fibres, which are longer than the body length, taper to a point at the rear, suggesting the tapering abdomen and tails of the natural nymph. Those that are tied Stewart-style (see below) are best fished upstream or across, allowing the movement of the current to work the soft hackles as the flies are carried downstream in a natural drift. The mobility of these soft fibres gives the fly the semblance of life, the one characteristic the fly dresser finds hardest to reproduce.

1 Dun Spider

COMMENT

W. C. Stewart was a Scottish trout fisher of the last century whose book *The Practical Angler* of 1857 went into a score of reprints over a hundred years. He seemed to do most of his fishing with just three wet flies, which killed thousands of trout in Scotland and the Borders. The Dun, Black and Red Spiders are still excellent patterns today. I doubt whether any of the three were dressed to represent a specific species but all are sufficiently generally impressionistic so that between them they cover most of the insects likely to be encountered.

DRESSING

Hook: 12–16 Code A, G3A, L2A or CS7.
Body: Well waxed yellow thread.
Hackle: Originally dotterel but a golden plover or ash-coloured soft feather is a substitute, lightly palmered over the front third of the body.

2 Red Spider

COMMENT

Stewart's spiders are all dressed with the specific hackle style of a soft feather palmered over the front part of the body. Stewart was a great exponent of fishing a team of wet flies upstream rather than the customary across and downstream. Dressed in such a way the current caught the soft hackle fibres and gave them some movement, giving the impression of life in the fly without it having to be moved by the angler. The 'buzz' of the moving fibres gives the impression of an emerging nymph when the flies are fished just below the surface.

DRESSING

Hook: 12–16 Code A, G3A, L2A or CS7.
Body: Well waxed yellow thread.
Hackle: Originally from the outside of a landrail's wing but a small red hen is a substitute, lightly palmered over the front third of the body.

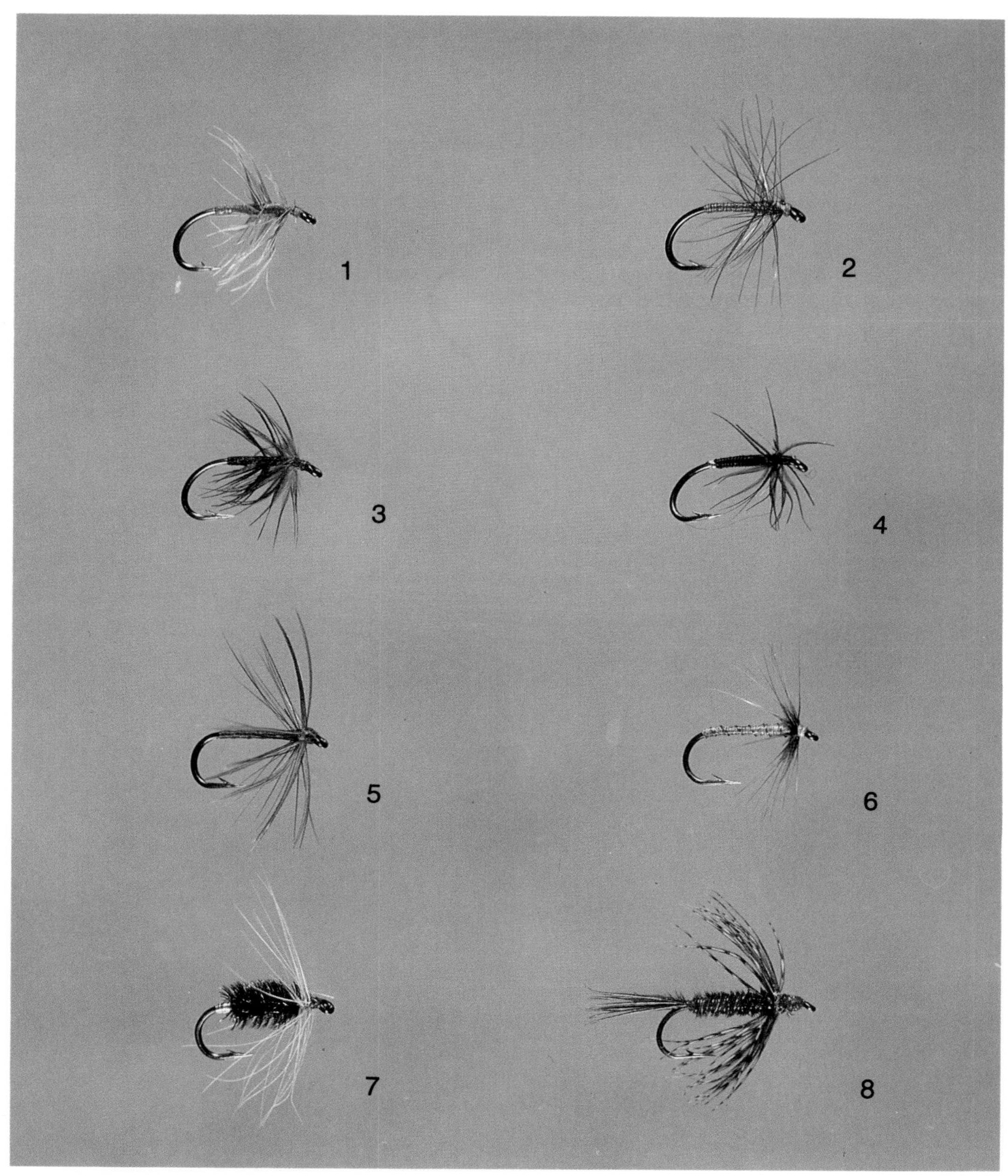

1 Dun Spider **2** Red Spider **3** Black Spider **4** Parry's Black Spider
5 Dark Olive Spider **6** Greenwell Spider **7** Kill Devil Spider
8 Endrick Spider

3 Black Spider

COMMENT

This fly was permanently on Stewart's leader and he described it as 'the most killing imitation we know'. The dressing given is Stewart's original, without the orange or red tip, which was a later addition from another source. The Red Spider was recommended in coloured water but the Black can bring results at any time. Any semi-palmered hackle feather should be tied in so that the longer fibres are nearer the head and the shorter ones towards the middle of the body.

DRESSING

Hook: 12–16 Code A, G3A, L2A or CS7.
Tip (optional): Orange or red floss or thread.
Body: Well waxed brown thread.
Hackle: Cock starling neck feather palmered over the front third of the body.

4 Parry's Black Spider

COMMENT

Few patterns can be more nondescript than a simple black hackled fly fished below the surface. They catch a great many trout, mainly because they are taken for a wide range of aquatic and terrestrial insects. On the upper reaches of freestone rivers throughout the country small black flies fished above or below the surface are always a reliable standby pattern. This dressing is a popular Welsh fly.

DRESSING

Hook: 12–16 Code A, G3A, L2A or CS7.
Tip: Flat silver tinsel.
Body: Black stripped quill.
Hackle: Dark starling.

5 Dark Olive Spider

COMMENT

Also known as the Dark Olive Bloa, it is a large dark olive imitation which is at least 150 years old. The natural is very common on many rivers and is probably the first fly of the season to put trout into a concentrated feeding mood. Later bloa versions omit the wing and/or include a lightly dubbed body of dark olive seal's fur on primrose tying thread. I am sure the lightly dubbed body improves the fly and certainly gives it some translucency.

DRESSING

Hook: 14–16 Code A, L2A or CS7.
Body: Lead-coloured thread or silk.
Wing hackle: Inside of a waterhen's wing.
Leg hackle: Dark-olive hen.

6 Greenwell Spider

COMMENT

Evolving from the winged wet Greenwell's Glory, this is a wingless spider variant to represent the range of olive and iron blue nymphs. One variation which improves the imitation when duns are hatching is to semi-palmer the hackle to give a better impression of a living insect.

DRESSING

Hook: 14 Code A, G3A, L2A or CS7.
Body: Well-waxed primrose thread.
Rib: Gold wire.
Hackle: Greenwell hen (ginger/black).

7 Kill Devil Spiders

COMMENT

This is a series of three wet flies originating in Derbyshire. With the long-fibred, relatively stiff hackles they are quite unlike the other spider patterns. They are general imitative patterns suggestive of a wide range of aquatic and terrestrial insects that end up below the surface. The Kill Devil Red Spider omits the tip and has a long-fibred natural red hackle. The black version also omits the tip and has a similar black hackle.

DRESSING

Hook: 14 Code A, G3A, L2A or CS7.
Tip: Gold or silver tinsel.
Body: Peacock herl.
Hackle: Long-fibred bright medium-blue cock.

8 Endrick Spider

COMMENT

I use the word 'fantastic' cautiously when applied to a fly but I am beginning to be less hesitant in applying it to this fly devised by John Harwood. In addition to being an excellent salmon and sea-trout pattern it is a very good general river and stillwater pattern. Its creator has caught 'thousands of sea trout and well over a hundred salmon on it, and brown trout up to nine pounds'. As a stillwater fly, I rate it higher than the ubiquitous Black and Peacock Spider. Many times it has spectacularly succeeded where other flies have failed. As a river fly its reputation grows every time I use it.

DRESSING

Hook: 10–14 Code A, G3A, L2A or CS7.
Thread: Orange.
Tail: Cock pheasant tail fibre tips.
Body: Copper wire underbody overlaid with cock pheasant tail fibres.
Rib: Silver wire.
Hackle: Grey partridge.
A variation has a copper wire rib and a brown partridge hackle.

Bloas

This series of flies are all North Country patterns originally for fishing the rivers and streams that run off the east and west slopes of the Pennines. Most are at least a hundred years old. They are still in use today and are extremely effective trout and grayling flies. All should be sparsely dressed with a shoulder hackle, or alternatively with a hackle semi-palmered halfway along the body. They are fished both upstream and downstream to represent nymphs, emerging and drowned duns and spent spinners.

The term 'bloa' is an old northern name meaning bluish, blue-dun or slate-blue colour.

1 Poult Bloa

COMMENT

This is a standard pattern which is used throughout the season, though it has been recommended for dull, cold days. It is generally accepted as being a useful imitation of the spurwings, pale wateries and blue-winged olive. As with many older patterns a number of variations have developed; some dressings have a dubbed body or include a rib. The term 'poult' means a young bird. Roger Fogg suggests that the slate-blue feather from the undercoverts of a young black grouse makes a better hackle.

DRESSING

Hook: 14–16 Code A, G3A, L2A or CS7.
Thread: Waxed yellow or primrose.
Body: Tying thread, optionally sparsely dubbed with ginger or natural red fur.
Rib (optional): Fine gold wire on the undubbed version.
Hackle: Slate-blue feather from a young grouse underwing or from the marginal coverts of a coot's wing.

2 Olive Bloa

COMMENT

Many of the various olives can be represented by this dressing and for that reason it can be usefully included on a three-fly leader throughout the entire season. Perhaps the commonest species on the northern rivers is the large dark or spring olive, of which this is a fair imitation of the ascending nymph. It is best fished in the early season between March and May when the natural might be expected to hatch. This is Roger Fogg's modern dressing for the very much older original.

DRESSING

Hook: 12–16 Code A, G3A, L2A or CS7.
Thread: Olive.
Body: Waxed olive thread.
Hackle: A small dull-grey hackle from the marginal coverts of a French partridge wing, coloured with a Pantone pen to a dull green-olive, palmered.

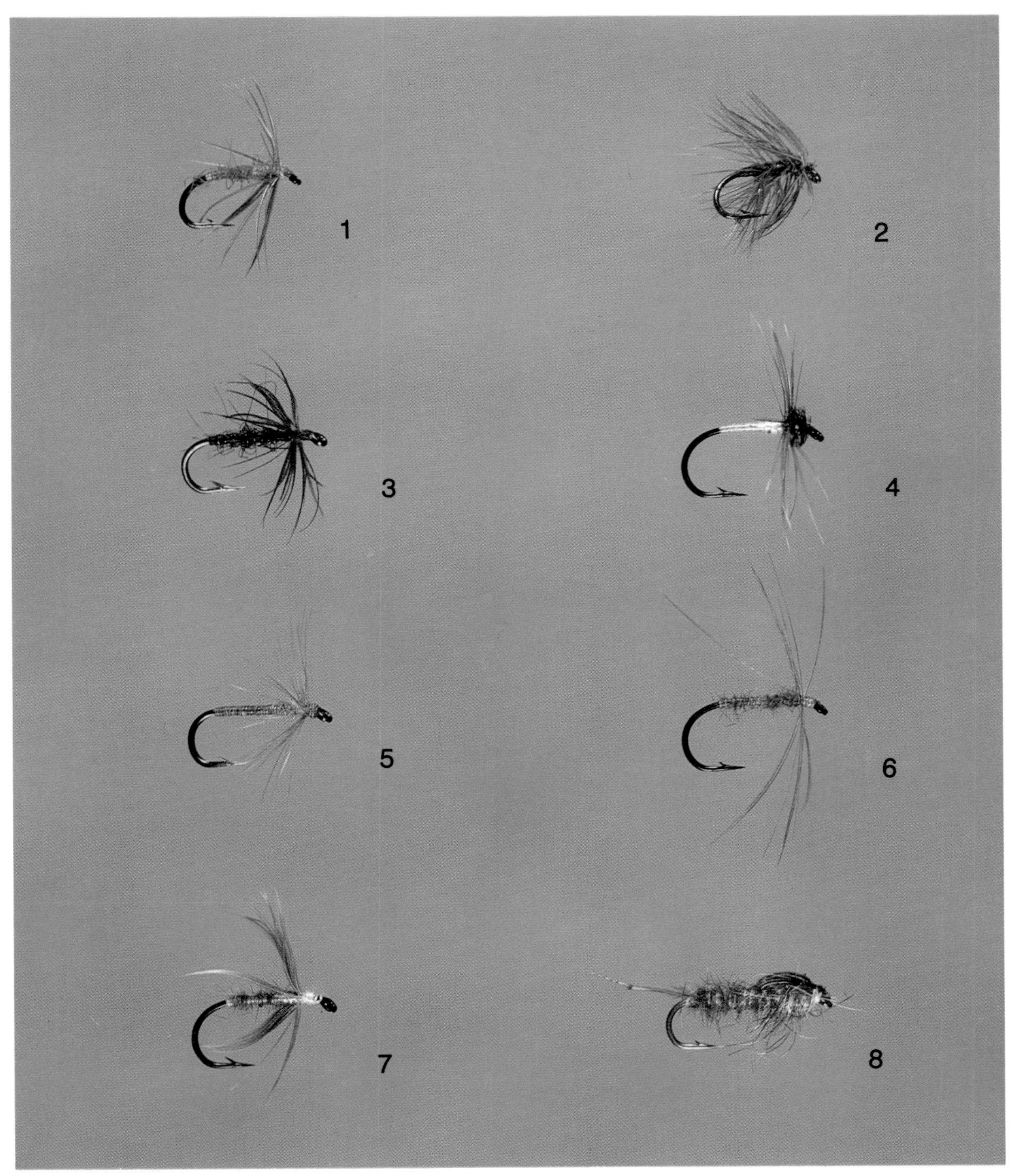

1 Poult Bloa **2** Olive Bloa **3** Dark Bloa **4** Starling Bloa
5 Yellow-Legged Bloa **6** Waterhen Bloa **7** Snipe Bloa **8** Bloa Nymph

3 Dark Bloa

COMMENT

This is a fly that seems to be a hackled version of Broughton's Point. It is a useful early-season pattern and probably a fair imitation of the nymph of the claret dun on stillwaters. It is an even better fly when tied with a Stewart-style semi-palmered hackle. This is a recommended dressing, though I should point out that earlier authorities winged the fly with the inside of a waterhen's wing and sometimes included tails, and one dressing changes the hackle to a dark-brown hen.

DRESSING

Hook: 14–16 Code A, G3A, L2A or CS7.
Thread: Claret or wine-coloured.
Body: Dark claret seal's fur substitute lightly dubbed.
Hackle: Black hen or a dark grey jackdaw's throat feather.

4 Starling Bloa

COMMENT

T. E. Pritt wrote a standard work on fishing the North Country rivers with his *Yorkshire Trout Flies* in 1885. Many of his patterns are still used today with substitutes for some of the now more obscure feathers. All are easy flies to tie, and this one with simple materials is still a good dressing. It looks as though it could well be a pale watery or small dark olive imitation and is a useful spinner imitation for the species that oviposit below the surface. Pritt recommended its use on cold May days and late in the evenings of June and July.

DRESSING

Hook: 14–18 Code A, G3A, L2A or CS7.
Body: Straw-coloured thread, optionally including a very small thorax of pale hare's ear fur.
Hackle: Lightest undercovert feather from a starling's wing.
Head (optional): Peacock herl.

5 Yellow-Legged Bloa

COMMENT

This is based on another of Pritt's patterns, which Roger Fogg suggests is a North Country Greenwell spider variant. It is a useful May and June fly, which suggests that it is effective as a nymph or emerger pattern of the yellow May dun, which is common at this time on many northern rivers, or the most distinctive of stoneflies, the yellow sally.

DRESSING

Hook: 14–16 Code A, G3A, L2A or CS7.
Body: Well-waxed primrose thread with an optional small thorax of pale olive seal's fur substitute.
Hackle: Light-ginger or pale-yellow hen.

6 Waterhen Bloa

COMMENT

Of all the Bloa series this is probably the best and most widely used. My guess is that more than three-quarters of North Country anglers carry it throughout the season. It is effective as an iron blue or dark olive imitation and is mainly used early and late season as a trout fly, and on into November as a grayling fly. Even if there are no flies on the water it is an excellent standby pattern to include on a three-fly leader when searching the pools and lies for trout. It is important with this and the other sparsely dubbed wet flies that when wet the colour of the underlying thread shines through.

DRESSING

Hook: 14–16 Code A, G3A, L2A or CS7.
Thread: Waxed yellow or primrose.
Body: Yellow thread sparsely dubbed with mole or blue water-rat's fur. Sometimes a tip of thread is left exposed.
Hackle: Undercovert or marginal covert feather from a moorhen's (waterhen) wing.

7 Snipe Bloa

COMMENT

With many of these old spider patterns, dressings with different names are very similar. The flies known as Snipe and Yellow, Light Snipe and the Snipe Bloa are almost the same fly with small variations. All the flies by these names are useful early and late in the season. They represent the paler upwingeds and the ovipositing *Baetis* spinners. I err in favour of the view that this dressing is probably improved by a very light dubbing of mole's fur or dyed seal's fur substitute.

DRESSING

Hook: 14–16 Code A, G3A, L2A or CS7.
Body: Straw-coloured or very pale primrose thread, optionally lightly dubbed with mole's fur.
Hackle: Pale blue-grey undercovert feather from a snipe's wing.

8 Bloa Nymph

COMMENT

John Davison was so impressed with the effectiveness of the Waterhen Bloa that he devised a modern weighted nymph based on the dressing. He tied the fly to give a general impression of the nymphs he found in the River Wharfe and other Dales rivers. It accurately matches the size, colour and translucency of the agile-darting type of nymph. The body should be only lightly dubbed so that the correct measure of translucency is achieved.

DRESSING

Hook: 16 long-shank Code H1A or 14 L2A.
Thread: Yellow.
Tail: Dark partridge fibres.
Body: Yellow thread lightly dubbed with mole's fur.
Thorax: Squirrel tail fur dyed yellow in picric acid.
Wingcase: Pheasant tail fibres.
Legs (optional): Partridge hackle.

AQUATIC FLIES

Introduction to Aquatic Flies

Trout feed on flies. It's what makes fly fishing so effective. The trout fisher has to learn something about entomology if any level of consistent success is to be hoped for. Collectively and at different stages of their life cycle aquatic flies are a major trout food source. I suspect that if the fly fisherman knows very little about the fly on the water his catch will be in direct proportion to his knowledge. Being armed with a copy of what flies might be hatching on your river during the period to be fished will mean being well equipped for the task. The fly fisher should be familiar with the life cycle and characteristics of the major species he might encounter. Except on an unfamiliar river there should be no excuse for not having at least a general copy of the important aquatic species. I've considered the sedges, stoneflies, alders, smuts and midges in their separate sections and that leaves only the Ephemeroptera, the upwingeds – the principal fly fishers' flies.

The source of the water and type of riverbed determine its alkalinity and influence which species inhabit a stream. Stones, mud, sand, gravel and weed all attract the nymphs of different species, as does the speed of the current. The shape of the nymphs gives some clue to their habitat: the broad flat ones live on stones, the slim agile-darters in weeds, and others live on moss and in silt. The nymphs grow by a series of moults of the outer skin until maturity is reached. Most species swim to the surface to emerge. Some make the journey to the surface a few times in the day or so prior to emerging, possibly to take on air to aid the splitting of the nymphal skin. When nymphs reach the surface film the skin of the upper side of the thorax and head splits for the dun to emerge on the surface and erect its wings. This point of emergence is a highly dangerous moment for the fly. The emerger has to fight to break the surface tension, free itself of the nymphal shuck, erect its wings in preparation for flight and wait a little time to dry. At the point of breakthrough trout find them easy targets as emergers and adults. A fair number also die naturally and become an easy, non-escaping food.

The factors affecting when hatches occur have been much debated. Humidity, barometric pressure, light, wind direction and strength are possible factors. It seems likely that temperature and temperature change are the largest single influences but it is a fairly vague theory with much further research needed. An interesting book, *The Ways of Trout*, by Leonard Wright Jr, explores the subject in some depth and is a fascinating read for the enthusiastic dry-fly fisher.

The characteristics common to all duns or subimagines are upright wings, a segmented body, six legs and two or three tails. Most species have four wings, one large pair and another very much smaller pair which the flydresser has no need to copy. In a few species the hindwings are absent. Most species are a fairly dull colour. The dun rests on the water with only its six legs for support. If the tails or any other part come into water contact there is a danger that it will not be able to shed the water for flight. If an accurate imitation of the emerged dun is sought, the artificial should be supported only by a leg imitation, with the tails and body held above the water. Few dun imitations actually achieve this ideal.

The duns fly to the shelter of vegetation, where, usually within the next forty-eight hours, the transformation to the final adult state, the spinner or imago, is completed. The skin splits and the spinner emerges. Its legs and tails are much longer, the body is brighter and the wings shiny, transparent and heavily veined. The males swarm over the water, where they are joined by the females for copulation. Air temperature and probably light intensity are important factors in the timing of this but most species have preferred times, places and altitudes. Swarming can take place at any time of the day but is most significant for the fly fisher in late evening and dusk. The mated females almost immediately start to lay their eggs and the males of a few species may die over the water.

The manner of oviposition, or egg laying, varies. Some females, such as the blue-winged olive, carry a distinctive egg ball under the rear of the abdomen; on others the last body segments are a different colour because of the eggs within. Some species lay their eggs in the water in a single batch by dipping the tip of the abdomen below the surface whilst in flight or when alighting briefly on the water. Some return a number of times. Many *Baetis* spinners climb down stakes and vegetation at the waterside and deposit their eggs on moss and stones below the surface. These subsurface spinners sometimes try to break back through the surface film but most die in the water and become easy prey for feeding fish. When spinners land on the surface they have their wings upright and only when the female has extruded her eggs and is exhausted are the wings in the spent horizontal position. All lie flush in the film, with their wings and bodies the key features for trout to see. During a good spinner fall trout feed quite leisurely on these flies they know will not escape.

Most fly fishers pride themselves on being able to identify the principal duns and spinners and knowing when they might be expected on the water. Lack of such knowledge leaves the fly fisher less than fully equipped. Even if one is unable to identify the hatching fly – and often one cannot without the aid of a magnifying glass – it should be a simple matter to collect a sample and match it for wing and body colour and size. The hatch matching and close imitation of some of the fine detail of each species gives a great deal of pleasure to many fly dressers and anglers and, indeed, this is what much of our pastime is all about. Most trout don't demand such fine detail and if medium-sized grey-winged olive-bodied duns are hatching they can generally be duped by a size 14 grey-winged olive-bodied artificial. Some of the dressings for the upwinged species have been specifically tied to represent that dun or spinner. Trout may of course be quite satisfied with a general imitation and not need so close a copy. Depending upon the water conditions, the size of the hatch, the education of the fish and its tendency to selectivity, accurate dressing may be required and some of the specific imitations will do just that. It may also, of course, give more pleasure and satisfaction to the fly-dressing trout fisher to recognise the natural fly, offer a fair imitation to a wary trout and dupe it.

Alder, Gravel Bed, Smuts

Of these three aquatic flies perhaps it is the alder that has attracted most attention from writers and fly dressers, and yet it is a fly I have rarely found the need to imitate. I've seen plenty of naturals near the water but I've never seen the adults taken. A larva dressing has proved useful but I guess that since it looks generally meaty and food-like it could be mistaken for a caddis larva or a large stonefly nymph. In my experience trout have taken far more interest in the gravel bed and the parachute-style fly below is an excellent imitation. Even more important are the smuts. If you enjoy a fly-fishing challenge these are the species to offer it. Their size makes the presentation of a suitably small imitation difficult. Trout can become so preoccupied with them that no other fly will work.

1 Alder Larva (Carnill)

COMMENT

The alder is a very common fly from late April until mid-June. The larvae, which at maturity are about an inch long, live in the debris on the riverbed. They crawl ashore to burrow in the damp river or lake margins, from which they emerge as adults a few days later. It is during this migration to the margins that trout take them and the subsurface artificial is best employed. This is a modern larva dressing from Bob Carnill.

DRESSING

Hook; 10 long-shank Code H1A.
Tail: Bunch of medium-brown cock fibres or one biot quill dyed light brown.
Body and thorax: Dark-chestnut seal's fur substitute.
Gills: A small pale-ginger hackle palmered and finished behind the thorax.
Legs: Brown partridge tied at the sides only behind the thorax.
Back and thorax cover: Plain or mottled brown fibres.
Rib: Oval gold over the abdomen and back.

2 Alder Adult

COMMENT

The adults are often mistaken for sedges at first glance. They are large dark, almost black flies with hard, shiny, roof-shaped wings that lack the hairs of the sedge wings. The adults are not normally found on the water as they lay their eggs on overhanging plants. Some may fall onto the surface by accident. Many patterns have been developed, most very similar to this pattern, which is loosely based on Charles Kingsley's and Richard Walker's dressings.

DRESSING

Hook: 10–12 Code A or L2A.
Thread: Black.
Body: Magenta-dyed peacock herl.
Wing: Any speckled brown hen feather, or brown mallard rolled and tied at a low angle.
Hackle: Black cock.

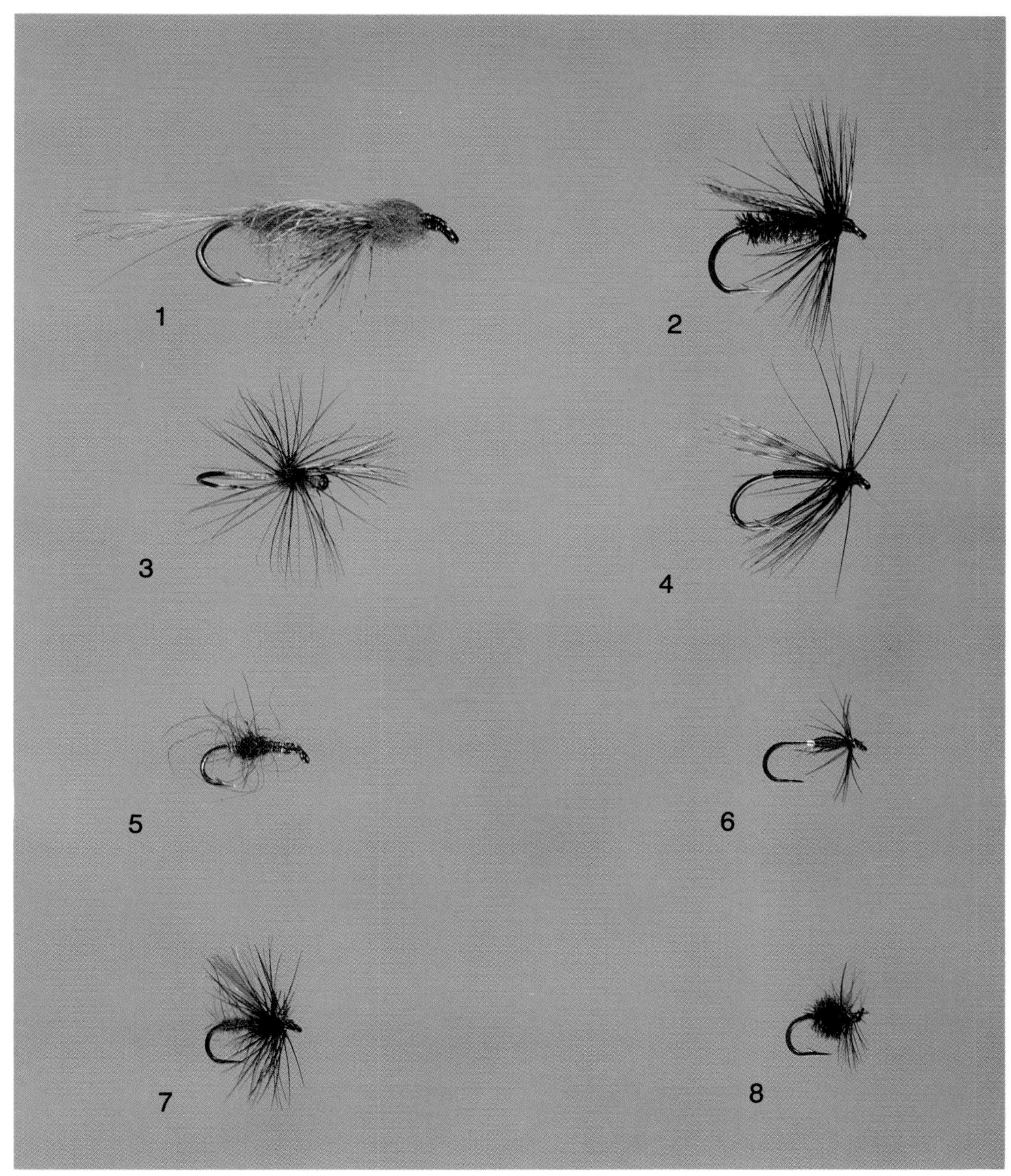

1 Alder Larva **2** Alder Adult **3** Gravel Bed **4** Clyde Sandfly
5 Jacobsen Smut **6** Mottram Smut **7** Black Jack **8** Goddard Smut

3 Gravel Bed (Fogg)

COMMENT

This is a flat-winged terrestrial species which is very often found in some numbers flying low over the surface as they swarm before mating. Inevitably many end up on the water. Some seem to dip down to the surface as though egg-laying. On some rivers their appearance attracts a lot of trout attention on warm days from late April until June. The body is brownish-grey and the wings are brownish and heavily veined. Overall they have the appearance of small craneflies and are easily recognisable. This is a parachute-hackled pattern from Roger Fogg.

DRESSING

Hook: 14 Code L3A or E6A.
Thread: Lead-coloured or grey darkened with dark wax.
Body: Lead-coloured thread with a thorax of mole's fur.
Hackle: Top-quality cock tied shiny side downwards.

4 Clyde Sandfly

COMMENT

This, as the name suggests, is a pattern from a region of Scotland where the gravel bed attracts a lot of trout activity. Its two alternative names no doubt derive from the fact that in its pupal state the gravel bed lives in damp sand or gravel on the river shore. They appear on many rivers and if the fly fisher is looking only for upwingeds or sedges he may well fail to notice the smaller gravel bed on the water. It is a very useful fly for the first half of the season.

DRESSING

Hook: 12–14 Code L3A or E6A.
Thread: Black.
Body: Black thread.
Wing: Hen pheasant centre-tail laid flat across the back.
Hackle: Long-fibred black cock.

5 Smut (Jacobsen)

COMMENT

When fish feed on these tiny flies emerging on the surface it can be a frustrating time. The larvae are impossible to imitate successfully but the adult fly, emerging from its pupal case, rises to the surface in a gas bubble. Sometimes these tiny flies will hang below the surface before emerging and trout find them very attractive. One key feature is the air bubble. It can be represented by silver wire, or – more successfully – by a body dubbing soaked in silicone, or by Antron fibres, which attract and hold air bubbles. This is Preben Torp Jacobsen's imitation.

DRESSING

Hook: 14 silvered wide-gape.
Thread: Brown.
Body: Blood-red cow's hair over a base of thin copper wire, tied in the middle of the shank for about a third of its length. This should be thoroughly soaked in silicone liquid so that air bubbles will adhere to the hair. Four or five turns of silver wire (0.15mm) at either end of the body.

6 **Smut** (Mottram)

COMMENT

This wet pattern belongs to John Cecil Mottram. It is simple to tie and can be very effective, particularly for smutting grayling. It should be fished just in the surface film. In many ways Mottram was a highly original theorist, with many of his ideas coming to fruition. More than seventy years ago he was suggesting no-hackle flies, calling them 'flies of the future'; turkey herls and bead eyes on lures; treating flies with floatant; advocating the use of tiny smuts and terrestrials long before the Americans; a nymph held in the film by a piece of cork (a suspender?), and much more.

DRESSING

Hook: 14–18 Code L2A or E6A.
Body: Black floss silk as a thorax only (I think it is improved by a tip of silver tinsel behind).
Hackle: One turn of a small starling breast feather.

7 **Black Jack**

COMMENT

As far as I am aware this dry fly was the creation of Bob Spink of York, a semi-professional fly tyer who gave me my first tying lesson. I think it was an unnamed fly so I christened it in 1981 in honour of Bob's lifelong friend, Jack Bardy, who was responsible for giving me my first rod and reel when I was aged 10. Between them these two have much to answer for. The fly is an excellent trout and grayling fly when either species is smutting. The natural adult smut is very small with a dark brown to black body and broad transparent wings held flat over the back.

DRESSING

Hook: 16–20 Code L3A or E6A.
Thread: Black.
Body: Dark-brown seal's fur substitute or poly dubbing.
Wing: Two small bunches side by side, originally dyed hackle fibres, one bunch bright red, the other yellow or light-green; I now use poly yarn.
Hackle: Black cock.

8 **Smut** (Goddard)

COMMENT

Smutting trout can be annoying and frustrating and when that happens you either end up defeated or hit it lucky with the right pattern and presentation. Never one to let the trout have the better of him, John Goddard came up with this pattern which allowed him to fish a small fly on a practical hook size. The body offers an acceptably small silhouette yet with a wide-gape hook it still offers a fair chance of holding the trout. Its creator describes it as being 'phenomenally successful'. It also has the distinct advantage of being easy to tie.

DRESSING

Hook: 18 Code B or L3B.
Thread: Black.
Body: Black ostrich herl with a very short flue (taken from near the tip of the feather) wound on the front half of the shank.
Hackle: Three or four turns of good-quality short-fibred black cock.

Stoneflies 1

The importance of stoneflies varies enormously between rivers. Hatches of the upwinged species and sedges are usually significant on all trout streams but the stonefly populations are so varied that on some rivers an imitation is never fished and on others the artificial is a good standby all year round. As a general rule the higher the altitude, the faster the gradient and river flow, the more stony the riverbed, the greater is the stonefly population. Only a few species prefer lowland, slower, weedy water. In addition to the patterns in these two sections a number of patterns can be found in the North Country sections.

1 Early Brown *(Protonemoura meyeri, Nemoura variegata)*

COMMENT

This is a useful early-season spider pattern for the northern rivers which the two small stoneflies of this name inhabit. The nymphs live among moss in fast-flowing water. The adults appear between February and May and have a distinctive pale bar across the top of the head. They are a small fly with a reddish-brown body and brown-grey wings. This is Roger Fogg's dressing.

DRESSING

Hook: 14–16 Code A, G3A, L2A or CS7.
Thread: Red spinner.
Body: Brown seal's fur substitute tied slim.
Hackle: Slate-coloured coot, palmered halfway down the body.

2 Willow Fly *(Leuctra geniculata)*

COMMENT

This is a widely distributed species and one of the few common chalkstream stoneflies. It is a late-season fly, appearing from August and into November. The adults are slim, 7–10mm long, with brownish wings and long antennae. I have never come across trout or grayling rising to the returning female, and the nymph imitation is much more use.

DRESSING

Hook: 14–16 Code A, L2A, C3A or CS7.
Thread: Orange.
Body: Orange thread lightly dubbed with brown fur leaving an optional tip of tying thread exposed.
Hackle: Brown partridge.
Head: Peacock herl.

1 Early Brown **2** Willow Fly **3** February Red **4** February Red (dry)
5 Yellow Sally **6** Yellow Sally (dry) **7** Light Spanish Needle
8 Dark Spanish Needle

3 February Red *(Taeniopteryx nebulosa, Brachyptera risi)*

COMMENT

Most stoneflies prefer fast water with a stony riverbed. The first of these species is an exception and the nymphs are found in the vegetation of slower rivers in parts of Scotland, Wales, the West Country, and the north of England. The second species is found on faster water. Roger Fogg's dressing is given and he recommends that it should be used as a top dropper in a team fished upstream.

DRESSING

Hook: 12–16 Code A, G3A, L2A or CS7.
Thread: Dark-orange.
Body: Mixed claret and brown seal's fur substitute, tied slim.
Rib: Dark-brown thread.
Hackle: Woodcock palmered over the front third.

4 February Red

COMMENT

The first species appears from February until April. The second will emerge as late as July. Both species are very similar, with red-brown wings and with the last three segments of the female's body red-brown. The only time the adult appears on the water is when the female returns to lay her eggs. When that happens this is the imitation to use.

DRESSING

Hook: 14 Code L3A, L2A or E6A.
Thread: Dark-orange.
Body: Red-brown seal's fur substitute.
Wing: Grizzle cock hackle tips tied flat acros the back.
Hackle: Natural red or grizzle cock.

5 Yellow Sally *(Isoper'*

COMMENT

The yellow sally is one of the commonest stoneflies. It is found throughout Britain except for East Anglia and in some areas of the Midlands. Stoneflies generally prefer to inhabit faster-flowing water in hilly areas, but this one is also found in lowland rivers with a sandy or stony bottom. This wet fly is based on an old Yorkshire dressing by T. E. Pritt. It is a useful pattern when the adults are in the air or when there is evidence of nymphal activity below the surface.

DRESSING

Hook: 14–16 Code A, L2A, G3A or CS7.
Thread: Primrose.
Body: Dubbed pale yellow fur or wool.
Hackle: Golden plover (mouse-coloured wit yellow tips) or pale yellow hen.

6 Yellow Sally

COMMENT

This is the easiest adult stonefly to recognise, with its yellow body and yellow-green wings. They appear from April until August. There are occasions, usually during the afternoons, when the returning females attract the attention of surface-feeding trout. This dressing for the dry fly includes tail fibres. No natural adult stonefly has tails, but the artificial balances better on the surface. The translucent synthetic wing material is a Traun River product.

DRESSING

Hook: 14 Code L2A, L3A or E6A.
Thread: Primrose.
Tail: Light-ginger cock fibres.
Body: Mixed yellow and brown seal's fur substitute (5:1).
Rib: Primrose thread.
Wings: Roman Moser stonefly wing across the back.
Hackle: Light-ginger cock.

7 Needle Flies *(Leuctra fusca, L. hippopus)*

COMMENT

These two are the smallest British stoneflies, widely distributed on stony-bottomed rivers. They are dark brown and, as their name suggests, very thin flies. One species emerges at the very beginning of the season from February to April and the other from August until October. This wet-fly dressing is known as the Light Spanish Needle. Both the needle-fly dressings given are also excellent grayling patterns.

DRESSING

Hook: 14–16 Code A, L2A, G3A or CS7.
Thread: Crimson.
Body: Crimson thread optionally very lightly dubbed with pale brown seal's fur substitute tied very slim.
Hackle: Snipe undercovert feather or small light starling feather.
Head: Peacock herl tied quite small.

8 Dark Spanish Needle

COMMENT

This is a similar fly to the Light Spanish Needle, both of which are popular North Country spider patterns which represent many of the smaller stoneflies. Both dressings have origins extending well beyond a century ago and have been killing trout on northern rivers with formidable reliability. This is T. E. Pritt's pattern, which for the purposes of fishing upstream is possibly improved by palmering the hackle halfway down the body in the style of W. C. Stewart.

DRESSING

Hook: 14–16 Code A, L2A, G3A or CS7.
Body: Orange thread darkened with wax.
Hackle: Feather from the darkest part of a brown owl's wing or dark-brown hen feather.
Head: Peacock herl.

Stoneflies 2

The nymphs are in many ways very similar to ephemeropteran nymphs except that they all have two tails, whereas the latter have three. They live on the underside of stones, a few species in weed, and are only found close to the riverbed, never swimming to the surface to emerge. The mature nymph crawls ashore to the stony margins where the nymphal skin splits for the adult to emerge. All adults have four hard, shiny wings, which are long and flat and when at rest lie flat over the body. The male's wings are much shorter than the female's. After mating the female returns to the surface to lay the eggs. Here the adult fly is an attractive target for surface-feeding fish.

1 Dark Moor Game

COMMENT

Moor game is an old Yorkshire name for the grouse. This is a useful old fly which I confess I haven't used, but I know of fly fishers who praise it highly. It is primarily a stonefly imitation and has been around for over 150 years. Two dressings exist. Pritt used a hackle from a hen red grouse but other authorities and our leading contemporary authority, Roger Fogg, suggest that a darker hackle is better and this is his dressing.

DRESSING

Hook: 14–16 Code A, L2A, G3A or CS7.
Thread: Orange waxed darker.
Body: Orange thread with a very fine dubbing of blue water-rat's fur.
Hackle: Very dark freckled feather from the 'knuckle' of a dark red grouse wing.

2 Brown Stonefly Nymph

COMMENT

What an excellent nymph this has proved for me, with river brown trout to three pounds nine ounces and grayling to two pounds three ounces falling for it. It has also consistently taken fish when there is no fly hatching and no other sub-surface pattern has worked. Because the nymph is leaded it can be fished deep, where the big fish often lie, particularly in the case of grayling. I've used it as a point fly on a downstream three-fly team on freestone rivers and as an upstream nymph on chalk streams and it rarely fails. It fishes point up, so avoiding snags. Roger Fogg gets the credit for devising it. I include tails.

DRESSING

Hook: 8–14 Code CS7 or G3A (I prefer long-shank 12–16 Code H1A).
Tail: The butts of two cock pheasant tail fibres.
Body: Lead-foil strips bound on top of the shank. (Dress the rest of the fly upside down.) Various shades of brown seal's fur substitute, built up at the thorax.
Hackle: Palmered brown hen over the abdomen only, with the upper and lower fibres trimmed away. The thorax top is clear-varnished to represent the wingcases.
Rib: Clear nylon monofilament.

1 Dark Moor Game **2** Brown Stonefly Nymph **3** Dark Creeper
4 Terrible Stone **5** Dark Stone **6** Adult Stonefly **7** Jansen Stonefly
8 Moser-Winged Stonefly

3 Dark Creeper

COMMENT

The old name for the three species of large stonefly nymph is the creeper, named after the manner in which they creep ashore. Some of these nymphs are an inch long and are eagerly devoured by trout. Some years ago I watched an elderly Yorkshireman fish his way upstream on a northern Dales river with his fly rod baited with the natural nymph. It was a deadly method and he enjoyed considerable success until his supply of bait expired. This is Taff Price's imitation, which will be more acceptable on fly-only waters.

DRESSING

Hook: 12–16 Long-shank Code H1A.
Thread: Brown.
Body: Brown seal's fur substitute.
Rib: Yellow silk.
Thorax: Dark hare's ear fur.
Wingcase: Dark turkey fibres.
Legs: Wingcase fibres turned beneath the body and trimmed.

4 Terrible Stone

COMMENT

This is a North American large stonefly nymph dressing from Al Troth. It is extremely realistic and worthy of use in any river the large stoneflies are known to inhabit. The hook should be bent slightly in the centre of the shank so that the two ends slope down slightly to give the impression of the moving swimming nymph. It can also be fished leaded.

DRESSING

Hook: 10–14 Long-shank Code H1A.
Thread: Black.
Tail and feelers: Grey goose quill fibres dyed dark-brown and tied in a V (cock pheasant tail fibres are a fair substitute).
Legs: Stripped black hackle stalks bent in the middle with the joint sealed with clear cement.
Body: Dark brown chenille, built up at the thorax, ribbed with a dubbing of mixed black and brown seal's fur substitute.

5 Dark Stone

COMMENT

Alan Hudson, who was at the time joint editor of *Flydresser*, the magazine of the Fly Dressers' Guild, sent me this pattern for the early-season stoneflies such as the early brown. It was devised for the Welsh border streams but it does very well as an early season general pattern on any rough stream. For this purpose it is best to include a tail of mixed black and grizzle cock fibres. Alan Hudson prefers to use two different hackle shades to give a variegated effect, which he is correct in believing is closer to nature than solid colours.

DRESSING

Hook: 14–16 Code L3A or E6A.
Thread: Black.
Tail (optional): Mixed black and grizzle cock fibres.
Body: Hare's ear fur.
Rib: Medium gold or silver tinsel.
Hackle: Badger cock in front, black cock behind.

6 Adult Stonefly

COMMENT

This is a general adult dressing to represent the returning ovipositing females. It is in many ways similar to some sedge designs. One of the key features is the flat wings in the style of the natural. The two feather slips for the wings should be stiff-fibred with their tips rounded off when tied in to give an accurate silhouette. Recommended wing feathers include hen pheasant wing or hen mallard body feather. Materials should be used to match the natural.

DRESSING

Hook: 10–16 long-shank Code E1A.
Thread: Brown or grey.
Body: Coloured polypropylene dubbing.
Rib: Palmered grizzle cock.
Wing: Two wing or body feather slips.
Hackle: Natural red cock wound over the wing roots.

7 Jansen Stonefly

COMMENT

Expert Dutch fly dresser Frans Jansen has produced this superb adult stonefly pattern based on an earlier Hal Jansen dressing from the USA. It is an excellent pattern for the large stoneflies. It floats very well and is very durable, and it certainly looks like the real thing. Fished in a riffle when the naturals are about, they are taken very confidently. They are, however, time-consuming to tie. Frans has come up with a cheap and effective wing material that can be naturally coloured and allows the light to shine through very effectively. The body deer hair can be a single colour or alternative bands.

DRESSING

Hook: 12–16 long-shank Code H1A.
Thread: To match the deer hair head.
Tail: Hair from a pig's bristle paintbrush or other dark stiff hair.
Body: Deer hair to match the natural tied in muddler style and trimmed slim.
Legs: Dark-blue-dun cock fibres.
Wing: Synthetic curtain material coloured brown and black patterned with waterproof markers.
Antennae: As for tail.
Head: Clear-varnished deer hair to match darkest body colour.

8 Moser-Winged Stonefly

COMMENT

Roman Moser's preformed stonefly wings are very effective and lifelike with their wing veining. Because they come in different shades and sizes they can be included on most adult stonefly imitations. The needle flies are probably just too thin to be tied in this style. The dressing opposite is suitable for imitating the early brown, medium and large stoneflies. Others can be represented by varying the colours of the materials and the hook sizes. The Yellow Sally on page 133 is an example.

DRESSING

Hook: 12–18 Code A, L3A or E1A.
Thread: Brown.
Body: Wound brown polypropylene yarn.
Wing: Traun River Stonefly wing.
Hackle: Furnace or Coch-y-bonddhu cock.

Midges

The unfortunate deterioration in water quality in some rivers has reduced the hatches of upwinged species and has meant that trout take a greater interest in aquatic insects more tolerant of pollution, such as the midges. Their hatches on some slow-moving rivers, even the chalk streams, are becoming very significant. John Goddard records one recent season's catch on rivers to his Suspender Midge Pupa as over 120 trout (mainly browns), many between three and five pounds. He comments further that he has rarely known trout take an artificial pattern with such confidence. Midge imitation on stillwater has been developed to a high level; perhaps now some of those patterns will be adopted and adapted by river fly fishers.

1 Black Midge Pupa

COMMENT

Although this dressing is black, it can be any colour to match the natural. They move in a wriggling motion and often rest hanging from the surface with a slight curl to the body which can be imitated in the dressing. When the pupae pause on reaching the surface film they sometimes adopt a horizontal position and swim for a few feet in that plane. Unintentional drag of the artificial is sometimes overlooked by trout and it may even make the artificial more lifelike. This dressing is a very simple one to be fished awash in the film.

DRESSING

Hook: 14–16 Code L2A, L3A or A.
Thread: Black.
Body: Black floss.
Rib: Fine silver wire.
Hackle: Black cock or hen.

2 Suspender Midge Pupa

COMMENT

John Goddard has done much to develop this design of fly. The Ethafoam ball ensures that the fly hangs suspended and the ball itself may be mistaken for part of the emerging adult breaking through the top of the nymphal or pupal shuck. Although this was primarily a stillwater pattern, it is very worth while for rivers (particularly slower-moving chalk streams) where trout sip the pupae from the surface film. Any midge pattern can be adapted to include the Ethafoam ball. John Goddard finds the green and the brown versions the most useful.

DRESSING

Hook: 14–18 Code L2A or A.
Thread: Dark-brown midge.
Tail (optional): White fluorescent wool tied slightly round the bend.
Body: Seal's fur substitute to match the natural colour.
Rib: Fine silver wire or lurex.
Thorax: Turkey herl fibres dyed brown, or peacock herl.
Head: A small Ethafoam ball enclosed in a fine white nylon mesh (ladies' tights are suitable).

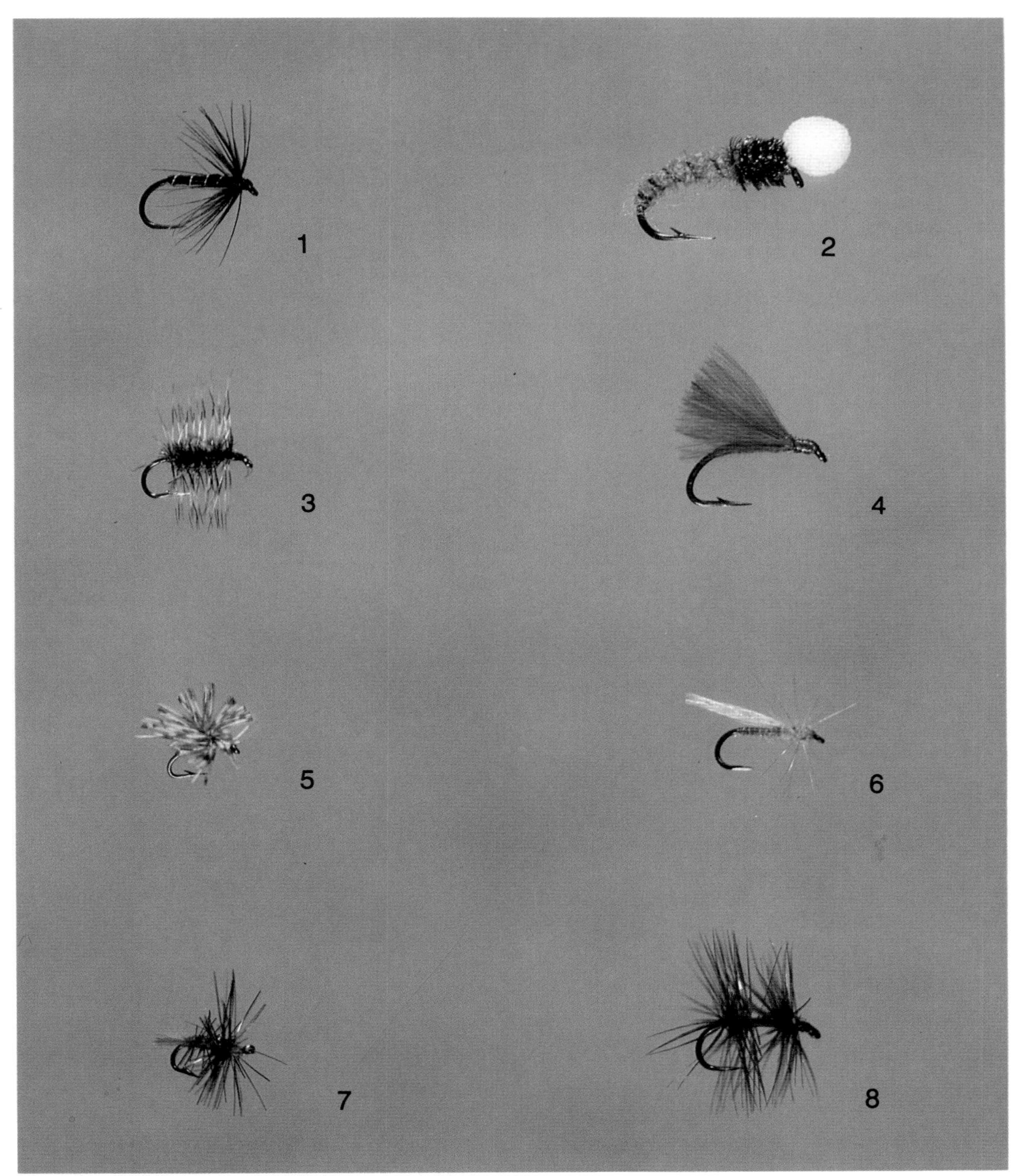

1 Black Midge Pupae **2** Suspender Midge Pupa **3** Griffiths' Gnat **4** F Fly **5** Shmidge **6** Low-Riding Midge **7** Red and Black Midge **8** Knotted Midge

3 Griffiths's Gnat

COMMENT

Widely acclaimed in the USA, it is beginning to have a following on some English waters. Fished awash in the film it provides a good impression of the half-pupa, half-adult insect. Fish all midge imitations on a fine leader of very soft nylon. If the trout won't take, then fish downstream. When fishing so small a fly it is likely to be the presentation that is at fault as much as the pattern, and downstream there is less chance of the leader spooking the fish.

DRESSING

Hook: 16–28 fine-wire Code L3A, L4A, E6A or K1A.
Thread: Black Spartan Micro.
Body: Peacock herl.
Hackle: Very short-fibred grizzle palmered down the body.

4 The F Fly

COMMENT

This is a Continental pattern which was developed by Marjan Fratnik from the earlier Moustique series. It utilises a duck feather which has largely been ignored by British and American fly dressers. I have seen its effectiveness on our chalk streams. Depending upon its size it could be taken for a midge or gnat and possibly a sedge. It is very successful in Europe for grayling, brown trout and rudd. There is no need to treat the fly to float as owing to the nature of the feather it floats like a cork. Dutch angling writer Kees Ketting also ties a very similar fly known as the Ketting Duck Fly.

DRESSING

Hook: 14–20 Code L3A, L4A or E6A.
Thread: Grey, brown, black or yellow Sparton Micro.
Body: Tying thread or natural heron herl.
Hackle: Fluffy grey feather from the sebaceous (preen) gland of a mallard, tied on top of the shank and trimmed to hook length.

5 Shmidge

COMMENT

Tiny flies can represent quite a large numerical proportion of a trout's intake on rivers at certain times. Sometimes on relatively slow water they'll ignore a hatch of duns and concentrate on something barely visible. These insects might be midges, smuts or other minuscule species. Because of the tiny amount of food each item represents, trout have a concentrated period on these to make up the volume they need. The rise is usually slow and leisurely, with fish merely sipping the fly in the film very gently. Various colours work for different species. The pattern is probably taken for emerging upwingeds as well.

DRESSING

Hook: 16–24 fine-wire Code L3A, L4A or K1A.
Body: Coloured tying thread.
Hackle: Generous turns of grey hackle or partridge or similar feather in parachute style and trimmed to size.

6 Low-Riding Midge

COMMENT

In Datus Proper's excellent book *What the Trout Said* (Knopf, 1982) he mentions this adult midge pattern which floats with its wings flat on the surface with the body hanging down like a hatching pupa. The Americans can teach us a great deal when it comes to midge fishing, not least in the presentation of flies as small as size 28. There are times when size is extremely critical, and it may be that if trout are rising to something small the artificial really does have to be of an equivalent size.

DRESSING

Hook: 16–28 Code L3A, L4A, E6A or K1A.
Thread: Sparton Micro to match the body colour.
Abdomen: Thinly dubbed fur.
Wings: Two small hackle-fibre points tied in a V over the abdomen.
Hackle: Two or three turns of cock hackle, bunched spent.
Thorax: Dubbed fur either side and over the wing and hackle roots.

7 Red and Black Midge

COMMENT

I can find no published references to this useful little fly. A very experienced elderly northern trout fisher gave me the dressing as being a successful one when midges were hatching. It has been a reliable fly for those circumstances and for smutting fish. The fly is also an excellent grayling fly and the red stimulus may be more important for this species.

DRESSING

Hook: 18–22 Code L3A.
Thread: Red Sparton Micro.
Tag: Bright-red floss.
Body: Bright-red floss with a palmered black cock trimmed short.
Hackle: Black cock (longer-fibred than normally required for the hook size) and trimmed.

8 Knotted Midge

COMMENT

This is one of the easiest dry flies to tie. For all its simplicity, it is a very successful pattern. Whether it's actually taken for the pair of mating midges which it is intended to represent is another matter since this all-black fly is also a good general terrestrial imitation. The fore-and-aft hackles also keep the body well clear of the water and give an effective light pattern to represent a small dun. On many occasions when I've needed a small fly because a fish has been sipping something I couldn't see, I've risen it on a knotted midge. A pattern I would not be without.

DRESSING

Hook: 14–20 Code L3A, L4A or E6A.
Thread: Black Sparton Micro.
Body: Black thread.
Hackles: Two small black cock hackles, one at either end of the body.

Emergers and Stillborns

The cataclysmic breakthrough by the mature nymph from the environment in which it has spent all its life to a totally new one is no easy transition. They don't all make it. Not only is the emerging dun which is struggling to leave its nymphal shuck and penetrate the surface film a prime target for a feeding trout, it also has to adapt itself from functioning as an aquatic nymph to being an airborne fly. The battle through the film as it sheds its old skin is a trauma that takes its toll. Many die in the process. The inch of water below the surface provides the most dangerous moment of the nymph's journey from the riverbed, even the most critical and vulnerable seconds of its life so far. Their vulnerability does not go unnoticed by trout, and particularly in the early stages of a hatch trout feed upon the emerging duns.

1 Walker's Hatching Nymph

COMMENT

This pattern of Richard Walker's can be fished either just below the film or, well soaked with floatant, on the surface. Although polypropylene materials were not specified by Richard Walker they enable the nymph to float better than other materials and the wing is more durable. If you want the nymph to float, use fine-wire hooks and add tails of widely spaced cock fibres held apart by a small ball of dubbing.

DRESSING

Hook: 12–16 Code L3A or E1A.
Tail: Cock hackle fibres.
Abdomen and thorax: Dubbed fur or polypropylene.
Wingcase: Feather fibres on the upper side of the thorax divided either side of the wing fibres.
Wing: A bunch of cock hackle fibres or polypropylene yarn to emerge from the top of the thorax.
Hackle: A short-fibred throat hackle to match the legs or underside of the natural.

2 Lawrie's Hatching Dun

COMMENT

The size and colour of the materials can be adapted to match any upwinged species. The soft hen fibres ensure that they sink below the surface. The wing hackle should be chosen to match the colour of the natural's wing, and the leg hackle should be a similar colour to the underside of the thorax or the legs. The hackle fibres of the wing should be cut away completely on the underside, and the upper hackle fibres of the leg hackle cut away. The fly is fished so that the tail and abdomen sink into the film but the hackles and thorax are treated to float.

DRESSING

Hook: 14–16 Code L3A, L4A or E6A.
Thread: Claret.
Tail: Three white or cream hen fibres.
Abdomen: Mole or water-rat fur.
Thorax: Dark-purple dyed rat's fur or seal's fur substitute.
Wing hackle: Medium slate-blue cock with the lower fibres cut away.
Leg hackle: Dark-blue cock with the upper fibres cut away.

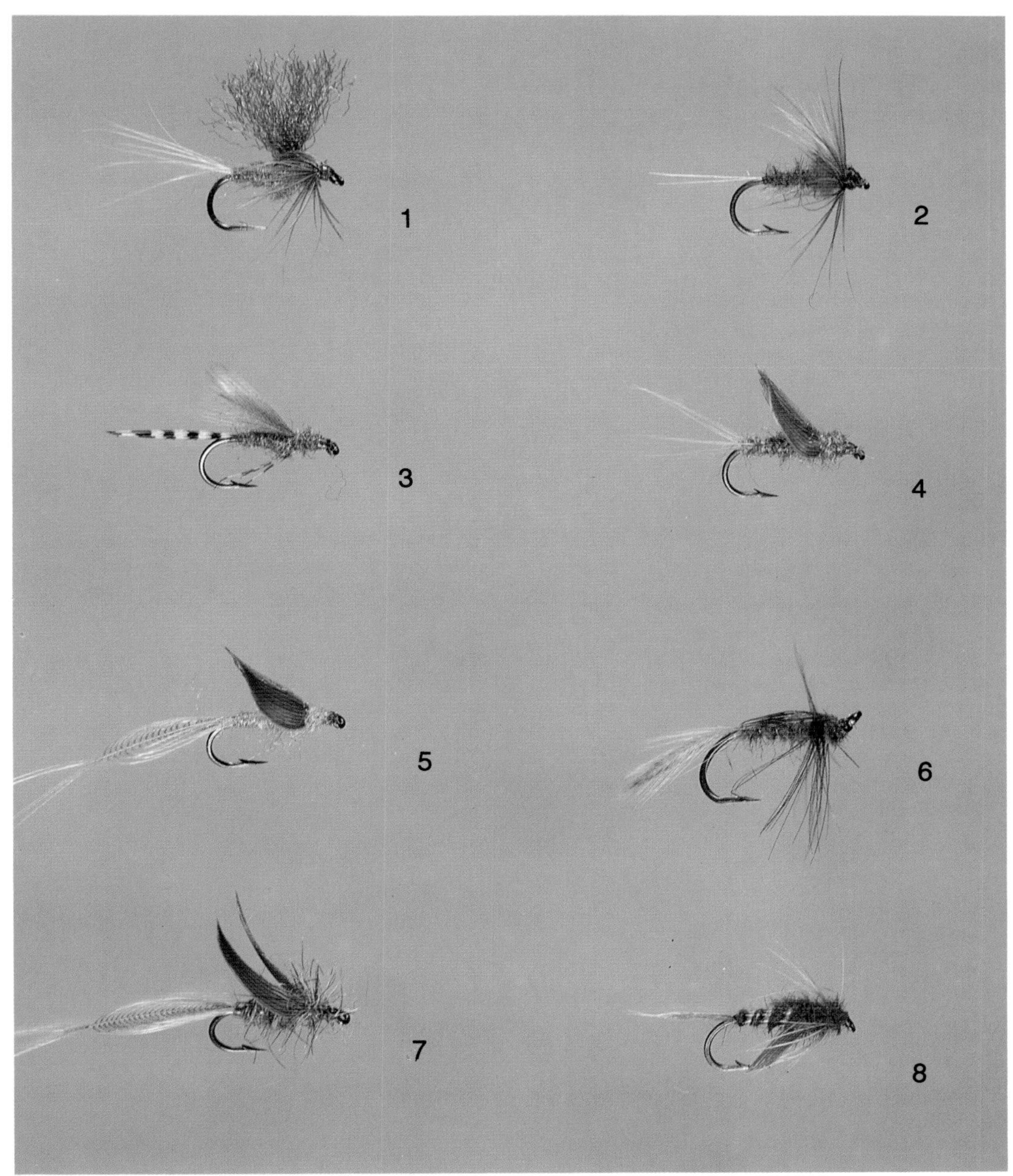

1 Walker's Hatching Nymph **2** Lawrie's Hatching Dun
3 Swisher and Richards' Wet Emerger **4** Swisher and Richards' Dry Emerger
5 Swisher and Richards' Stillborn Freewing **6** Swisher and Richards' Stillborn Trapped Wing
7 No-Hackle Gold-Ribbed Hare's Ear Emerger **8** Jardine's Emerger

3 Swisher and Richards' Wet Emerger

COMMENT

'If we were confined to select one pattern, and one pattern only, to catch the maximum number of fish during hatch situations, that pattern would undoubtedly be an emerger type. . . . We often use the emerging pattern to solve many of the difficult stream problems that we encounter. It could easily be called a "wet" dry fly or a "dry" wet fly. Whatever you call it, the emerger is really versatile.' Quote from Doug Swisher and Carl Richards. Whether fished on heavy hooks near the bottom or on fine-wire hooks as floaters this is a very adaptable pattern.

DRESSING

Hook: 14–16 Code E1A, L3A or L4A (dry) or G3A or CS7 (wet).
Thread: Olive.
Tail: Barred wood duck fibres.
Body: Dubbed fur or polypropylene Fly-Rite.
Wings: Dark-grey hen hackle tips, wide and webby.
Legs (optional): Dyed partridge hackle or wood duck fibres to match the natural.

4 Swisher and Richards' Dry Emerger

COMMENT

This pattern is very similar to the No-Hackle Duns, the main difference being that the wings are much shorter, being no more than three-quarters of the body length. The wing length, according to the creators of the pattern, is the secret of their effectiveness. The fly should be well soaked in floatant to ensure that it stays a dry emerger.

DRESSING

Hook: 14–16 fine wire Code L4A.
Tail: Two widely spaced bunches of cock hackle fibres separated by a small ball of body dubbing.
Body: Dubbed fur or polypropylene Fly-Rite.
Wing: Grey duck shoulder feather or short duck quill segments.

5 Swisher and Richards' Stillborn Freewing

COMMENT

It was Doug Swisher and Carl Richards who really highlighted the need to represent the stillborns and emerging duns. They studied the way in which duns hatched in their impressive aquaria and devised a number of patterns to imitate the different ways in which the duns are trapped or stillborn. They experimented with a wide range of alternative materials to represent the trailing nymphal shuck. This first pattern incorporates a feather shuck with the no-hackle design. All are system patterns to be adapted to match the naturals in colour and size.

DRESSING

Hook: 14–18 Code L4A.
Thread: To match the body colour.
Tail: Centre part of a hackle. All except the top few fibres are pulled back on themselves. The untouched top fibres trail to the rear.
Body: Dubbed fur or polypropylene yarn.
Wing: Short rear-sloping duck primary wing segments.

6 Swisher and Richards' Stillborn Trapped Wing

COMMENT

The second type of stillborn has a flattened unerected wing across the back. It is designed to represent those stillborns that ride the water at an angle with the thorax supported higher by the legs but without any wings erect. The trailing shuck is represented by an appropriately coloured hen hackle tip.

DRESSING

Hook: 14–18 Code L3A, L4A or E6A.
Tail: Hen hackle tip.
Body: Dubbed fur or polypropylene yarn.
Trapped wing: A section of feather fibres or wing quill (to match the natural) tied in flat over the back and bound in at each end. The rear is tied in first, then the dubbed body and hackle, then the front of the wing.
Hackle: Stiff short-fibred cock with the upper fibres cut away.

7 No-Hackle Gold-Ribbed Hare's Ear Emerger

COMMENT

The Gold-Ribbed Hare's Ear when tied as a floating nymph or fished in the film is already a good impression of many emerging upwingeds and sedges. This dressing takes the imitation a step further with the addition of a trailing nymphal shuck and sidewinder wings. Another useful development of the GRHE that has done very well for me is to tie it in the suspender style (see next plate).

DRESSING

Hook: 14–16 Code L4A.
Thread: Yellow.
Tail: Centre part of a hackle. All except the top few fibres are pulled back on themselves. The untouched top fibres trail to the rear.
Body: Dubbed fur from the base of a hare's ear.
Rib: Flat gold tinsel.
Wing: Two short rear-sloping or upright duck primary wing segments.

8 Jardine's Emerger

COMMENT

Charles Jardine is one of our most thoughtful river fishers. He has studied some of the North American innovations and has adapted them for English streams. This is his system pattern for the emerging dun. The colours of the materials should be varied to represent the species on the water.

DRESSING

Hook: 14–16 fine wire Code L3A, L4A or E6A.
Thread.: Crimson.
Tail: Lemon wood duck or light-blue dun fibres.
Abdomen and thorax: Dubbed mixed rabbit and mole's fur.
Rib: Stripped quill.
Emerging wing: Two grey mallard slips tied short and rear-facing either side of the body at the rear of the thorax.
Hackle: Lemon wood duck tied either side of the thorax only.

Emergers & Floating Nymphs

It has been noted that some upwinged species, such as the blue-winged olive, suffer more than most when trying to break free of the nymphal shuck. It also seems likely that the same species has a varying success rate on different rivers. This is probably due to the likelihood that on faster-flowing rivers or broken water any collection of fine particles that make up the surface scum will be broken up and dispersed, making the breakthrough easier. On a slow-moving river the build-up of particles in the film will be greater, increasing the surface tension, so that the failure rate for the hatching fly will be greater. Consequently, stillborns and trapped emergers seem to be more common on slow-moving chalk streams than on most freestone rivers. The patterns listed are designs and should be tied in appropriate colours for different species.

1 Jardine's Floating Nymph

COMMENT

When I received this fly from Charles Jardine I used it three times within the week. One trip to a northern chalk stream and two to a small freestone river resulted in fourteen trout on this pattern. The fish weren't concentrating on floating nymphs but they liked the look of this. Trout see something that is nymph-like but on the surface. They take it because it looks like a stillborn nymph that won't escape. It sometimes works when fish are nymphing just subsurface and they respond to the silhouette. This is a blue-winged olive imitation. Suitably coloured materials are used for other species.

DRESSING

Hook: 14 Code L3A or E1A.
Tail: Wood duck fibres.
Body: Dark-olive Orvis Antron/hair mix tapering from the rear.
Rib: Fibres of white synthetic parcel string or a translucent substitute.
Thorax: A dubbed ball of grey Poly II (polypropylene).
Parachute hackle: Golden-olive cock wound round the base of the thorax.

2 Floating Nymph

COMMENT

This is an American design for the small upwinged species and is useful to represent our smaller *Baetis* species. The thorax ball represents exaggerated mature wingpads or the wings themselves before erection. The hackle-fibre legs imitate the natural's legs but in reality they are an insignificant feature in the trout's view of the floating nymph. Their main purpose in the dressing is to act as outriggers to aid the nymph's balance. The usual dressing calls for widely spaced hackle-fibre tails; this dressing uses the modern alternative of Microfibetts or Magic Spinner Tails.

DRESSING

Hook: 14–16 fine-wire Code L4A or E1A.
Thread: Olive.
Tail: Widely spaced tan Microfibetts (Orvis) or Magic Spinner Tails (Traun River Products).
Abdomen and thorax: Naturally dyed fur or poly dubbing tapering to the rear.
Thorax ball: A dubbed ball of grey polypropylene.
Legs: Four or five olive cock fibres each side, tied in at the base of the ball, before the thorax is completed, with a small drop of cement.

1 Jardine's Floating Nymph **2** Floating Nymph **3** Suspender Nymph
4 Loop-Wing Emerger **5** Flymph **6** Parachute Nymph
7 Soft-Hackle Emerger **8** Pheasant Tail Emerger

3 Suspender Nymph

COMMENT

The method of suspending the nymph in the film by an Ethafoam ball in a nylon mesh was first devised by an American, Theodore Rogowski, and popularised in the UK by Neil Patterson, John Goddard and Brian Clarke. The imitation is quite realistic, with the suspension ball at the head representing the emerging adult coming through the split nymphal skin. Any nymph pattern can be adapted by the inclusion of the enmeshed ball. Be aware if colouring the Ethafoam ball not to use a Pantone pen as the ink reacts with the Ethafoam. This is a general olive nymph pattern.

DRESSING

Hook: 14 Code E6A or L2A.
Thread: Brown.
Tail: Greenwell hackle fibres (ginger/black).
Body: Olive-dyed goose feather fibres.
Rib: Fine gold tinsel or wire.
Thorax: Dark-olive or olive-brown seal's fur.
Wingcase: Brown feather fibres with tips tied in for legs.
Suspender ball: Small Ethafoam ball in a nylon mesh (ladies' tights) and optionally coloured light-grey or blue-grey with an indelible pen.

4 Loop-Wing Emerger

COMMENT

This is an American pattern for the fly exactly in the process of emerging. The wing is visibly in the process of erection. The whole of the fly should float on the surface and to ensure this it should be well treated in floatant and tied on a fine-wire hook. The legs are tied horizontally for balance rather than imitation. The poly yarn wing is available in a number of shades suitable for matching any natural wing. An alternative wing material is looped Magic Spinner Wing fibres. This is a March brown or late March brown emerger tied with a rabbit fur body.

DRESSING

Hook: 12–14 Code E1A, E6A, L3A or L4A.
Thread: Orange or tan.
Tail: Widely spaced cree cock fibres.
Abdomen and thorax: Mixed olive-dyed and brown rabbit's fur or seal's fur substitute or poly dubbing.
Wing: A single upright loop of tan polypropylene yarn strands.
Legs: Four or five cree cock fibres or barred Microfibetts tied either side of the body and cemented in before winding on the final thorax dubbing.

5 Flymphs

COMMENT

American, Vernon S. Hidy devised this half-fly, half-nymph pattern to represent the struggling insect trying to break through the surface film. On rougher water the flies should use stiffer hackles and on moderately paced water soft-to-medium hen hackles. All are tied rear-sloping and should have just the right flexibility to be achieved by the current to simulate the living nymph. Hidy spins the fur on two strands of thread and ties it in separately. The flymphs are fished in the top couple of inches of water. The dressing below is an iron blue flymph.

DRESSING

Hooks: 14–16 long-shank Code E1A.
Thread: Claret or black.
Tail: Dark-blue-dun fibres.
Body: Mole's fur tapering to the rear.
Hackle: Dark-blue-dun hen, starling or coot.

6 Parachute Nymph

COMMENT

There are two basic designs of parachute nymph, both with hackles lying flat on the surface supporting the nymph below. The first design is a parachute hackle on top of the nymph body. This is rather like a wingless parachute dry fly, the nymph body is held below the surface by the hackle. The second design, illustrated, has a long-fibred shoulder hackle which lies flat on the surface *supporting the body vertically below.* The hackle should be treated to float and the body to sink. This is a general olive dressing.

DRESSING

Hook: 14–16 Code E1A or L3A.
Thread: Yellow
Tail: Olive hackle fibres.
Body: Light-coloured hare's ear fur.
Rib: Fine gold wire.
Thorax: Dark-coloured hare's ear fur.
Wingcase: Dark feather fibres.
Hackle: One or two turns of long-fibred grizzle cock.

7 Soft-Hackle Emerger

COMMENT

If you believed all you read in some American books you would think that this was one of their newer dressings. In reality the North Country wingless spider patterns when fished awash in the film have been representing the emergers in a very similar fashion. The soft, mobile hen hackles or feathers from a suitable game bird are used in both styles. The only difference is that the American soft-hackle emerger should be fished dry, well soaked in floatant and tied on fine-wire hooks. Carl Richards says it is the deadliest pattern he uses when trout are taking emergers.

DRESSING

Hook: 14–16 Code L3A, L4A or E1A.
Thread: To match the body dubbing.
Tail: Widely spaced cock hackle fibres.
Body: Fine natural fur or synthetic dubbing (polypropylene or Antron/Hare mix).
Hackle: Soft game bird (*see* North Country sections) or hen hackle.

8 Pheasant Tail Emerger

COMMENT

Two superb flies of proven trout-catching ability are the Pheasant Tail nymph and the floating Pheasant Tail, each excellent in its own domain, one below and the other above the surface. It seemed an obvious gap to fill when there was no emerger or hatching pattern to fish in the film. Hans van Klinken has produced his dressing for that situation, with the parachute hackle supporting the pheasant tail body suspended below. The white polypropylene yarn wing is highly visible to both trout and angler. Although I have given this just a season's trial it has proved to be a very good fly.

DRESSING

Hook: 12–16 Code E1A or L3A, or 22 Code K12ST.
Thread: Tan.
Tail: Pheasant tail fibres.
Abdomen: Cock pheasant tail fibres tapering to the rear.
Rib: Fine gold wire.
Thorax: Peacock herl.
Hackle: Cock in various natural red-brown shades.
Wing: White poly yarn.

Blue-Winged Olive, Olive Upright & Dusky Yellowstreak

In the southern counties the blue-winged olive *(Ephemerella ignita)* is very likely the most widespread and most prolific upwinged fly and therefore one of the most important of all the trout fishers' natural flies. It is also widely distributed in the rest of the country. The adults are fairly distinctive medium-to-large flies with their erect wings slightly sloping back at an angle, quite unlike other upwingeds.

The dun of the olive upright *(Rhithrogena semicolorata)* is overall very similar to the blue-winged olive but slightly smaller. The nymphs are stone-clingers and distribution is restricted to the western half of Britain. The adults appear in the late afternoons and evenings from late April until July. General olive imitations or blue-winged olive patterns are adequate imitation.

The dusky yellowstreak *(Heptagenia lateralis)* inhabits small stone streams and is concentrated in the west and parts of the north and Scotland.

1 Blue-Winged Olive Nymph (Jacobsen)

COMMENT

The nymph is fairly inactive except for the ascent to the surface. It is a moss-creeping type, living wherever moss covers the riverbed. This dressing is from Preben Torp Jacobsen, who based it on an earlier G.E.M. Skues pattern which called for cow's hair the colour of dried blood. This does not come from red-coloured cows but from the black varieties which have a touch of red in them. Jacobsen comments that in the winter and spring, just before the moult, the wool is very soft and easy to dub.

DRESSING

Hook: 14 Code CS7 or L2A.
Thread: Hot orange.
Tail: Three or four brown-speckled partridge hackle fibres.
Abdomen: A small amount of otter's fur spun on the thread or rust Antron/Hare blend as a substitute.
Thorax: Soft cow's hair (*see* text).
Hackle: Small dark-blue-dun hen hackle.

2 Blue-Winged Olive Nymph (Edwards)

COMMENT

This dressing comes from Oliver Edwards, who doesn't just tie beautiful flies but devises flies that catch trout. Such nymph-fishing authorities as Oliver Kite and Frank Sawyer denied the need for a suitable leg imitation on nymphs but I confess that leg fibres like these brown partridge fibres seem to give the necessary suggestion of life and movement as the current works through them. I think most nymph patterns benefit from leg imitations and, even if I'm completely wrong and Sawyer was right, then the leg fibres will still behave naturally.

DRESSING

Hook: 18–20 Code L2A.
Thread: Orange.
Tail: Dark mottled partridge tail.
Abdomen and thorax: Sandy hare's ear fur.
Rib: Finest gold wire (on abdomen only).
Legs: Dark partridge hackle.
Wingcase: Dark pheasant tail fibres in two clumps.
Head: Dubbed sandy hare's ear, smeared with varnish, tightened into a spindle and wound on.

1 BWO Nymph (Jacobsen) **2** BWO Nymph (Edwards) **3** Hatching BWO
4 BWO Dun (Righyni) **5** BWO Dun **6** Sherry Spinner
7 No-Hackle Sherry Spinner **8** Dusky Yellowstreak

3 Hatching Blue-Winged Olive

COMMENT

Emergence can take place almost anywhere on the river but it is frequently in areas just below well broken water. It has been observed that the blue-winged olive suffers more than most upwingeds when trying to break through the surface tension to emerge as an adult. No reason has been offered for this high failure rate but the nymphs wriggle and struggle to break through. This is one occasion when a suitable stillborn or emerging pattern is more likely to succeed. This is loosely based on the Swisher and Richards emerger with the trailing nymphal shuck still attached.

DRESSING

Hook: 12–14 Code L3A.
Thread: Hot orange.
Shuck: Any dun or olive hackle (for tying method see the pattern on page 144).
Body: Olive or mixed brown and olive seal's fur substitute or rabbit's fur.
Wing: A single bunch of slate-blue polypropylene yarn half the normal height.
Hackle: Blue-dun or olive cock with the lower fibres clipped flat.

4 Blue-Winged Olive Dun (Righyni)

COMMENT

The adults can be expected on the water as early as May on some southern rivers but usually from mid-June through to October or November. They generally appear in the evenings and sometimes in the afternoons. In October and November I have seen quite large hatches condensed into a ten-minute period in the early afternoon and grayling in the river have been very free risers to them. The dressing illustrated was tied by Reg Righyni, who had considerable success with it for both and grayling. They are also the only olive adults to have three tails, a feature most trout fishers are aware of but no trout has ever noticed.

DRESSING

Hook: 14–16 Code A, E6A or L3A.
Thread: Yellow.
Tail: Blue-dun hackle fibres.
Body: Pinkish-beige opossum fur lightly dubbed.
Hackle: Blue-dun followed by a red game-cock hackle.

5 Blue-Winged Olive Dun

COMMENT

The colour of the abdomen differs between the sexes; the male's is orangy or orange-brown, and the female's is olive-green, darkening to rusty-brown as the season progresses. The grey-blue wings tilt back slightly over the body. It used to be the consensus that trout rising to the duns left a distinctive kidney-shaped boil on the surface. This is fiction and not fact; trout rise no differently to these duns than to any others. A kidney-shaped boil may result if a trout takes an emerger hanging in the film – a not unusual occurrence with this fly.

DRESSING

Hook: 12–14 Code A, E6A or L3A.
Thread: Olive or black.
Tail: Dark-dun cock fibres.
Body: Dark-olive thread or olive-dyed rabbit's fur.
Wing: Grey duck wing quills.
Hackle: Dark-dun cock.

6 Sherry Spinner (Rice)

COMMENT

This angler's name for both the male and female spinner came from their distinctive sherry-red abdomen colour, but it should be noted that the colour varies from olive-brown to a brighter red. This variation, according to J. R. Harris, is because the abdomen of the female changes from olive-brown to deep red with age. The mated female also carries a round green egg sac at the rear of the abdomen. The wings are transparent, with pale brown veins, and the tails are olive-grey with light-brown rings. This is Freddie Rice's dressing, which has its hackle optionally clipped flat.

DRESSING

Hook: 14 Code A, L3A or E6A.
Thread: Light yellow.
Tail: Natural buff-barred cree fibres or the same dyed light-olive.
Tip: Light-yellow rayon floss.
Body: One dark and one light moose mane hair, the lighter dyed olive-brown or shades of sherry through to pinkish-red, wound together to represent the segmented body.
Wing: Pale-ginger cock fibres wound and bunched spent.
Hackle: Natural light-red cock.

7 No-Hackle Sherry Spinner

COMMENT

The hackled spinner dressing does not wholly satisfactorily represent the spent female spinner. When the natural fly has extruded its eggs it drifts helplessly downstream with its wings and body flush in the surface film. Only when it first arrives on the surface is the thorax held clear of the water, so the imitation of the spent spinner must be flat on the surface with the key features being the body colour and the wings.

DRESSING

Hook: 14 Code L3A or L4A.
Thread: Sherry spinner.
Tail: Two widely spaced bunches (3 or 4 fibres each) of white cock fibres or two white Microfibetts.
Body: Reddish-brown seal's fur substitute or poly dubbing (Fly-Rite rust #5)
Wing: White poly yarn or bunched white cock hackle fibres tied spent.

8 Dusky Yellowstreak

COMMENT

The stone-clinging nymphs are usually found quite close to the water's edge. The medium- to large-sized adults emerge between May and September. They have dark-grey wings, two tails and a dark grey-brown body. A distinguishing feature of the dun and spinner is the yellow streak on each side of the front of the thorax. The spinner has an olive-brown body. A Dark Watchet is a suitable wet and emerger pattern and a Pheasant Tail for the female spinner. I suggest this dressing for the dun.

DRESSING

Hook: 14 Code L3A or E6A.
Thread: Brown.
Tail: Blue-dun cock fibres or widely spaced grey Microfibetts.
Body: Any grey feather herls.
Rib: Strong brown thread.
Hackle: Mixed dark-blue-dun and grizzle cocks.

Small Spurwing, Large Spurwing and Dark Olive

Both species of spurwings *(Centroptilum luteolum* and *C. pennulatum)* are so named because of the small spur-shaped hindwing. Without this aid to identification, which can be seen only with the aid of a low-powered magnifying glass, the dun is very similar to the pale watery and small dark olive. Perhaps the most noticeable feature of the large spurwing duns is that when at rest the wings are held apart in a wide V, in contrast to other upwinged duns, whose wings are always more or less vertical. This is the only clue to identification at any distance.

The dark olive *(Baetis atrebatinus)* is localised in its distribution, confining itself to alkaline streams in the south and a few northern rivers. Elsewhere it is very rare. The duns are very similar to the large dark olive but are only medium-sized. Smaller patterns of the former are often quite adequate imitations.

1 Spurwing Nymph (Waites)

COMMENT

The nymphs of both species can be considered together for fly-fishing purposes. They are agile-darting types, probably the most agile of all upwinged species, inhabiting weedbeds or moss in slow-moving water and occasionally lakes. This modern nymph pattern comes from Tony Waites, head keeper for the Driffield Anglers' Club water of the Driffield Beck, probably the most alkaline water north of the southern counties. Donald Overfield has suggested that the dressing might be improved by the inclusion of a wingcase of heron herl.

DRESSING

Hook: 14–18 Code L2A or G3A.
Thread: Grey.
Tail: Three natural heron herl tips.
Body: Fine silver fuse-wire covered with three natural heron herls.
Rib: Fine silver fuse-wire.
Wingcase (optional): Natural heron herl.

2 Spurwing Nymph (Skues)

COMMENT

No book representing river trout flies can fail to include a few of the patterns of G. E. M. Skues, who did so much to restore the place of subsurface flies on the chalk streams. A number of Skues's dry and nymph patterns are still used, though some have been improved with modern materials. This is Skues's spurwing nymph dressing, better known in 1940s as the blue-winged pale watery. It is interesting how this and the previous nymph dressing differ in their coloration. Both are said to imitate the same nymph and no doubt both are effective.

DRESSING

Hook: 14 Code L2A or G3A.
Thread: White.
Tail: Pale-blue hen hackle fibres.
Body: White lamb's wool, tapering to the rear.
Hackle: Dark-blue hen.

1 Spurwing Nymph (Waites) **2** Spurwing Nymph (Skues)
3 Small Spurwing Dun **4** Small Spurwing Spinner **5** Large Spurwing Dun
6 Large Spurwing Spinner **7** Dark Olive Dun **8** Dark Olive Spinner

3 Small Spurwing Dun

COMMENT

With the exception of Wales, distribution is widespread in alkaline water. They hatch from early May, reaching a peak in June and thereafter declining until early October. During the first two to three months they emerge at all times of the day and later the hatches are confined to late afternoon. The medium-sized duns have pale or blue-grey wings and two grey tails. The male's abdomen is pale olive-grey with a brown-olive underside. The female dun has a watery-olive abdomen with a pale olive underside.

DRESSING

Hook: 14–16 Code L3A or E6A.
Thread: Pale-yellow.
Tail: Cream cock hackle fibres.
Body: Mixed cream and pale-olive seal's fur substitute or poly dubbing (3:1).
Wing (optional): Light-grey polypropylene yarn set upright, or bunched light-grey feather fibres.
Hackle: Cream cock (or pale blue-dun cock on the wingless version).

4 Small Spurwing Spinner

COMMENT

Both spinners attract considerable trout interest. The female is usually known as the little amber spinner because of its pale to reddish-amber upper abdomen. The underside is pale creamy-yellow with the last two segments dark amber. The wings are colourless and the tails almost white with a tinge of olive. Sometimes the swarms of male spinners are blown onto the surface. It has a translucent white abdomen with the last three segments reddish-brown. The underside is grey-white. This is an imitation of the commoner female spent spinner and emphasises the underside colouring.

DRESSING

Hook: 14–16 Code L3A or E6A.
Thread: Hot orange.
Tail: Widely spaced cream cock fibres.
Body: Cream variant (Fly-Rite #25) poly dubbing with a built-up tip of waxed orange thread.
Hackle: White or cream cock in parachute style on top of the body.

5 Large Spurwing Dun

COMMENT

Distribution is restricted to localised areas of the south, the north and the Usk area of Wales. The medium-to-large adults emerge on slow-moving water from late May until September, with June being the most prolific. The wings are dark blue-grey and at rest are often held in a V shape. The abdomen is pale olive-grey or olive-brown with the underside paler. The last three segments on the male's abdomen are amber. The two tails are grey. Trout find them attractive and will take the duns despite the hatches often being sparse.

DRESSING

Hook: 14 Code L3A or E6A.
Thread: Cream.
Tail: Cream cock fibres.
Body: Olive-grey or olive-tan seal's fur substitute or poly dubbing (Fly-Rite pale morning dun #31).
Wing: Grey or blue-grey polypropylene yarn set upright.
Hackle: Cream or pale olive cock.

6 Large Spurwing Spinner

COMMENT

The female spinner, also called the large amber spinner, is very similar in overall appearance to the small spurwing spinner, except that it is significantly larger. The underside of the deep-amber abdomen is quite pale, almost an off-white olive. Most imitations try to represent the amber colouring accurately whereas what trout are most likely to see is the very pale under-abdomen. The male spinner has a near-translucent white abdomen and one pattern can imitate them both. When dressing a spinner imitation, bear in mind that the body of the spent female is drained of much of its original colour.

DRESSING

Hook: 14 Code L3A or E6A.
Thread: Orange.
Tail: Widely spaced pale blue-dun fibres.
Body: Mixed amber and cream seal's fur substitute or poly dubbing (1:2).
Wing: Bunched white cock fibres, or white polypropylene yarn, or clear Antron fibres, tied spent.

7 Dark Olive Dun (Clegg)

COMMENT

In the localised areas of its restricted distribution the dark olive is an important fly. The medium-sized duns emerge in April and May and again from September to early November. On my home stream in North Yorkshire it is an important April fly, appearing in larger numbers than the nationally more familiar large dark olive, to which it is almost identical except in size. It has grey wings, a dark olive-brown abdomen and two grey-olive tails. This is a dressing from Thomas Clegg.

DRESSING

Hook: 14 Code L3A or E6A.
Thread: Olive.
Tail: Dark-olive-dyed cock fibres.
Body: Dubbed dark-olive wool.
Rib: Electron-white fluorescent floss.
Hackle: Slate-blue and dark brown-olive cock hackles wound together.

8 Dark Olive Spinner

COMMENT

I have not seen the female spinner on the water and the likelihood is that along with other *Baetis* species it climbs below the surface to oviposit. Neither John Goddard, J. R. Harris nor other authorities are conclusive about its egg-laying behaviour. The female spinner has transparent wings, an olive-grey tail and a dark reddish-brown abdomen with a light-olive underside. This is a pattern to be fished just below the surface in the manner of a spent female having failed to struggle back through the film.

DRESSING

Hook: 14 Code L3A or E6A.
Thread: Olive.
Tail: Widely spaced light-olive hackle-fibres or Microfibetts.
Body: An underbody of a single layer of copper wire at the thorax covered with mixed olive and rusty seal's fur substitute.
Rib: Fine gold wire.
Wing: Clear Antron or clear Orvis poly wing fibres.

Iron Blue and Purple Dun

With the exception of some parts of the south-east there is barely a part of Britain that does not have one of these two species. They are common on most trout streams throughout the country. They begin to appear in late April and can be expected any time until November. One feature about their times of emergence is that they often appear on cold, blustery days when no other species are on the water. This is particularly useful for the dry-fly fisher, who on such days would probably be left without a hatch of fly. In addition to the patterns below, the Snipe and Purple, Watchets and some of the Bloas are excellent wet flies.

The purple dun *(Paraleptophlebia cincta)* is very similar to the iron blue *(Baetis niger, B. muticus)* except that the former has three tails. The same artificials can be used for both. They are found in the west of the country, Wales and parts of the north.

1 Iron Blue Spider

COMMENT

Crimson is a colour that is associated with this species but it nowhere appears in the natural nyphm or dun. Richard Walker and G. E. M. Skues suggested that some fly species have key colours, not necessarily obvious to the human eye but recognisable by trout. Sometimes the female spinners or duns display these colours. If crimson is incorporated in the iron blue imitation, particularly in the thread underlying the semi-translucent dubbed body, the attraction of the artificial is increased.

DRESSING

Hook: 14 Code A, CS7 or G3A.
Thread: Crimson.
Tip: Crimson floss or tying thread.
Body: Lightly dubbed mole's fur.
Hackle: Inside of a moorhen's wing or snipe.

2 Iron Blue Nymph

COMMENT

The nymphs are small agile-darting types. The dressing given here is one of a number of similar patterns, which all vary slightly. Skues adapted what he learned from the northern wet-fly fishers and began to tie nymphs for the southern chalk streams with soft small-fibred hackles. His pattern, similar to the one detailed, omits the wingcase and has a hackle of just one or two turns of very short cock jackdaw throat hackle.

DRESSING

Hook: 14–16 Code G3A, L2A or CS7.
Thread: Claret.
Tail: White cock fibres.
Body: Mole's fur with a tip of tying thread exposed at the rear.
Thorax: Mole's fur.
Wingcase: Black crow or moorhen wing.
Legs: Wingcase fibres tied beneath the body.

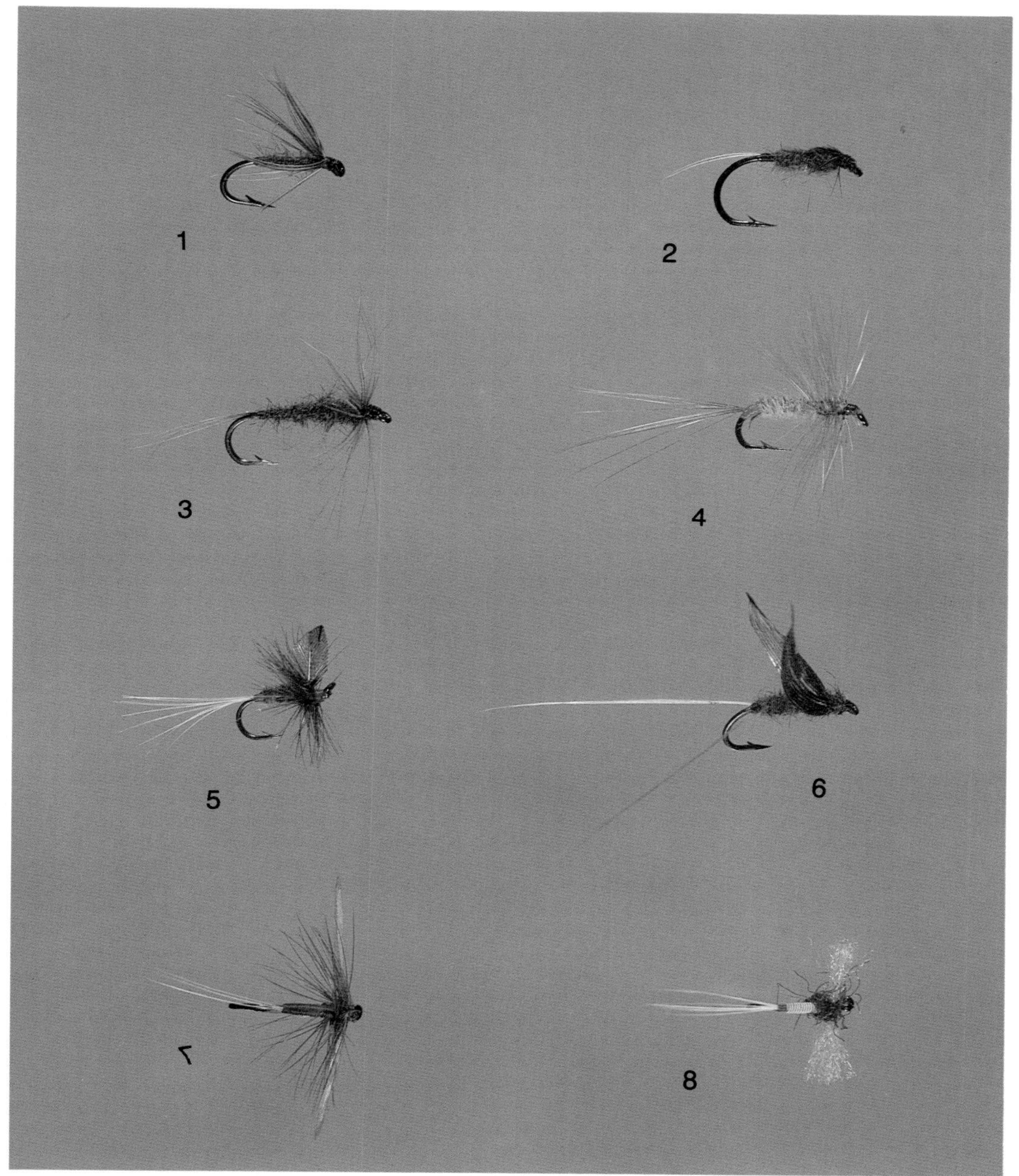

1 Iron Blue Spider **2** Iron Blue Nymph **3** Iron Blue Flymph
4 Iron Blue Dun (Russell) **5** Iron Blue Dun (Warrilow)
6 No-Hackle Iron Blue Dun **7** Houghton Ruby **8** Jenny Spinner

3 Iron Blue Flymph

COMMENT

This dressing is based upon V. S. Hidy's design for the in-between stage when the fly is in the process of emerging from its nymphal shuck as a winged adult. It is fished just below the surface. Stiffer hackles should be used on rough water and soft hen hackles on the smooth glides. The E1A Hooper dry fly hooks are ideal for this style as they are both long-shank and 4× fine wire to aid floating.

DRESSING

Hook: 14–16 long-shank Code E1A.
Thread: Claret.
Tail: Dark-blue-dun fibres.
Body: Mole's fur.
Hackle: Dark-blue-dun hen, starling or coot.

4 Iron Blue Dun (Russell)

COMMENT

Whenever the duns hatch they always attract trout attention. Trout reaction to other upwinged species varies. They invariably ignore some dun species; others are sometimes attractive and on other occasions ignored, but a hatch of iron blues will almost without exception induce trout to feed at the surface. Because they sometimes hatch on cool, damp days the duns are often on the water some little while drying before taking flight. They are an encouraging sight for the dry-fly fisher. This is Pat Russell's dressing and the fly illustrated is tied by him.

DRESSING

Hook: 16 Code L3A or A.
Thread: Crimson.
Tail: Dark-slate-blue cock hackle fibres.
Tip: Neon-magenta thread.
Body: Dark heron herl.
Hackle: Dark-slate-blue cock, two short-fibres hackles palmered from halfway down the body to the head.

5 Iron Blue Dun (Warrilow)

COMMENT

The duns are easy to recognise, being quite small with distinctive blue-black or grey-black wings. They can barely be mistaken for any other species. The colour of the two sexes varies slightly: the male has a grey-black body and the female's is a dark brown-olive. The legs are dark-olive and olive-brown respectively and the two tails olive-grey or dark-grey. This imitation is from Ian Warrilow. It uses burnt wings shaped in a wing burner. They should be tied to curve outwards.

DRESSING

Hook: 14–16 Code E1A or L3A.
Thread: Crimson.
Tail: White cock fibres.
Tip: Crimson thread.
Body: Natural dark heron herl.
Wing: Burnt dark-dun saddle hackles (Metz shade).
Hackle: Dark-dun cock.

6 No-Hackle Iron Blue Dun

COMMENT

The no-hackle design of fly seems to work best for me in its smaller sizes, when trout are possibly prepared to ignore the absence of a realistic light pattern on the surface and rise because of the stimulus of a clear view of the wings and body. This small species is well suited to this type of fly design. Fine-wire hooks should always be used for this style. The dressing uses the option of Microfibetts or Magic Spinner Tails for the tail fibres. A much cheaper but no less effective alternative is to use nylon fibres from an artist's paintbrush.

DRESSING

Hook: 14–16 Code L3A or L4A.
Thread: Crimson.
Tail: Two widely spaced sparse bunches of dark-slate cock hackle fibres, or two Microfibetts, or Magic Spinner Tails.
Body: Dark grey-blue natural fur or poly dubbing (Fly-Rite #7).
Hackle: Dark-grey duck primary wing or moorhen wing sections.

7 Houghton Ruby

COMMENT

This is an imitation of the female spinner devised for the southern chalk streams but it is successful on all rivers. In common with many of the *Baetis* spinners these females crawl below the surface on stakes and the like – even on an angler's waders if you are lucky. Despite this behaviour, the floating fly is very effective. The female spinner, which is also known as the little claret spinner, has transparent, colourless wings and a dark claret-brown abdomen with a paler underside. The tails are pale grey. Another imitation is the Sunk Spinner on page 42.

DRESSING

Hook: 12–14 Code L3A.
Thread: Crimson.
Tail: Three white cock hackle fibres.
Body: Rhode Island Red hackle stalk dyed crimson.
Wing: Two light-blue-dun hackle tips tied spent, or sometimes semi-spent.
Hackle: Rhode Island Red cock.

8 Jenny Spinner

COMMENT

This is an old fly fishers' name for the male spinner, which unlike most male spinners sometimes finds its way back onto the water. It is quite distinctive with its two long white-grey tails and translucent white abdomen, of which the last three segments are browny-orange. The male spinners always swarm during the day and the females' egg laying invariably takes place before the evening. Some dressings have a wing of white cock hackles but these are not very durable. This is Ian Warrilow's more durable imitation.

DRESSING

Hook: 14 Code L3A.
Thread: Crimson.
Tail: White cock hackle fibres (widely spaced Microfibetts are an alternative).
Tip: Crimson thread.
Body: Stripped white hackle stalk.
Thorax: Rich brown Antron.
Wing: Cream poly yarn.

Caenis or Broadwing and Small Dark Olive

Of the six *Caenis* species three are found in slow-moving rivers. They are equally well known by their more appropriate name, the Angler's Curse, which signifies the frustration often experienced in trying to persuade trout feeding on them to take the artificial. They are easily recognisable by their overall whitish colouring and because they are the smallest of the upwinged species.

The small dark olive *(Baetis scambus)* is common and widely distributed, except in Scotland. They are found in chalk and limestone rivers and also the upper reaches of less alkaline streams. Both the nymphs and adults are very small, often not much larger than caenis.

1 Caenis Nymph (Carnill)

COMMENT

The nymphs inhabit the top layers of the silt, mud and moss on the riverbed and are found in midwinter only when they swim to the surface to hatch. Bob Carnill devised this dressing for stillwater use but there is no reason not to use it on rivers. The wingcase is of biot quills tied with the broad ends facing rear over the body. They are trimmed and rounded so that they extend halfway down the body.

DRESSING

Hook: 14–16 Code G3A.
Thread: Brown.
Tail: Three brown partridge hackle fibres or tail fibres.
Body: Drab-brown swan, goose or heron herl.
Rib: Stripped peacock quill.
Thorax: Hare's ear fur.
Wingcase and thorax cover: Biot quills from the narrow side of a heron primary feather (*see* text).
Legs: Partridge fibres.

2 Caenis Nymph

COMMENT

In contrast to the detailed imitation of Bob Carnill's, I am including this easier-to-tie impressionist nymph. The natural nymph is not as white as this but when the underlying or principal colour of the adults is displayed or exaggerated in a nymph dressing it often works well. Fished close to the surface or awash in the film it suggests the emerging adult.

DRESSING

Hook: 16 (or tied short on a 14) Code L2A.
Thread: White.
Tail: Three brown partridge fibres.
Body: White or cream seal's fur substitute or Fly-Rite dubbing #12.
Rib: Fine oval silver tinsel.
Hackle: Sparse grey partridge.

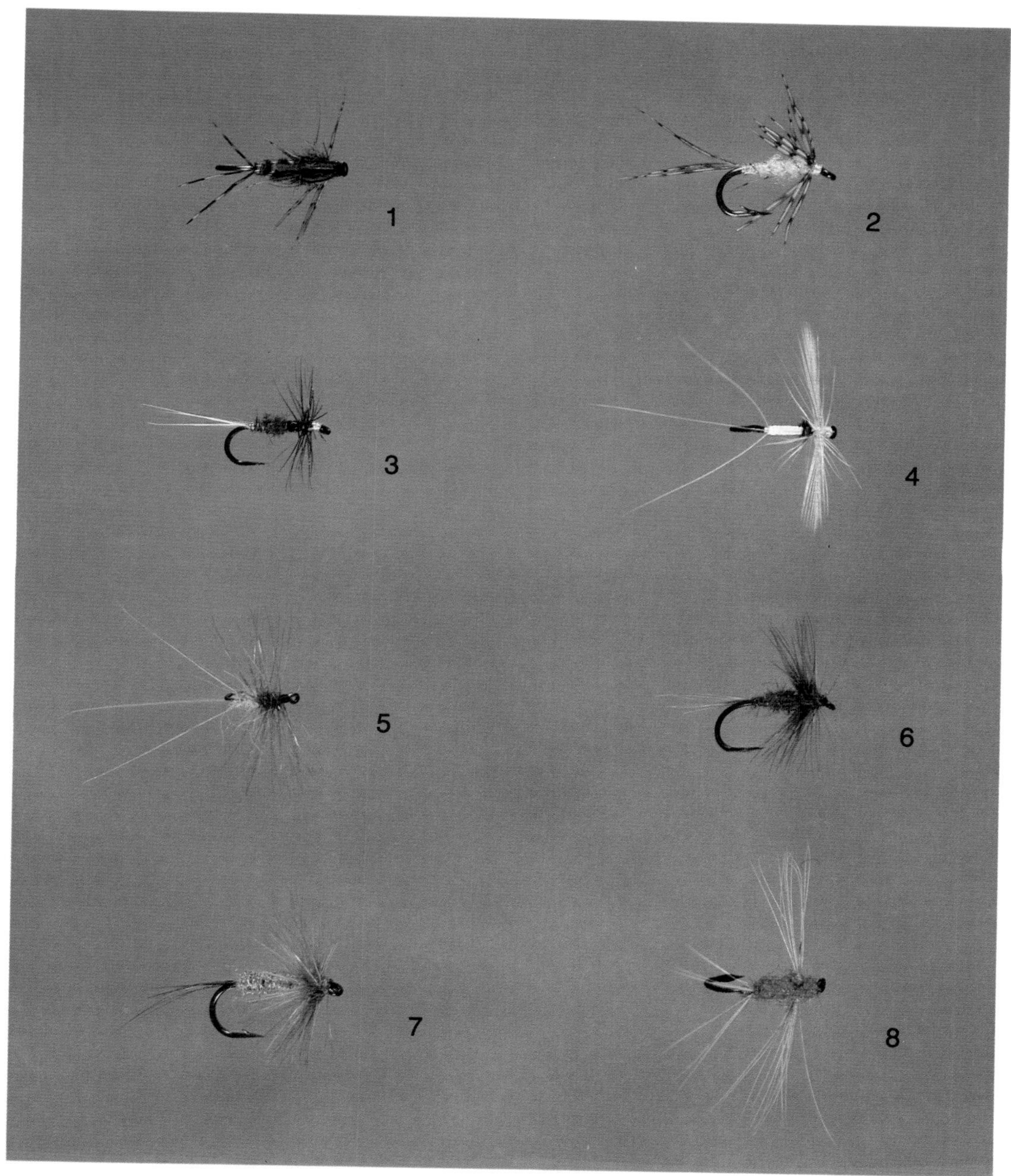

1 Caenis Nymph (Carnill) **2** Caenis Nymph **3** Caenis Dun (Sawyer)
4 Caenis Spinner (Canham) **5** Caenis Spinner (Jardine)
6 Hatching Small Dark Olive Special **7** Small Dark Olive Dun
8 Small Dark Olive Spinner

3 Caenis Dun (Sawyer)

COMMENT

The adults are first seen in May and can continue into September. In addition to the evening hatches, they are one of the few species which emerge in the early morning. If trout are rising in the hours after dawn it is probably to spent spinners of the previous evening's activity or to caenis duns. Hatches can be enormous. They have three tails, cream-coloured bodies and broad whitish wings. Some species have a darker, near-black thorax. This is Frank Sawyer's dressing. Here it is tied on a size 16 to aid illustration.

DRESSING

Hook: 18–20 Code L3A.
Thread: White midge thread.
Tail: Short cream cock fibres.
Body: Mole's fur.
Thorax: Stripped black ostrich herl, shiny side uppermost.
Hackle: Three turns of a tiny dark blue-dun cock.

4 Caenis Spinner (Canham)

COMMENT

The adult stage of the caenis life cycle is the shortest of all ephemeropterans, lasting only about ninety minutes. When a hatch of duns occur they almost immediately begin the process of transposing into spinners as soon as they find dry land, or even on an angler's clothing. The spinners are whiter than the duns and the males have very long tails. Fine white polypropylene dubbing makes an excellent spinner body. This is a pattern with an unusual body material from Stuart Canham, recommended by John Goddard.

DRESSING

Hook: 18 Code L3A.
Thread: White midge thread.
Tail: Three widely spaced white cock hackle fibres.
Body: White polythene.
Thorax: A single turn of brown condor herl substitute or turkey herl.
Wings: White hen hackle cut with the smallest wing-cutter and tied spent.
Hackle: Short-fibred white cock trimmed flat along the bottom edge.

5 Caenis Spinner (Jardine)

COMMENT

Despite the big hatches of duns sometimes experienced, particularly on stillwaters, it is the returning female spinners that attract most interest from the trout. The spinner fall can be considerable with a very large number of naturals for trout to choose from. It is the sheer numbers of naturals that reduce the chances of the artificial's success. With any large fall of spinners, feeding trout need not move far from their position in the stream to feed; they let spinners come to them. The artificial needs to be cast very accurately so that it drifts directly over the fish. This is Charles Jardine's dressing.

DRESSING

Hook: 16–18 Code L3A or L4A.
Thread: White midge thread.
Tail: Three widely spaced white nylon paintbrush fibres or Microfibetts.
Abdomen: Cream-dyed rabbit's fur or Antron/hair mix.
Thorax: Brown or black rabbit's fur or Antron/hair mix.
Hackle: One or two high-quality very pale blue-dun or white cock wound through with four or five turns, trimmed with a V on top and bottom.

6 Small Dark Olive Hatching Special

COMMENT

The nymphs are very small agile-darting types inhabiting weed beds, moss and stones. Any of the general olive-imitating patterns will be adequate for the nymph imitation. The two-tailed adults are also very small, with medium to dark grey wings. The abdomen is pale yellow-olive or grey-green-olive, with the last two segments yellowish. This is Terry Griffith's dressing for the hatching dun.

DRESSING

Hook: 16–18 Code L3A.
Tail: Very short blue-dun fibres.
Body: A short body of mole's fur.
Rib: Finest gold thread.
Hackle: Rhode Island Red cock (medium-red) with a blue-dun in front.

7 Small Dark Olive Dun

COMMENT

The main hatches can be expected between May and August with the peak in July and August, which gave them their once-popular name of July Dun. They are not unknown in March or as late in the year as November. Emergence, which is sometimes in very large prolonged hatches, is usually in the afternoon and evening. It is a very important hatch on some rivers, particularly the chalk streams. Small versions of any general olive dressings are usually sufficient imitation.

DRESSING

Hook: 16–18 Code L3A or E6A.
Thread: Yellow.
Tail: Blue-dun cock fibres.
Body: Mixed light-olive (Fly-Rite #15) and Adams grey (Fly-Rite #26) polypropylene dubbing.
Hackle: Olive cock with blue-dun in front.

8 Small Dark Olive Spinner

COMMENT

In common with many *Baetis* species the female spinners return to oviposit their eggs below the surface by crawling down stakes or anything half in and half out of the water. The returning and spent females below the surface are taken by fish, often without any surface movement betraying their feeding. However, some spinners swim back to the surface and struggle to break through the film. Here the spent and weary flies make an easy target. The female, also known as the little red spinner, has a dark-brown or mahogany-red abdomen, transparent wings and two greyish-white tails.

DRESSING

Hook: 16–18 Code L3A.
Thread: Brown.
Tails: Two widely spaced sparse bunches of pale blue-dun fibres.
Body: Rusty-red seal's fur substitute or polypropylene dubbing (Fly-Rite #5) dubbed after the wing is tied in.
Wing: Pale blue-dun cock wound and bunched in the spent position with figure-of-eight turns of thread.

March Brown, Late or False March Brown and Large Brook Dun

The two March brown species *(Rithrogena germanica* and *Ecdyonurus venosus)* are so similar that only in this century have they been separately identified. The nymphs and adults can be distinguished from the other species only by a close examination, which no trout would be able to make. So similar is the large brook dun *(Ecdyonurus torrentis)* that it can be represented by the same patterns.

The March brown is restricted in its distribution to fast-flowing rivers in localised areas of Wales, the West Country, the north of England and Scotland, appearing in March and early April. The late March brown is more widely distributed and much more common than its near-namesake. The months of its emergence from April to June are a sure indicator that the adults are late March browns. The large brook dun prefers smaller stony rivers and appears from late March to July.

1 March Brown Nymph

COMMENT

The natural nymph is a flat, broad, stone-clinging type and is dark bronze-green. They inhabit the stones and rocks of the riverbed and leave this relative safety only to make the journey to the surface to emerge. The nymph should be fished during a hatch period or before one is anticipated. If the correct shape of the nymph is to be imitated the artificials should also be broad and flat. The Draper Flat-Bodied Nymph hooks are useful for this purpose.

DRESSING

Hook: 12–16 Code HS3T, E1A or CS7.
Tail: Three widely spaced strands of cock pheasant tail fibres.
Body: Cock pheasant tail.
Rib: Gold wire.
Thorax: Hare's ear fur with the upper and lower fibres trimmed flat.
Wingcase: Woodcock wing feather fibres.
Legs: Small brown speckled partridge hackle.

2 March Brown Nymph (Ruane)

COMMENT

Both John Goddard and J. R. Harris suggest that the mature nymphs of the late March brown move into the shallower warmer waters on the edge of the river, probably in preparation for crawling onto rocks to emerge in the manner of a stonefly. There may well be some benefit in fishing a nymph pattern in the margins when the adults are in the air or might be expected. This is an unusual dressing from Terry Ruane, which has also proved to be a useful stillwater fly.

DRESSING

Hook: 12–14 long-shank Code H1A.
Thread: Brown.
Tails: Three hen pheasant centre-tail fibres.
Body: Light-brown Furry Foam.
Gills: White ostrich herl, tied double.
Thorax and head: Dark-brown Furry Foam.
Legs: Brown partridge hackle, tied Defoe style at the sides only.

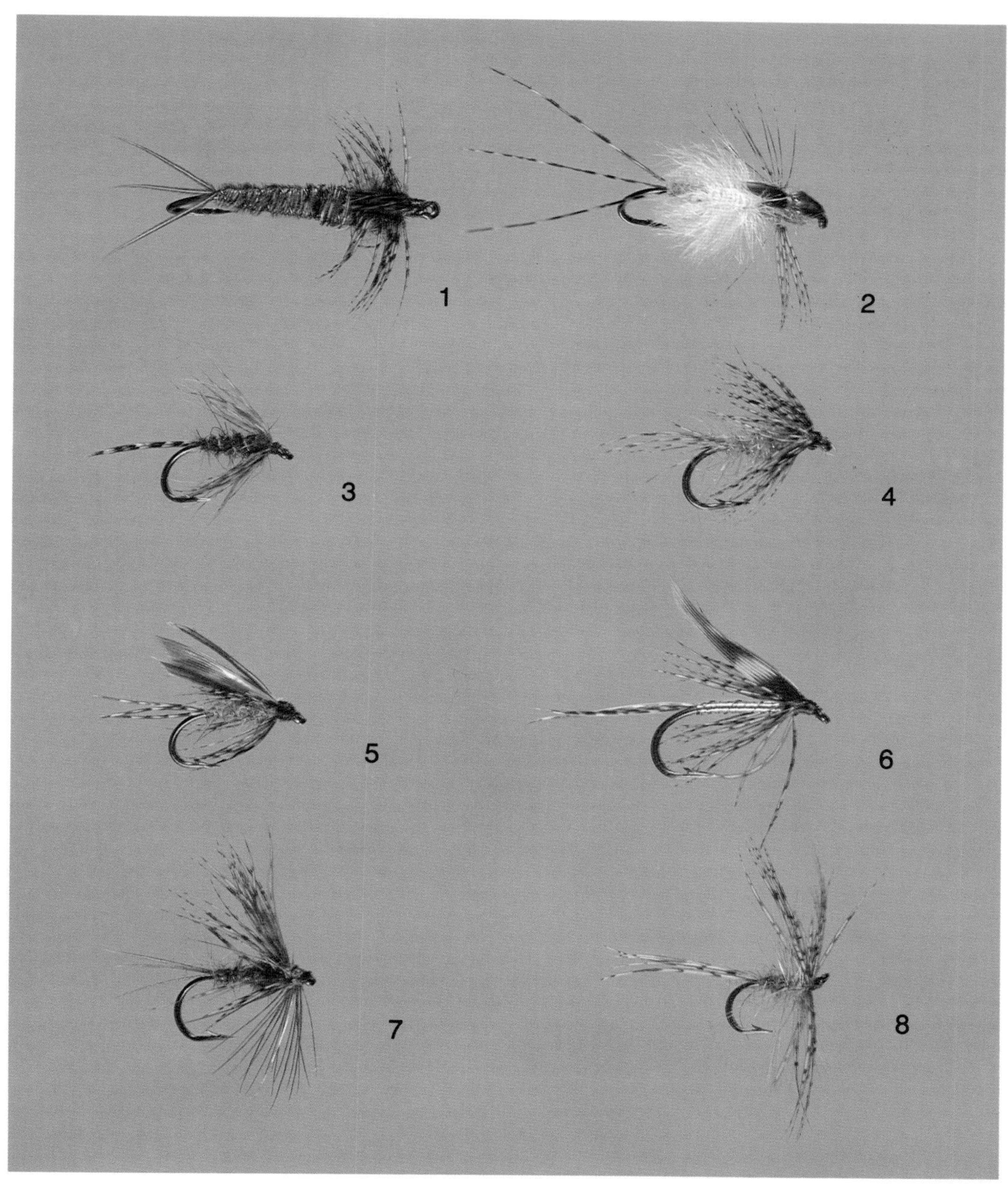

1 March Brown Nymph **2** March Brown Nymph (Ruane)
3 March Brown Spider **4** March Brown (Hancock) **5** Winged March Brown
6 Gold March Brown **7** Hatching March Brown
8 March Brown Dun (Pepper)

3 March Brown Spider

COMMENT

This is based on the northern style of dressing a wet fly with a sparse soft-fibred hackle feather. It is an excellent general early-season pattern, even on rivers that never experience a March brown hatch. If the hackle is wound Stewart-style, semi-palmered, the dressing is a good imitation of the emerging dun and generally suggestive of a number of species.

DRESSING

Hook: 12–14 Code A, CS7 or L2A.
Thread: Brown or primrose.
Tail: Speckled partridge tail fibres.
Body: Dark hare's ear fur mixed with brown or claret seal's fur substitute (4:1).
Rib: Silver wire or primrose thread.
Hackle: Dark speckled partridge.

4 March Brown (Hancock)

COMMENT

Cyril Hancock was well known in the Midlands for his angling column in the *Birmingham Post*. He devised this wet fly for the Welsh Dee and Usk, two of the few rivers that experience hatches of the true March brown.

DRESSING

Hook: 12–14 Code A, CS7 or L2A.
Thread: Brown or black.
Tail: Brown partridge fibres.
Body: Yellow seal's fur substitute.
Rib: Round gold tinsel.
Hackle: Brown partridge hackle.

5 Winged March Brown

COMMENT

This is a traditional winged wet pattern used wherever the two species are found and even on rivers where there is never a March brown to be seen. Not only does it represent the nymphs or emerging adults, it is also sufficiently impressionistic to be mistaken for a sedge pupa or shrimp.

DRESSING

Hook: 12–14 Code CS7, J1A or A.
Tail: Partridge tail fibres.
Body: Brown seal's fur substitute or sandy hare's ear fur.
Rib: Fine gold wire.
Wing: Brown partridge or hen pheasant.
Hackle: Brown partridge.

6 Gold March Brown

COMMENT

I wonder whether this pattern is actually taken for the natural fly of this name. It seems to be more of an attractor pattern. I have no experience of fishing it during a March brown hatch or at a time when they might be anticipated. However, it is a very good general river pattern and is sometimes acceptable as a hatching sedge pupa when fished close to the surface when sedges are leaving the river.

DRESSING

Hook: 10–14 Code CS7, J1A or A.
Thread: Brown or black.
Tail: Partridge tail fibres.
Body: Flat gold tinsel.
Rib: Oval gold tinsel or wire.
Wing: Partridge tail or hen pheasant wing.
Hackle: Brown partridge.

7 March Brown Hatching Dun (Lawrie)

COMMENT

The large-sized adults usually emerge at the tail of faster, broken water, most frequently around midday and in the early afternoon. For some reason trout seem to prefer the emerging nymph in the surface film to the fully winged adult and at such times a wet fly fished close to the surface catches many more fish than a fully dry fly. This observation is borne out by angling evolution, which has produced dozens of subsurface imitations but a mere handful of adult patterns. This W. H. Lawrie's emerging pattern to be fished in the film.

DRESSING

Hook: 12–14 Code L3A.
Thread: Yellow or orange.
Tail: Three short cock pheasant tail fibres.
Body: Medium hare's ear fur.
Rib: Fine gold wire.
Thorax: Sepia seal's fur substitute.
Wing hackle: Dark partridge feather with the lower fibres cut away.
Leg hackle: Dark-red cock hackle with the upper fibres cut away.

8 March Brown (Pepper)

COMMENT

The natural dun has dark-to-pale-fawn wings with heavy dark-brown veining, the female being lighter than the male. The abdomen is dull dark brown with straw-coloured rings. The two tails are dark brown-grey. The female spinner has transparent dark-veined wings and a dark red-brown body with straw-coloured rings. The late March brown female spinner is slightly larger and the body is of a deeper red than the March brown. It is known as the great red spinner. This is Tony Pepper's dun imitation, which he says is also very useful again at the end of the season.

DRESSING

Hook: 14–16 Code A, L2A or L3A.
Thread: Purple.
Tail: Speckled brown partridge breast fibres.
Body: Hare's ear.
Hackles: Honey cock with a speckled brown partridge breast feather in front.

Pale Watery and Pale Evening Dun

The pale watery *(Baetis fuscatus)* is widely distributed in the south of England and elsewhere on alkaline rivers. The female duns are very similar in overall colouring to the medium olive and small dark olive and are frequently distinguished from these only by careful examination. The male duns are easier to differentiate by their yellow eyes. Good hatches will often extend into late October and stimulate grayling into surface feeding.

The pale evening dun *(Procloëon bifidum)* is also fairly similar to the pale watery and is often found on the same rivers. Overall they are a very pale fly, probably the palest of all duns. To aid the angler's identification it is the only river dun without hindwings, although no trout is aware of this fact.

1 Pale Watery Nymph

COMMENT

The nymphs are the agile-darting type, preferring to live amongst weedbeds. The adults begin to emerge in May and an increase in nymphal activity can be expected during this month. An excellent nymph pattern is Frank Sawyer's Grey Goose Nymph; if you prefer a traditional wet fly the Poult Bloa is excellent. This is a hackled nymph dressing.

DRESSING

Hook: 14–16 Code G3A or L2A.
Thread: Primrose.
Tail: Ginger hackle fibres.
Abdomen: Thinly dubbed mixed cream and olive (3:1) seal's fur substitute.
Thorax: Mixed ginger and cream (2:1) seal's fur substitute over an optional weight of turns of copper wire.

2 Pale Watery Dun (Walker)

COMMENT

The duns primarily hatch during the day from May to October, reaching a peak towards the end of this period. The size of the duns varies between medium and small. They have pale-grey wings and two grey tails. Both the male and female have a pale grey-olive abdomen, with the last two segments pale-yellow or yellow-olive. The male has distinctive yellow eyes. This dressing is one of Richard Walker's, which he highly recommended for both trout and grayling.

DRESSING

Hook: 16 Code L3A or E6A.
Thread: Primrose.
Tail: Fibres of the hackle used.
Tip: Primrose tying thread, to which may be added a few drops of clear cellulose to give it an amber tint.
Body: Swan secondary herl tinted palest greenish-grey.
Wing (optional): Honey-dun cock fibres bunched upright, or bleached starling wing.
Hackle: Honey-dun or deeply tinted cream cock.

1 Pale Watery Nymph **2** Pale Watery Dun (Walker)
3 Pale Watery Dun (Rice) **4** Goddard's Last Hope
5 Pale Watery Spinner (Warrilow) **6** Pale Watery Spinner
7 Pale Evening Dun (Kite) **8** Pale Evening Dun

3 Pale Watery Dun (Rice)

COMMENT

Thirty years ago the term pale watery was used to include the small dark olive, small and large spurwings and often the pale evening dun. Now these are correctly recognised as being separate species and angling entomologists have tied patterns to represent each of them. Do trout recognise them for what they are? I suspect that one good general dressing will dupe most trout most of the time. Freddie Rice ties this pattern.

DRESSING

Hook: 14–16 Code L3A or E6A.
Thread: Light-yellow.
Tail: Light-blue-dun or pale honey-dun cock fibres.
Tip: Unwaxed tying thread.
Body: Two or three herls of light-grey heron, white swan or goose wing dyed palest olive.
Hackle: Palest olive or pale honey-dun cock.

4 Goddard's Last Hope

COMMENT

John Goddard suggested this imitation of the dun, which is also a suitable pattern for any of the small pale flies, including the caenis. Light-coloured body herls are used for the early-season pattern, and darker herls from mid-June onwards. The lighter version is illustrated. When the fly was devised in the 1960s condor herl was readily available. It is now on the prohibited list but suitable alternatives are marketed as condor herl substitutes.

DRESSING

Hook: 16–18 fine wire Code L3A or E6A.
Thread: Pale yellow.
Tail: Bunch of dark-honey-dun hackle fibres.
Body: Buff-coloured condor herl substitute, or Norwegian goose breast feather fibres.
Hackle: Short-fibred dark-honey-dun cock.

5 Pale Watery Spinner (Warrilow)

COMMENT

The female spinners are highly distinctive with their pale golden-brown or golden-olive abdomens, which give rise to their common name of golden spinner. The last three body segments are darker, the wings are transparent and the tails greyish-white. I have seen very few spinners returning to the water and I've not been aware of trout taking them. However, on streams with good hatches I've no doubt the spinner imitation is of value, if the number of patterns is a guide. This is Ian Warrilow's dressing.

DRESSING

Hook: 14–16 Code L3A or E6A.
Thread: Cream.
Tail: Honey hackle fibres.
Abdomen: Stripped yellow hackle stalk.
Thorax: Ginger Antron.
Wing: Cream poly yarn, spent.

6 Pale Watery Spinner

COMMENT

The female spinners return to the water in the evenings. Many of the *Baetis* female spinners return below the surface to lay their eggs but there is a difference of opinion about whether *Baetis fuscatus* do. I have seen the spinners ovipositing on the surface and angling entomologists also record the same, but other entomological authorities suggest that the spinners crawl into the water to oviposit in addition to egg laying on the surface. I'd welcome any readers' observations. This is another modern pattern to represent the spinner in the process of egg laying.

DRESSING

Hook: 14–16 Code L3A or E6A.
Thread: Pale orange.
Tail: Widely spaced white cock fibres or white nylon paintbrush fibres.
Body: Golden-amber (Fly-Rite #14) poly dubbing with the rear of the abdomen golden-olive (Fly-Rite #8).
Wing: Clear Antron fibres or white poly yarn.

7 Pale Evening Dun (Kite)

COMMENT

These medium-sized duns appear in the evenings of July and August, sometimes hatching almost until dusk. They have a preference for the slower-moving reaches of the river. The wings are pale grey and the abdomen very pale straw-coloured. The two tails are olive-grey. The male dun has distinctive yellow eyes. The dressing is Oliver Kite's. I think he was the first person to tie a pattern to specifically imitate the species.

DRESSING

Hook: 14–16 Code L3A or E6A.
Thread: White.
Tail: Cream cock fibres.
Body: Grey goose herls, doubled and redoubled at the thorax.
Hackle: Cream cock.

8 Pale Evening Dun

COMMENT

A spinner imitation is of no practical value as the spinner fall is rarely seen and very likely takes place after dark. John Goddard records the duns as often hatching alongside the blue-winged olive and trout taking the pale evening duns in preference. There's no doubt that trout can express a preference when there is a choice of surface food. Perhaps pale evening duns hatch in greater numbers than the blue-winged olive (the bigger the hatch, the more likely trout will concentrate on the commonest species – not the biggest insects), or perhaps they taste better.

DRESSING

Hook: 14 Code L3A or E6A.
Thread: Yellow.
Tail: Cream cock fibres.
Body: Cream variant Fly-Rite #25 poly dubbing.
Wing (optional): Light-grey polypropylene yarn set upright.
Hackle: Cream cock.

Mayfly 1

A good hatch of mayfly *(Ephemera danica, E. vulgata)* is deemed precious in the eyes of all trout fishers. It is an exhilarating sight to see the air heavy with thousands of these large duns and every trout and grayling in the river rising with abandon. No other hatch attracts so much attention or induces trout to surface-feed so freely. For a week or so each season on rivers fortunate enough to have good hatches trout gorge themselves on this annual banquet. Even the bigger, wiser fish that have previously viewed with suspicion each artificial fly now seem to be consumed with gluttony and throw caution to the wind. Often during the first days of the hatch trout do not rise too readily but by the time hatches peak they rise freely and the difficulty becomes one of persuading a fish to take the artificial alongside so many naturals.

1 Mayfly Nymph

COMMENT

So important has been the imitation of the adults that the mayfly nymph has been largely overlooked by fly tyers. At the end of the last century the first imitation was tied but few patterns have been offered until relatively recently. Courtney Williams' dictionary fails to offer a dressing in 18 pages of text about the species. Perhaps Oliver Kite's view prevailed: 'When they feed greedily on these big nymphs in this way, catching them on a large artificial can scarcely be dignified by the name of sport. Those who want fish rather than sport can catch them in this way'!

DRESSING

Hook: 10–14 long-shank Code H1A.
Thread: Brown.
Tail: Pheasant tail fibres.
Underbody (optional): Lead foil or wire.
Abdomen: Mixed cream and light-brown seal's fur substitute (3:1) with a palmered brown cock hackle over the front half with the underfibres cut away.
Rib: Strong brown thread over the abdomen.
Thorax: As for abdomen.
Wingcase: Pheasant tail fibres with the tips turned down as legs.

2 Walker's Mayfly Nymph

COMMENT

These large nymphs burrow in the mud or silt of the riverbed. On some rivers they have been observed ascending to the surface and returning again in the fortnight before the main hatch. The species are widely distributed on waters that provide a suitable habitat for the nymphs. Their size (sometimes over an inch long) and their overall creamy-dun colouring with brown marking makes them easily distinguishable from other species. The artificial is well worth fishing in the weeks either side of the main hatch. This dressing of Richard Walker's is the best so far devised.

DRESSING

Hook: 10–14 long-shank Code H1A.
Thread: Brown.
Tail: Pheasant tail fibres.
Abdomen: Light yellowish-buff angora wool over an optional lead foil underbody, with tw bands of pheasant tail fibres near the tail.
Rib: Brown nylon thread over the abdomen
Thorax: As for the abdomen, with the fibre: picked out.
Wingcase: Pheasant tail fibres, with the en turned down for legs.

1 Mayfly Nymph **2** Walker's Mayfly Nymph **3** Suspender Mayfly Nymph **4** Poly May Dun **5** Lively Mayfly **6** Edwards' Mayfly **7** Mayfly Dun 1 **8** Mayfly Dun 2

3 Suspender Mayfly Nymph

COMMENT

This is John Goddard's and Brian Clarke's dressing for the insect on the point of leaving its nymphal skin. It hangs at an angle just below the surface supported by the buoyant Ethafoam. The larger the Ethafoam ball, the higher in the film the nymph is supported. The ball should be tied in after the tail fibres and before the rest of the materials. A ready-mixed alternative for the body dubbing is polypropylene Fly-Rite #25 cream variant. Oliver Kite would not be impressed with its use or its effectiveness!

DRESSING

Hook: 12 long-shank Code H1A or E1A.
Thread: Brown.
Tail: Three tips of cream-coloured ostrich herl.
Abdomen and thorax: Mixed white, tan and yellow seal's fur substitute (2:1:1).
Rib: Brown monocord or tying thread over the abdomen.
Wingcase: Ethafoam ball in a nylon mesh and indelibly coloured brown.

4 Poly May Dun

COMMENT

John Goddard spent some time over three or four seasons achieving the right silhouette and colours for this and his Poly May Spinner pattern. He commented that these 'really are killers. I now need no other fly even for the most sophisticated of trout, except occasionally for Neil's.' (This is a reference to Neil Patterson's Deerstalker.) The bulky tail fibres represent the nymphal shuck clinging to the newly emerged dun.

DRESSING

Hook: 10–12 wide-gape Code A or E1A.
Thread: Primrose.
Tail and wings: Natural calf's tail hair dyed gold, laid along the shank and tied in an upright V.
Body: Cream-coloured polypropylene yarn, wound not dubbed.
Hackle: Three or four turns of black cock either side of the wing roots.

5 Lively Mayfly

COMMENT

This and the variation on page 77 are based on a North American dressing by Chauncy Lively, amended by Charles Jardine, who comments that they are the only mayfly dressings he uses. He also adds that he has known them to be taken in preference to the naturals. Any artificial that looks more realistic or attractive than the real thing must be good! The two versions were extremely successful on the River Test section for the English team on their way to victory in the 1987 World Championships. A V is cut through the body hackle underneath to achieve the correct silhouette.

DRESSING

Hook: 10 light-wire down-eye Code L2A or L3A.
Thread: Green.
Tail: Three pheasant tail fibres.
Extended body: Light deer hair (10–15 fibres) or moose mane ribbed with green thread.
Thorax: Cream/yellow Fly-Rite poly dubbing (illustrated) or Orvis Antron/hare blend.
Wing: Wood duck fibres bunched and separated by figure-of-eight turns of thread.
Body hackle: Grizzle cock.
Head hackle: Golden-olive cock.

6 Edwards' Mayfly

COMMENT

Oliver Edwards ties this dressing on the Swedish Dry Fly hook, which enables it to be fished point up and with the abdomen just touching the surface like the natural. The parachute hackle and wide-spread tails ensure a stable presentation. The silver underbody also makes the abdomen appear translucent. The wing is from a feather with fibres of equal length each side of the quill. Strip the lower fluff and clip off the tip. Fold it over at the quill and bind to the vertical post; it should be about ¾inch tall. Wind the two hackles up the post and finally dub the thorax.

DRESSING

Hook: 10 Swedish Dry Fly Code K3A.
Tail: Four strong moose mane or deer hairs.
Abdomen: Equally mixed ivory seal's fur and fine ivory poly dubbing over silver lurex.
Rib: Light-brown rayon or nylon floss in two broad bands at the rear.
Wing: Silver mallard breast or flank feather dyed very pale yellow, or lemon wood duck.
Hackles: Mixed pale-blue-dun cock and a pale-lemon-yellow-dyed grizzle.
Thorax: Mixed ivory and light-brown poly dubbing.

7 Mayfly Dun 1

COMMENT

The first hatches appear towards the end of May with a peak in the first two weeks of June and diminishing hatches thereafter. It is not common but quite possible for occasional adults to appear as late as September and even October. *E. danica* hatches on faster-flowing streams throughout the day, with a preference for the afternoons. *E. vulgata* is commoner on slow-moving muddy streams but there is only an insignificant difference between the species.

DRESSING

Hook: 10–12 long-shank Code E1A or D5B
Thread: Claret.
Tail: Pheasant tail fibres.
Body: Natural raffia with two palmered badger cock hackles cross-wound.
Hackle: Light-olive-dyed cock.

8 Mayfly Dun 2

COMMENT

The alternative angler's name for the dun is the green drake. The colouring of the duns varies regionally. Some hatching on my local stream have a distinctive olive hue but this is absent in other duns hatching the same day on the same water. This is an American dressing for the more olive duns. Generally the abdomen colour varies between yellow-cream in the females and greyish-white in the males. The male's wings are grey tinged with yellow and have heavy brown veining. The female's are grey with a blue-green tinge with black veins. They have three tails.

DRESSING

Hook: 10–12 long-shank Code E1A.
Thread: Olive or yellow.
Tail: Moose fibres.
Body: Olive polypropylene ribbed with yellow floss, or olive-dyed rabbit fur.
Wing: Goose or duck wing quills.
Hackle: Olive-dyed grizzle cock.

Mayfly 2

I've little doubt that more dressings for both mayfly duns and spinners have been devised than for any other upwinged species and this is reflected in the number of patterns I have included. In addition to these imitations other less specific dressings are also used to good effect as mayfly imitations, notably the White Wulff and Blonde Wulff. Also see the Straddlebug.

1 One-Feather Mayfly

COMMENT

This unusual design is highly praised by members of Romsey Fly Fishers, who now consider it their No. 1 Mayfly choice and refer to it as the RFF Mayfly. It is based on an idea by an American, André Puyans, and amended by Pat Russell. The fly floats very well with a relatively small hook. The mallard feather body, tail and wing needs a little explanation. A whole feather is used. A V of fibres forms the tail and the bulk of the feather the body, with the fibres swept forward in two upright bunches in a V for the wings.

DRESSING

Hook: 12 Code L3A.
Thread: Yellow.
Body: Yellow Furry Foam wound round the shank
Tails, overbody and wing: One bronze mallard feather.
Hackle: Hot orange cock.

2 Walker's Mayfly Dun

COMMENT

Richard Walker commented that the presence of orange in a mayfly dun dressing sometimes makes it highly attractive. He observed that in a sparse hatch when almost every dun passing over a trout was taken this dressing wasn't so good, but in a dense hatch, with numerous naturals to chose from, orange-hackled patterns were singled out by trout, even to the extent of ignoring naturals to reach it. The additional orange hackle can be added to any dressing to improve its appeal. This is Richard Walker's tying.

DRESSING

Hook: 8–10 long-shank Code E1A.
Thread: Brown.
Tail: Pheasant tail fibres.
Body: Very pale buff turkey tail fibres or substitute with two bands of pheasant tail near the rear.
Hackle: Speckled duck feather dyed pale green or a pale-green-dyed cock, followed by a ginger cock and a short-fibred hot orange cock.

1 One-Feather Mayfly **2** Walker's Mayfly Dun **3** Deerstalker
4 French Partridge Mayfly **5** Mayfly Spinner **6** Poly May Spinner
7 Russell's Mayfly **8** Plastazote Mayfly

3 Deerstalker

COMMENT

Neil Patterson's pattern is rated very highly. Although it lies flush in the film exactly like the natural spent female there is little danger of it becoming saturated and sinking. The horizontal deer hair fibres are buoyant and they trap air bubbles when bound on. The finished fly might look big, ungainly and unattractive, but believe me, it works very well indeed.

DRESSING

Hook: 10 long-shank Code E1A or H1A.
Thread: Brown.
Tail: Pheasant tail fibres about twice the body length.
Body: White deer hair laid along the shank with the tips protruding beyond the bend.
Rib: Generous turns of thread and silver wire.
Hackle: Palmered black over the thorax, severely trimmed. Long-fibred natural red cock through the front part of the black cock and bound in spent bunches.

4 French Partridge Mayfly

COMMENT

There are a number of well proven patterns using a French partridge feather as a shoulder hackle, some of which seem to share a common name but vary in their dressings. This has most of the commonest materials and is widely praised by those who use it.

DRESSING

Hook: 12 long-shank Code E1A.
Thread: Black or brown.
Tail: Cock pheasant tail fibres.
Body: Natural raffia with a palmered olive cock hackle.
Rib: Gold wire.
Hackle: French partridge feather.

5 Mayfly Spinner

COMMENT

The female spinner, also called the grey drake, or the spent gnat after oviposition, has a pale-cream abdomen, of which the last three segments are streaked brown. The wings are transparent with a blue tint and brown veins. The slightly smaller male spinner's wings have a brownish tint. It is the imitation of the returning or spent females that can offer the most exciting fishing when in the evenings the females descend *en masse* and when, by the end of an evening after a heavy spinner fall, every backwater and eddy is awash with the dead spent spinners.

DRESSING

Hook: 12 long-shank Code E1A.
Thread: Black.
Tail: Pheasant tail fibres.
Body: White floss silk.
Rib: Thick black thread or stripped black quill.
Hackle: Long-fibred badger cock fully wound or tied in spent bunches.

6 Poly May Spinner

COMMENT

John Goddard devised the spinner imitation to complement his dun pattern. He writes: 'It is a fallacy to suppose that the natural spinners always float on the surface with both wings flat on the surface on all waters that I fish. I would say that 65 per cent float along with one wing vertical'. He devised this dressing, which cocks one wing in the air and has the other flat on the surface.

DRESSING

Hook: 10–12 wide-gape Code A or L2A.
Thread: Black.
Tail: From three to five long black cock fibres or black nylon mono.
Body: White polypropylene yarn, wound not dubbed.
Wing: Mixed black and natural off-white calf's tail tied in a very wide V.
Hackle: Three or four turns on either side of the wing roots of a relatively short-fibred black cock hackle.

7 Russell's Mayfly

COMMENT

This is Pat Russell's spent dressing, based on an earlier Frank Speak pattern tied up by Jackie Wakeford. It is a buoyant fly and remarkably durable. Pat relates a remarkable story of how he was fishing on the Itchen and casting through some overhanging branches to what looked like the largest rainbow trout in the river. Stalking the fish, he cast the fly but wasn't able to see the target area. On the sound of the rise he struck and using an 8-foot rod and a 4lb point he played out the fish, which twice took 70 yards of line and backing. The large rainbow turned out to be a 13½-pound salmon!

DRESSING

Hook: 10 long-shank Code E1A or DB5.
Thread: Black.
Tail: Twelve or more light-brown cock fibres.
Body: A strip of polyethylene foam.
Rib: Natural red cock hackle stalk.
Hackle: Badger cock.
Wing: Two bunches of dyed slate-blue cock hackle fibres forward-slanting and divided.

8 Plastazote Mayfly

COMMENT

Chris Kendall has taken advantage of the buoyant properties of Plastazote as the body material to keep the fly afloat. The white colour suits the egg-laying female spinner but the same material can be coloured with an indelible pen to match the more olive hue of some duns. This dressing represents the spinner newly returned to the water, but because the fully spent natural lies flush on the surface it is a good idea when imitating these to cut away the lower hackle fibres.

DRESSING

Hook: 8–10 long-shank Mayfly up-eye Code DB5.
Thread: Dark brown.
Tail: Cock pheasant centre-tail fibres.
Body: Plastazote cut into strips and wound.
Rib: Dark-brown floss.
Wing: Lightly marked teal, tied spent.
Hackle: Light-brown cock.

Large Dark Olive and Yellow May Dun

Both these species are quite distinctive flies, never to be confused with any other duns. The large dark olive (*Baetis rhodani*), also known as the early olive or large spring olive, is widely distributed throughout the country, with the best hatches on fast-flowing rivers. They are the earliest important fly on many rivers, with large hatches appearing even before the trout season opens.

The yellow may dun (*Heptagenia sulphurea*) is quite a common species. I have been on rivers with fantastic hatches when almost every yard had a dun on it and the air was heavy with them but not a trout rose anywhere. Some authorities confirm that this is not unusual, yet I know of fly fishers who have seen trout rise freely to them and have found the artificial very effective.

1 Large Dark Olive Nymph (Price)

COMMENT

The nymph is an agile-darting type to be found clinging to rocks and stones, or, in the slower parts of the river, on weeds and moss. In addition to the many general olive nymph imitations, Taff Price devised this more specific dressing.

DRESSING

Hook: 12–14 Code L2A, CS7 or G3A.
Thread: Yellow.
Tail: Dark-olive hackle fibres.
Body: Mixed olive seal's fur substitute and hare's ear fur.
Rib: Fine gold wire.
Thorax: Brown seal's fur substitute.
Wingcase: Dark-olive swan or goose fibres.
Legs: Tips of the wingcase fibres, or olive cock fibres.

2 Large Dark Olive Nymph (Edwards)

COMMENT

The agile-darting nymphs are slim and translucent and at the time of maturity have prominent wingpads. This superb dressing by Oliver Edwards is the best I have seen to represent any of the agile-darting species. It is exactly the right size, shape and colour and it is translucent. Compare it with a natural! Tying sequence: tail; abdomen, tie in wingcase and leg feather; thorax; leg feather; wingcase and wingcase strip. Before the leg feather is laid on the thorax, smear a thin line of glue or varnish on the thorax, and again before the wingcase. Optional weight can be added at the thorax.

DRESSING

Hook: 18 long-shank Code H1A.
Thread: White, which after winding under the abdomen is coloured dull orange.
Tail: Badger hair dyed medium-olive.
Abdomen: Olive flexibody or olive-dyed polythene strip in overlapping turns.
Wingcase: Dark turkey feather fibres with a narrow strip of abdomen material down the middle.
Legs: Small speckled partridge feather dyed or coloured medium-dark olive.
Thorax: Olive-brown hare's belly fur.

1 Large Dark Olive Nymph (Price) **2** LDO Nymph (Edwards) **3** LDO Dun **4** LDO Dun (Rice) **5** LDO Dun (Jacobsen) **6** Yellow May Dun Emerger **7** Yellow May Dun 1 **8** Yellow May Dun 2

3 Large Dark Olive Dun

COMMENT

The medium-to-large adults first appear in late February and usually end before May, and in some years they reappear in October. They often emerge on cool damp spring days and consequently they spend some time on the surface drying their wings before flight. They are an attractive and easy meal for trout and they usually tempt trout into the first surface-feeding spree of the season. Even on quite early cold spring days a midday hatch can be expected. The wings are pale grey; the abdomen is olive-brown or olive-green, with a paler underside in the female. It has two tails.

DRESSING

Hook: 12–14 Code L3A or E6A.
Thread: Olive.
Tail: Grey cock fibres, Microfibetts or Magic Spinner Tails.
Body: Natural or synthetic olive dubbing (Fly-Rite #29 is used in the illustration).
Wing: Pale-grey polypropylene yarn set upright.
Hackle: Olive and ginger cocks wound together.

4 Large Dark Olive Dun (Rice)

COMMENT

This is Freddie Rice's dressing for the dun. It uses starling wing quills, which are a popular winging material and are used on many upwinged patterns. Tying the two slips of wing in is not easy and I prefer the no less effective single bunch of poly yarn or bunched wing fibres. I confess that the wing quills look more natural to the human eye. The body in this tying is of white moose-mane dyed dark mahogany, browny-olive or dark-grey olive, lighter in the spring and autumn.

DRESSING

Hook: 14 Code L3A or E6A.
Thread: Olive.
Tail: Light-blue-dun hackle fibres.
Body: Generous layers of tying thread covered with dyed moose-mane hair (*see* text).
Wing: Paired slips of pale starling primaries.
Hackle: Medium-olive cock.

5 Large Dark Olive Dun (Jacobsen)

COMMENT

A few years ago I enjoyed a correspondence with the world famous Danish trout angler and fly tyer Preben Torp Jacobsen. He sent me this imitation. It is tied with three hackles, which makes it a very good floater. The reason for the generous hackling is that it was tied to cope with surface pollution from local trout farms. The female spinner, known as the large red spinner, is of doubtful value to the fly fisher. It is rarely on the water in sufficient quantity to attract trout interest. It oviposits below the surface and a suitable wet pattern should be used.

DRESSING

Hook: 12–14 Code L3A or E6A.
Thread: Amber.
Tails: Ginger cock hackle fibres.
Body: Two natural and two olive-dyed heron herls twisted together.
Rib: Fine silver wire.
Hackles: Medium-sized pale-olive cock and a small ginger cock wound together, with a larger rusty dun at the head.

6 Yellow May Dun Emerger

COMMENT

Oliver Edwards produced this emerger when he found trout taking the emerging nymphs with just the first signs of the wings. The partially stripped partridge hackle is tied stalk to the rear on top of the shank. Pull the stalk through so there is enough for the thorax cover. The forward-facing fibres will form the legs. Cut out the middle ones, leaving about six each side. Bind in the doubled Raffene. Dub the thorax over the wing roots and either side of the legs. Pull the thorax cover forward and bind in.

DRESSING

Hook: 16 Code H1A.
Thread: Pre-waxed yellow.
Tail, thorax cover and legs: Grey partridge hackle fibres dyed pale sulphur-yellow.
Abdomen: Natural or synthetic fur dyed pale sulphur-yellow, covered by overlapping turns of 2mm-wide clear polythene strip.
Thorax: Same fur as the abdomen.
Emerging wings: Light-brown Raffene trimmed to shape and size.
Head: Varnished yellow thread.
Eyes (optional): Black head cement.

7 Yellow May Dun 1

COMMENT

The nymphs are flat stone-clingers and are sometimes found on thicker weed stems. The medium-to-large adults emerge in the afternoons and evenings throughout the season but are most prolific between May and July. Other sources suggest that the hatches can be quite sparse but I have known very big hatches on the Yorkshire Dales rivers. It has a reputation for being unpopular with trout but I know that on some rivers it is eagerly taken and can be an important fly. The nymph should be fished during a hatch or just before one might be expected.

DRESSING

Hook: 12–14 Code L3A or E6A.
Thread: Olive-yellow.
Tail: Badger or yellow cock fibres.
Body: Olive-yellow tying thread or floss.
Hackle: Yellow-dyed cock.

8 Yellow May Dun 2

COMMENT

The two-tailed duns are easy to recognise with their pale yellow wings and yellow bodies. The female spinner has transparent wings with a pale yellow leading edge and brown veins. Its body is pale yellow. The eyes of both duns and spinners are very distinctive, being blue-black but fading with age to become a very attractive pale blue. I've not heard of the female spinners being taken with any conviction.

DRESSING

Hook: 12–14 Code L3A or E6A.
Thread: Yellow.
Tail: Yellow cock.
Body: Pale sulphur-yellow seal's fur substitute or poly dubbing (Fly-Rite pale-watery yellow #38).
Wing: Upright or slightly forward-slanting bunch of pale yellow cock fibres, or mixed white and yellow.
Hackle: Yellow cock.

Medium Olive, August or Autumn Dun and Yellow Evening Dun

The three medium olive species (*Baetis vernus, B. tenax, B. buceratus*) are very much alike and between them are widely distributed, particularly in alkaline weedy rivers. One species prefers small stony streams at a higher altitude. They are unknown in Wales and Ireland. Where they are found they are an important trout fishers' fly.

The August or autumn dun (*Ecdyonurus dispar*) prefers rivers with stony beds and is found in South Wales, the West Country and quite widely in the northern counties. As its name suggests, it is a late-season fly.

Yellow evening duns (*Ephemerella notata*) have a fairly localised distribution in the western half of England and Wales.

1 Medium Olive Nymph

COMMENT

The agile-darting nymph is found among weeds and on stones in both fast and slow water. Any olive nymph pattern is likely to work since the various natural olive nymphs are very similar. This is G. E. M. Skues' pattern for the southern chalk streams, where the natural is an important fly.

DRESSING

Hook: 14 Code A, G3A or CS7.
Thread: Waxed primrose.
Tail: Pale-blue cock hackle fibres.
Abdomen: Olive-dyed heron herl.
Rib: Fine gold wire.
Thorax: Blue squirrel's fur.
Hackle: Short-fibred dark-blue cock, two turns at most.

2 Medium Olive Dun (Hudson)

COMMENT

The medium-sized adults first begin to hatch in mid-May and continue regularly until the end of June and spasmodically thereafter until October. Their usual emergence time is in the late morning and early afternoon. The adults have medium-grey wings, a brown to yellowy-olive abdomen with a paler underside, and two grey tails. Many of the general olive imitations will suffice but this is a highly regarded pattern from Alan Hudson.

DRESSING

Hook: 14–16 Code L3A or E6A.
Thread: Black.
Tails: Plymouth Rock fibres.
Body: Rabbit's fur, a mixture of underfur and guard hairs.
Hackle: Plymouth Rock cock.

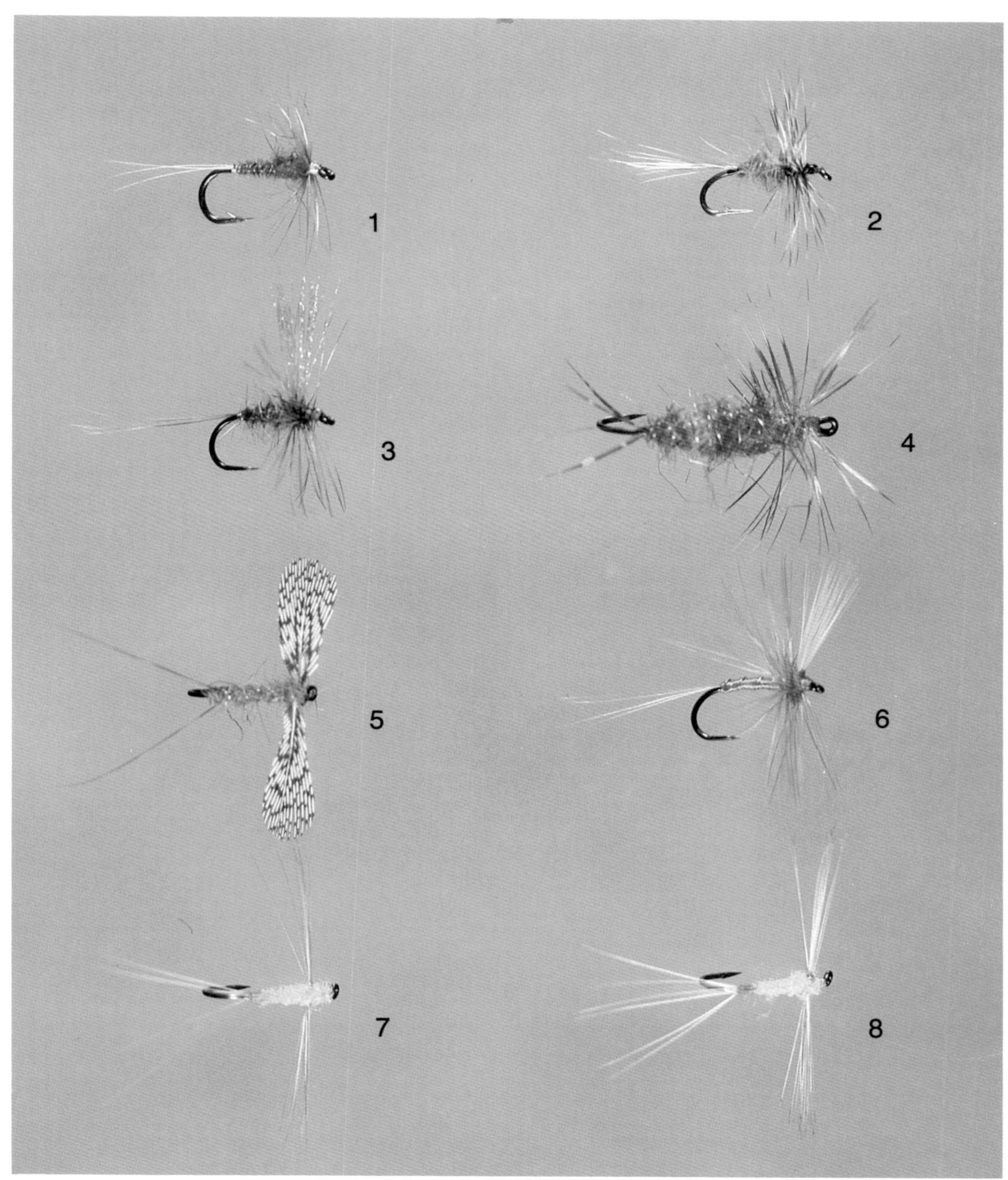

1 Medium Olive Nymph **2** Medium Olive Dun (Hudson)
3 Medium Olive Dun **4** August Dun Nymph **5** August Dun Spinner
6 Yellow Evening Dun (Harris) **7** Yellow Evening Spinner
8 Lunn's Yellow Boy

3 Medium Olive Dun

COMMENT

Hare or rabbit's fur is an excellent material for the olive-bodied duns and I made use of it for this olive imitation I tied up when experimenting at the fly vice, as all fly tyers do. I have been impressed by the Magic Spinner Wing fibres produced by Traun River products; they are translucent and give the impression of the light, highly delicate natural's wings. The fibres are available in a range of natural colours and can be used for all sorts of winging styles. This is a good general olive imitation. The emerger can be imitated with a parachute hackle wound round the wing base.

DRESSING

Hook: 14–16 Code L3A or E6A.
Tail: Blue-dun cock hackle fibres.
Body: Hare's ear fur.
Rib: Fine gold wire.
Wing: A single bunch of grey Magic Spinner Wing fibres tied upright.
Hackle: Greenwell cock wound at the shoulder or in parachute style.

4 August Dun Nymph

COMMENT

The mature nymph is quite large and is the flat stone-clinging type inhabiting stony-bedded rivers. Only when the mature nymph swims to the surface to emerge will it be found other than in the bottom inch of the stream. When tying any of the stone-clinging nymphs an accurate body shape and silhouette is easy to achieve if you use Partridge Draper Flat-Bodied Nymph hooks, code H3ST. The hollow body of these double-shanked hooks can be packed with fine lead wire for extra weight without suffering from the extra bulk above the shank.

DRESSING

Hook: 14–16 Code H3ST.
Thread: Yellow.
Tail: Yellow guinea-fowl fibres.
Body: Mixed brown and pale-yellow seal's fur substitute with a few fibres picked out through the rib.
Rib: Fine gold wire.
Hackle: Sparse turns of golden plover (ash-coloured feather with yellow tips) over the front fifth of the body.

5 August Dun Spinner

COMMENT

The large adults emerge from July to October, with their most prolific period in August. Both the duns and spinners are so similar to the late March brown that only an examination of the wing veins makes identification certain. The female spinners, also known as the great red spinner, has a reddish-brown abdomen and transparent wings with dark-brown veining. The tails and legs are brown. This is a modern spinner dressing that needs to be dressed on the finest wire hooks to aid floating. The partridge wings imitate well the veins of the natural's wings.

DRESSING

Hook: 12–14 Code L4A.
Thread: Claret.
Tail: Brown Microfibetts (Orvis) or Magic Spinner Tails (Traun River Products).
Body: Reddish-brown seal's fur substitute or poly dubbing (Fly-Rite rust #5).
Rib (optional): Fine gold wire.
Wing: Light partridge breast feathers tied concave side down.

6 Yellow Evening Dun (Harris)

COMMENT

The nymphs are moss-creepers, which tend to avoid the faster parts of a river. There is no published pattern to represent them. The duns are of medium-to-large size and appear, as their name suggests, in the late evenings and dusks of May and June. They have pale yellow-grey wings with yellow or pale yellow bodies, of which the last three segments of the males' are pale amber. The three tails are yellow with brown rings. Overall they are similar to the larger two-tailed yellow May dun. This is J. R. Harris's dressing slightly adapted by the alternative wing fibres.

DRESSING

Hook: 14 Code A, L3A or E6A.
Thread: Hot orange.
Tail: Ginger cock fibres.
Body: Orange rayon floss.
Rib: Fine gold wire.
Advanced-wing: Bunched pale-yellow cock fibres or light-yellow golden pheasant breast fibres tied forward-sloping.
Hackle: Ginger cock.

7 Yellow Evening Spinner

COMMENT

Distribution of the species is not widespread, though they are quite common in Wales. The male spinner, like those of most species, dies over land and is not seen on the water. The female spinner has transparent wings with a yellow leading edge. The body is yellow-olive with the last three segments brown-olive. The legs are olive-yellow and the tails yellow with red-brown rings.

DRESSING

Hook: 14 Code L3A, L4A or E6A.
Thread: Orange.
Tails: Widely spaced yellow or cream cock fibres or Microfibetts.
Body: Pale yellow-olive seal's fur substitute or poly dubbing (Fly-Rite olive sulphur #23), with the tying thread visible at the rear.
Wing: Bunched honey cock fibres in the spent position.

8 Lunn's Yellow Boy

COMMENT

The Test river keeper William Lunn produced many patterns to which he gave names which offered no clue to their use or the natural they imitated. It has been suggested that this is an olive spinner imitation, but to me that has no credibility. The suggestion of yellow in the name may offer a hint. It is unlikely that Lunn tied the fly as a yellow evening spinner but it serves as a fair representation, with the pale-orange tying thread giving a hint of the change of colour of the last three body segments.

DRESSING

Hook: 14 Code L3A or L4A.
Thread: Pale orange.
Tail: Pale-buff cock fibres.
Body: White hackle stalk dyed yellow or yellow seal's fur substitute.
Wing: Pale-buff cock hackle fibres bunched and tied spent.

SEDGES OR CADDISFLIES

Introduction to Sedges or Caddisflies

If the fly fisher can identify and name half a dozen of the nearly 200 British and 800 American species of the order Trichoptera, I suspect he is doing better than most anglers. Beyond the grannom, caperer and one or two locally numerous species many sedges are simply referred to by their size and colour and all the trout fisher has to know is that the small reddish-brown sedge he sees on his local river is well represented by a Little Red Sedge. The low priority of species identification is not a reflection of the importance of the caddis, which is on the trout menu at all stages of its life cycle. As larva, pupa, newly emerged adult and egg-laying female it attracts trout attention.

The grub-like larvae build round themselves protective cases of vegetable debris and material from the riverbed. A few are free-swimming and some build a net between stones, in which they live on the food ensnared. They vary in size from a few millimetres to well over 2 inches. At this stage they appear very prominently in trout and grayling diets. Grayling are primarily bottom feeders and they consume the cased larvae in quantity.

Within its case the larva spins a silken cocoon around itself in which the wings and legs are formed beneath its pupal skin. After some months the pupa chews through the case wall and emerges. It drifts downstream for some distance, perhaps up to 25 feet or more, depending upon the current speed, and then it swims to the surface. Trout feed on these emerged pupae on the bottom and near the surface. Very few are taken in midwater. Trout rarely take up positions in midwater anyway; most of the food is either on the bottom or on or just under the surface. Relatively few trout seem to follow the swimming ascending pupae and take them as they are rising unless they are intercepted just below the surface. They choose to feed when food comes easiest to them. In this case it is when the newly emerged pupa drifts downstream and as the pupa hangs below the surface film, struggling to emerge as an adult. The pupae of a few species crawl ashore to emerge on dry land but the vast majority, and all those of interest to the fly fisher, emerge on open water. Sometimes during a sedge hatch trout can go through a period of frenzied activity, rolling and even jumping. The temptation is to fish a high-floating pattern when often one would do far better with a pupal imitation because the trout are invariably gorging themselves on the struggling pupae in the film. The relatively immobile targets provide easy feeding.

One of the key features of the natural pupa is the brightness of the air bubbles trapped beneath the transparent sheath which surrounds its body. A major breakthrough in the imitation of the pupa came with the introduction of Du Pont's Antron, a nylon filament which is both translucent and reflective. Gary LaFontaine discovered the material's effectiveness in this role and put the fibres through rigorous laboratory and field testing. The lastest Antron yarn fibre is square in cross-section, with four holes running through each fibre. Each side reflects the light much better than a circular fibre. Because of the physical properties of Antron it also attracts and holds air bubbles, unlike any other material used in tying pupal imitations. The product known as Sparkle Yarn incorporates a blend of clear and coloured Antron filaments and can be used to simulate the pupal body accurately.

The behaviour of adult sedges on the surface varies. Some lie passively; others do not delay and take to the wing quickly; some skitter over the surface across and upstream before flight. The dry-fly fisher can represent these adults with a suitable pattern. Just as important to any success as the size and colour of the artificial is its behaviour on the water. Just as adult sedges adopt different positions and have varying degrees of movement, so too must the imitation. Some sedges are quite pale on emerging but darken with age. All have four wings, of varying degrees of hairiness, carried in a tent shape over the body when at rest. Many species have prominent antennae, up to three times the body length. Their size varies from a few millimetres to over an inch in length.

The returning egg-laying female is sometimes of more interest than the newly emerged adult. A few species crawl below the surface and there is little the fly fisher can do to imitate these, nor those that drop their eggs in flight. Most species land on the water. The landing varies from a gentle ripple-free touch-down to a splash as a female of a species which dives below the water drops from an altitude of a few feet. Some skitter or hop across the surface. Each must be imitated in its own way. There is not much point in offering a dead-drift presentation if the natural is zig-zagging upstream, or vice versa.

Because newly emerged adults and ovipositing females have various behaviourial characteristics, their light patterns on the mirrored undersurface and through the window are quire different from each other. Some rest quite motionless on their six legs, sitting quite high on the surface; other returning females rest in the film; some have their abdomens below the surface or are trying to break through the film, and others will be running or skating. The resulting light pattern varies from the six dimples from the legs through to a confused mixture of streaks of light as a highly active insect tries to break through the surface tension. When selecting an imitation to copy the fly on the water, remember that if an inactive fly is being represented size, shape, silhouette and colour are important features. In the active insect the fly's movement and light pattern are often the triggers to the rise.

During the last twenty years fly tyers have taken a much closer interest in tying more faithful imitations. For generations trout fishers made do with palmered flies with a rolled feather wing over the back. They fooled trout quite satisfactorily. Even the simple wingless palmer fly fished dry or awash in the film can be an acceptable imitation of some caddis. What trout anglers are opening their eyes to is that, just as earlier generations went through an enlightenment, or rather a series of enlightenments from Halford to Goddard, as to the accurate imitation of individual species of upwingeds and the different stages of their life cycle, so now the caddis is receiving the same treatment.

Caddis Larvae and Pupae

Most caddis larvae remain almost immobile on the riverbed or in weeds; only a few are free-swimming. The larvae, for all that they are housed in what one would expect to be indigestible cases of stones, gravel and vegetation, are a major food source for trout and grayling. Even though cased larvae move at an almost undetectable pace, when the artificial is fished slowly along the riverbed it catches very many fish.

When trout take pupae they do so after the pupae have broken free of the case and are drifting along the bottom for a few yards prior to swimming to the surface to emerge. It is just after they leave the larval case that they are eaten, and as they hang just below or in the surface film. Relatively few are taken in midwater. One of the key features of the pupa is the transparent sheath filled with air bubbles round the body.

1 Cased Caddis

COMMENT

This Bob Carnill pattern is principally a stillwater fly which in its smaller sizes has worked very well for me on rivers. I regularly fish the Driffield Beck for autumn grayling. Often many of those big fish just won't look at a fly until it is drifted along on exactly their level. This might mean 5 or 6 feet deep. A heavily leaded long-shank size 14 caddis larva often works when other patterns fail. Weighting the shank so that the fly fishes hook point uppermost is useful for avoiding snagging weed or the riverbed.

DRESSING

Hook: 10–16 long-shank Code H1A.
Thread: Black.
Body: Lead wire wound over with two-toned fur from the leading edge of a hare's ear.
Thorax: White swan or goose herl (to represent the larva).
Legs: Black hen sparsely wound as a collar.
Head: Black-varnished thread tied quite large.

Caddis Larva

COMMENT

One of the keys to a successful cased caddis imitation is accurate representation of the case, which is usually built up from material on the river-bed. This means that some are made from sand, tiny stones, twigs or green vegetation. Derek Bradbury tied this pattern using mottled contrasting feather fibres, which accurately simulate the case of tiny stones and sand. I suspect that it was devised as a stillwater fly but as a river pattern it has done very well. My good friend Nick Bradley, who tied up many of the patterns for this book, can claim a four-pound fourteen-ounce brown trout on it from the River Costa.

DRESSING

Hook: 12–18 long-shank Code H1A.
Thread: Brown.
Underbody (optional): Fine lead wire.
Body: Golden pheasant centre-tail feather fibres with a small dubbing of hare's ear fur in front.
Rib: Gold wire.
Legs: A single turn of brown partridge hackle.
Head: Peacock herl.

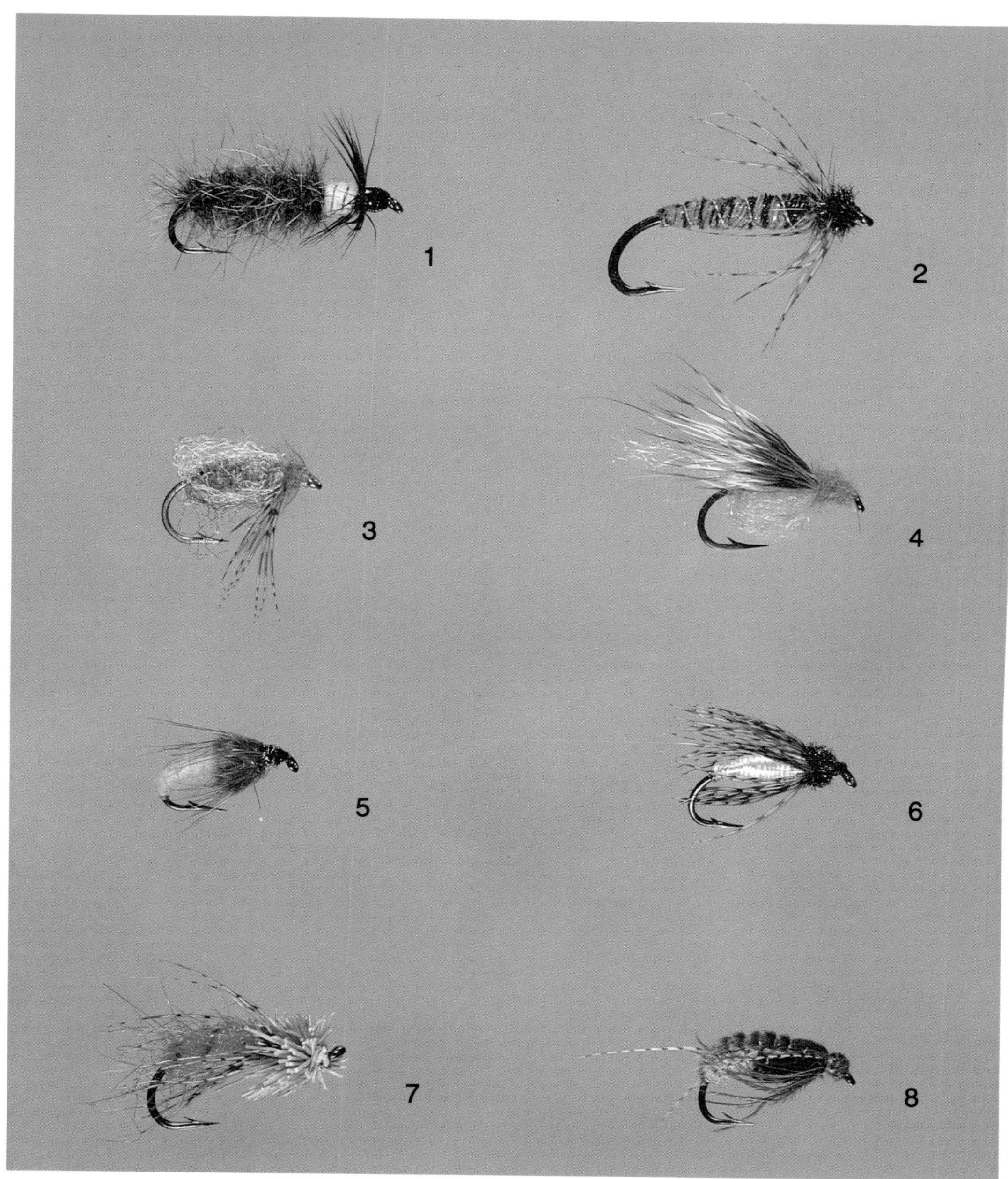

1 Cased Caddis (Carnill) **2** Caddis Larva (Bradbury)
3 Deep Sparkle Pupa **4** Emergent Sparkle Pupa **5** Latex Pupa
6 Mono Sedge Pupa **7** Hatching Sedge Pupa (Roberts)
8 Hatching Sedge Pupa (Edwards)

3 Deep Sparkle Pupa

COMMENT

When the pupa eats its way through the larval case it drifts downstream with the current as it builds up the gas beneath its skin before swimming to the surface. Most pupal imitations are fished just below the surface. This is Gary LaFontaine's weighted pattern to be fished along the riverbed. It is an ideal pattern to fish with the Leisenring lift. It should be tied in appropriate colours. The Sparkle Yarn overbody should be tied in above and below the shank at the rear and combed out. This should cover the body in a sparse envelope.

DRESSING

Hook: 10–14 Code A, G3A, CS7 or GRS2A wound with copper or fine lead wire.
Overbody: Sparkle Yarn (in this dressing mixed clear, olive and orange) (see text).
Underbody: Sparkle Yarn and natural fur (this dressing mixed cream, olive, clear and orange and red squirrel fur).
Hackle: Long soft hackle fibres along the lower half each side (partridge in this dressing).
Head: Marabou herl (dark orange).

4 Emergent Sparkle Pupa

COMMENT

For the British trout fisher this is probably the most useful of Gary LaFontaine's patterns. It represents the pupa just under the surface. Its success is due to the special features of Antron. Gary quotes its achievements as 'twenty-eight browns on twenty-eight consecutive casts on the Beaverhead River; sixteen trout on sixteen consecutive casts and seventy trout altogether in one afternoon on the White River in Arkansas; twenty trout in a few hours on a morning when everyone was moaning about the poor fishing on Henry's Fork in Idaho'. It is well worth trying on our rivers.

DRESSING

Hook: 10–14 Code A, L2A or CS7.
Overbody and underbody: Coloured Sparkle Yarn tied as for the Deep Sparkle pupa above, with some fibres trailing to the rear to represent the loosening sheath.
Wing: Natural or black deer hair tips.
Head: Coloured marabou fibres wrapped round the thread and wound to the eye.

5 Latex Pupa

COMMENT

Roger Fogg developed this pattern to represent the pupae of one tiny species emerging on a still pool. Many sedges are extremely small and fly fishers have tended to neglect their imitation, both as pupae and as adults. Roger ties these as small as a size 20. When other dressings of the correct size and colour failed, these fluorescent latex imitations worked well. The orange version has orange latex over fluorescent orange wool. The latex should be ribbed under tension from the bend with the tension relaxing towards the thorax.

DRESSING

Hook: 12–20 Caddis hook Code K4A or K2B.
Thread: Brown.
Body: Fluorescent lime-green floss wound with natural cream-coloured latex.
Thorax: Chestnut-brown ostrich herl.
Hackle: Chestnut-brown hen.

6 Mono Sedge Pupa

COMMENT

This pattern is best fished to float just below the surface to imitate a caddis on the point of emergence. One of the key features is the transparent monofilament abdomen which, particularly when viewed from below, gives a fair representation of the translucent natural pupa.

DRESSING

Hook: 12–14 Code A, L2A or CS7.
Thread: Brown, green or white.
Body: An underbody of tying thread overlaid with clear, colourless nylon mono, tapering to the rear.
Hackle: Partridge hackle tied rear-sloping.
Head: Peacock herl.

7 Hatching Sedge Pupa (Roberts)

COMMENT

I have made use of the buoyant deer hair as a muddler-style head to ensure that the fly hangs in the film in the manner of the natural pupa preparing to break through on the surface. A few turns of lead wire at the rear of the body ensure that the pupa hangs vertically. The seal's fur body should be well picked out and the deer hair should not be very densely packed and have a few longer fibres underneath. The smaller sizes (14–16) work best on rivers.

DRESSING

Hook: 10–16 Sedge hook K2B.
Thread: To match the body.
Body: Orange, green, brown or beige seal's fur substitute.
Rib: Fine gold tinsel or wire.
Hackle: Brown partridge tied as a rear-sloping collar.
Head: Natural deer hair in muddler style and roughly trimmed.

8 Hatching Sedge Pupa (Edwards)

COMMENT

Oliver Edwards came up with this excellent dressing based on his experiences of the pupae trout were gorging themselves on in some of the Yorkshire Dales rivers. Apart from the overall colouring, one of the key features is the dropping wingcases, which this pattern imitates with its accurate silhouette. The wingcase Raffene (well soaked in water) is tied in before the thorax, then the thorax is dubbed and the Raffene then looped each side of the thorax. The butts of the pheasant tail fibres are wrapped as the head.

DRESSING

Hook: 12–14 Code K4A or CS7.
Abdomen: Light-green Fly-Rite poly dubbing.
Abdomen back: Dark-green-dyed swan shoulder fibres ribbed with fine gold wire.
Wingcases: A loop of dark-brown or near-black Raffene either side of the thorax.
Thorax: Sepia and brown seal's fur.
Legs and head: Cock pheasant tail fibres (crumpled for effect).
Antennae: Wood duck or dyed mallard breast fibres.

Emergent and Adult Sedges

Many British sedge patterns have been loosely based round one or two standard designs, with simply a variation in size and materials to enable different coloured species to be represented. Perhaps as fishing pressure increases some of the more specific imitations like those in the second section adult sedges may be needed.

Because sedges appear on the water at all times of the day they are an excellent search pattern when there is no sign of surface-feeding fish and individual trout cannot be spotted. Floating a Little Red Sedge or an Elk Hair Caddis over the likely lies is a useful tactic, particularly on the faster sections of a river where trout have to make up their minds quickly about food passing overhead.

1 Klinkhåmen Special

COMMENT

This is an emerging caddis pattern from the Dutch angler, Hans van Klinken, who originally tied it for grayling feeding in the film. It is an excellent pattern and has caught trout and grayling all over Europe. Hans caught a grayling of 19½ inches from the Welsh Dee on it when there were no large flies on the water. He comments that the fly is much like an iceberg: it gives best results when 90 per cent is under water. The uncharacteristic white polypropylene yarn wing makes it more visible than other emergers. I now use the fly extensively and it caught almost 100 fish for me in its first season. Very highly recommended.

DRESSING

Hook: 12–22 Caddis hook Code K4A or K12ST given a slight downward bend halfway along the body.
Thread: Black or yellow.
Body: Light-tan poly yarn, lightly dubbed over an underbody of a layer of the wing material.
Thorax: Peacock herl.
Wing: White poly yarn.
Hackle: Chestnut cock tied in a parachute round the wing base.

2 Walker's Red Sedge

COMMENT

Many excellent flies came from the late Richard Walker. This general dark adult sedge imitation is a good pattern for when the great red sedge is in the air. It is common on rivers throughout the country between May and July, and it is the largest British sedge. Walker's pattern really imitates the mated female with the egg sac at the rear of the abdomen.

DRESSING

Hook: 10–12 Code A or L3A.
Thread: Tan.
Tip: Arc-chrome wool.
Body: Clipped chestnut ostrich herl or chestnut pheasant tail fibres.
Wing: Natural red cock fibres clipped level with the bend.
Hackle: Two long-fibred natural red cock hackles.

1 Klinkhåmen Special **2** Walker's Red Sedge **3** Grannom
4 Bradley's Roman Moser Caddis **5** Grey Sedge **6** G&H Sedge
7 Little Red Sedge **8** Black Sedge

3 Grannom

COMMENT

This is a widely distributed species which is often the first caddis of the season to appear in any numbers. On rivers where it does appear it becomes a very important fly. It is a medium-sized fly with fawn-grey wings. The mated female is the easiest to identify with its green egg sac. They will be seen from April until June but only on weedy rivers, as the larvae live in the weed beds. Hatches often occur around midday. This is Pat Russell's dressing.

DRESSING

Hook: 14 Code E6A or L3A.
Thread: Green.
Tip: Fluorescent green wool.
Body: Natural heron herl.
Wing: Blue-dun cock fibres, optionally clipped level with the bend.
Hackle: Ginger cock.

4 Bradley's Roman Moser Caddis

COMMENT

From the Austrian Roman Moser come sedge wings (Traun River Products) which are pre-shaped and are simply cut out, folded and tied in. They might not appeal to the purists or the impecunious but a very effective wing results. The pre-formed wing can be used on many existing sedge patterns. Use materials and wings in colours to match the naturals. This is Nick Bradley's dressing based on Skues's Little Red Sedge. It is a superb general pattern and in Nick's hands caught nineteen trout in a day to the one fly, all for the loss of just one antenna. It is highly recommended.

DRESSING

Hook: 22 Code K12ST.
Thread: Brown.
Body: Dark reddish-brown poly dubbing (Fly-Rite #28), palmered with a natural red cock hackle, slightly trimmed.
Rib: Fine gold wire.
Wing: Traun River Sedge Wing.
Hackle: Generous turns of natural red cock with the lower fibres trimmed in line with the body hackle.
Antennae (optional): Two single bronze mallard fibres coated in Beecham's Newskin.

5 Grey Sedge

COMMENT

This general grey adult imitation was devised by John Veniard. It can be used to represent two similar common grey species: the grey flag and the grey or silver sedge. The grey flag adults are about ⅓inch long with grey wings and blackish markings. The grey or silver sedge is slightly larger and has silver-grey wings and appears from June to September.

DRESSING

Hook: 12–14 Code E6A or L3A.
Thread: Grey.
Body: Grey seal's fur substitute.
Rib: Silver wire.
Wing: Grey squirrel tail fibres.
Hackle: Grizzle cock.

6 G & H Sedge

COMMENT

Although this has gained a reputation as a stillwater fly, it is also a good river pattern with a considerable following in North America. Created by John Goddard and Cliff Henry, it is a very buoyant general imitation which offers an excellent silhouette and a green underbody. Green figures highly in the coloration of a number of species at the emerging pupae/hatching adult stage. The body fur is twisted between two lengths of green thread and tied in at the rear before the deer hair. This is pulled taut under the body.

DRESSING

Hook: 12–14 long-shank or standard Code A, E6A or L2A.
Body: Deer hair spun on along all the body and trimmed, tapering towards the eye. The underside fibres are cut away and parts of the side to give a sedge silhouette.
Lower body: Dark-green seal's fur substitute.
Hackle: Two rusty-dun cock hackles trimmed at the top. The hackle stems can be used as antennae.

7 Little Red Sedge

COMMENT

G. E. M. Skues named and publicised this general small dark sedge dressing. I've fished it on chalk streams and freestone rivers in England and Europe and on some Western American rivers and it has risen fish with uncanny regularity. As a trout fly I use it from May onwards, and as a grayling fly I've seen it work when no other dry fly would persuade them to rise. It is such a good standby that if I had to be restricted to just six dry flies this or the Bradley Roman Moser Sedge would be one of them.

DRESSING

Hook: 12–16 Code E6A or L3A.
Thread: Hot orange.
Body: Darkest hare's fur with a palmered short-fibred red cock.
Rib: Fine gold wire.
Wing: Landrail wing (red-brown partridge tail is a substitute), bunched and rolled and sloping well back over the tail.
Hackle: Five or six turns of deep-red cock in front of the wings.

8 Black Sedge

COMMENT

Both the black sedge and black silverhorn sedges can be adequately represented by the one pattern. Both emerge during the daytime between June and September and are of an overall black appearance with long antennae. In its smaller size the pattern works well even when no black sedges are about since small black flies are often mistaken for a number of terrestrial species.

DRESSING

Hook: 12–14 Code E6A or L3A.
Thread: Black.
Body: Black or dark-coloured wool or chenille.
Wing: Black moose hair or deer hair tied flat and clipped square.
Hackle: Black cock.

Adult Sedges 1

Adult sedges have always been of interest to trout and to the fly fisher, but it is in North America that the huge hatches of adults and falls of egg-laying females are experienced. There the caddis imitation is of much greater importance. Fly tyers of that continent have been much more enterprising in finding suitable styles of dressing to match the different characteristics and their behaviour. The sheer numbers of caddis on American waters has meant that trout anglers have developed much more specific imitations of stages in the adult life cycle than we would normally use. Any of the following patterns can be adapted to cover British species by variations in the colours of the materials and hook sizes.

1 Henryville Special

COMMENT

This is a pattern that has crossed the Atlantic both ways. The fly is based on an older English dressing and is now one of the most widely used American caddis imitations. It has again begun to have a following on English waters. Carl Richards and Doug Swisher described it as 'the greatest hackle pattern we have ever used; it can be fished drag-free, skittered, or even wet and dragging'.

DRESSING

Hook: 10–16 Code A, E6A or L3A.
Thread: Grey.
Body: Olive silk with a palmered grizzle hackle.
Wing: Two grey duck wings quill sections either side of the body, over wood duck fibres.
Hackle: Natural brown cock over the wing roots.

2 Spent Partridge Caddis

COMMENT

This is a Western American pattern to represent the smaller spent female sedges lying exhausted on the surface after depositing their eggs. It should be fished in the film, where its excellent silhouette is a key trigger to the trout. It was devised by Mike and Sheralee Lawson. A few years ago I had the pleasure of fishing the Yellowstone with Mike while he was being filmed for a video. On a day when there were few fish surface-feeding Mike used a caddis pattern as a search fly and this did the trick. The film crew were kept happy.

DRESSING

Hook: 14–22 Code L3A or K12ST.
Body: Olive fur.
Wing: Mottled fibres of a brown partridge feather tied flat across the back.
Hackle: Brown cock palmered over the head and optionally trimmed flat on the top and bottom.
Head: Peacock herl.

1 Henryville Special **2** Spent Partridge Caddis **3** Elk Hair Caddis
4 Flat-Wing Sedge **5** Delta-Wing Sedge **6** Dancing Caddis
7 Diving Caddis **8** Thompson Foam Caddis

3 Elk Hair Caddis

COMMENT

The Elk Hair Caddis is an adaptation by Al Troth, one of America's finest fly tyers, of the Hairwing Caddis, originally a bass fly. It is widely used across that continent and has in the last few years become a more common sight on British and European rivers. It is principally a system fly to represent many different sedges with materials of different colours. The deer or elk hair makes the fly almost unsinkable. If you want to carry only a single adult sedge imitation this is highly recommended.

DRESSING

Hook: 12–18 Code E6A or L3A.
Thread: To match the body colour.
Body: Mixed natural or synthetic fur to match the required colour and (optionally) palmered with a short-fibred ginger or furnace cock.
Wing: Fine grey or tannish-cream elk hair tied round the upperside of the body.
Head: Clipped wing roots.

4 Flat-Wing Sedge

COMMENT

This is an effective imitation of the newly emerged sedge at rest on the surface. The flat wing offers a realistic silhouette. It also works well when trout are demanding a low-floating pattern in the film, when they are taking the dead spent females. The design works best in size 14 and below and an alternative style should be used for larger flies. Before it is tied in, the wing, stripped of its fluffy base, is pulled through fingers coated with celluloid varnish or vinyl cement, which narrows, thickens and stiffens the feather.

DRESSING

Hook: 14–16 Code L3A or E6A.
Body: Dubbed fur with a palmered short-fibred cock hackle. The upper fibres are cut away completely and the lower fibre trimmed shorter.
Rib: Fine silver or gold wire.
Wing: A wide, soft feather such as a partridge, woodcock or crow body feather, prepared as described in the text and cemented in place.

5 Delta-Wing Sedge

COMMENT

When Larry Solomon devised this fly it was the first to specifically imitate the spent and exhausted females in the film. If trout are really choosy for the low-floaters, the lower hackle fibres should be cut away completely to allow the body to rest on the surface. Then it should be well soaked in floatant. The wings are improved and more durable if they are celluloid-varnished or coated with vinyl cement or Beecham's Newskin. This and other low-floating spent flies are ideal for slower calm water.

DRESSING

Hook: 14–18 Code L3A or E6A.
Body: Light-olive mink fur or coloured polypropylene.
Wing: Two grey hen hackle tips tied in a delta shape (see text).
Hackle: Brown cock.

6 Dancing Caddis

COMMENT

Gary LaFontaine's book *Caddisflies* is the standard reference work. He devised this pattern to represent a wide range of naturals and their different behaviour. This dressing takes into account silhouette, wing spread, light patterns from the legs and wing edges of a skating sedge, and the insect body for those naturals in the film. The colour of the materials should match the natural fly. The fly floats upside-down, point up. Gary LaFontaine's revised version is illustrated. The original used a Swedish Dry Fly hook and had a hackle with the lower fibres trimmed in line with the body.

DRESSING

Hook: 12–8 salmon dry-fly hook or Code D5B.
Body: Yellow fur.
Rib: Clipped black hackle.
Wing: Light-brown deer or elk hair.
Head: Dubbed grey or brown fur over the wing roots.

7 Diving Caddis

COMMENT

I have never found the need to fish the imitation of the returning female caddis diving through the surface to lay its eggs, but some species do oviposit in this manner and a suitable pattern may be worth a try. Gary LaFontaine devised this imitation using Antron fibres to represent the air bubble some caddis take down with them. The fibres themselves hold air bubbles better than other materials and together reflect light in an almost identical way to an air bubble. Use colours to match the naturals.

DRESSING

Hook: 10–16 Code A, G3A or CS7.
Thread: Brown.
Body: Antron Sparkle Yarn (a mixed dubbing of chopped-up clear and dyed fibres).
Rib (optional): Tying thread.
Underwing: Soft hackle fibres such as grouse, partridge or wood duck rolled into a wing shape.
Overwing: 20–30 fibres of clear Antron over the underwing.
Hackle: One turn of a suitably coloured cock hackle.

8 Thompson Foam Caddis

COMMENT

This is an unusual sedge imitation tied by aquatic entomology graduate Ken Thompson. The thin Ethafoam back which overlaps the sides of the body gives the impression of the translucent edges of the adult's wings. The pattern is probably best used when the returning females are on the water laying their eggs. The fur body should match the natural and the Ethafoam can be coloured with a waterproof marker pen. Illustrated is my grannom version. Some of the recommended sizes for North America are as small as size 28!

DRESSING

Hook: 12–16 Code L3A or E1A.
Thread: To match the body colour.
Body: Dubbed natural or synthetic fur.
Half-wing: Mink hair tied in as a tail.
Back: White or coloured Ethafoam.

Adult Sedges 2

In addition to the general characteristics of size, silhouette and colour, a further important attribute – often ignored – is behaviour. Too many sedge imitations are fished in a straight drift. Thankfully they often rise trout, but sedge behaviour varies considerably. Some newly emerged adults flutter their wings, some skitter upstream. The egg-laying females produce widely different images in the trout's window and differing light patterns. Some rest on the surface quietly with the abdomen under the water; others are flush in the film; some are fully spent; some try to break through the surface to swim to the riverbed; others skate and dance. Trout take these insects in a manner and speed appropriate to their behaviour. The artificial must also emulate the natural's behaviour.

1 Ruane Sedge

COMMENT

Terry Ruane is one of Britain's best professional fly tyers. He has not been afraid to look to North America and Europe to examine their most successful pattern designs. Nor has he been reluctant to experiment with synthetic and unusual materials. He has produced this adult sedge design which can be adapted with materials of different colours to match other species. One of the key features is the wing edges, which produce a characteristic light pattern on the surface.

DRESSING

Hook: 12–10 Code L3A or E1A.
Thread: Green.
Body: Fly-Rite insect-green poly dubbing.
Wings: Light-brown Fly-Rite Poly II cut to shape.
Antennae: Dark bristles from a paintbrush.
Legs: Dyed green deer hair swept under the body.

2 Polysedge

COMMENT

This is a development of the Swedish pattern called Rackelhanen. Similar patterns developed simultaneously in North America. This variant is by Hans van Klinken, who uses a white polypropylene wing. Hans is a fanatical grayling angler (grayling to five pounds on dry fly) and has devised some excellent trout and grayling flies which also work well on our waters. This is probably taken for an ovipositing female. The body colour is important and should match the natural's. The whole fly can be treated to float or just the wing, which can also colour-match the natural.

DRESSING

Hook: 10–20 fine-wire Code L3A or L4A.
Thread: Yellow or black.
Body: Light-tan poly dubbing, lightly dubbed.
Wing: Cream, white or coloured poly yarn.

1 Ruane Sedge **2** Polysedge **3** Balloon Sedge
4 Goddard's Poly Caddis **5** V-Wing Caddis
6 Para-Poly Sedge **7** Squirrel Tail Sedge **8** Microcaddis

3 Balloon Sedge

COMMENT

As with most of the adult sedge patterns in these two sections, this is a style of fly rather than a specific dressing. Suitable colours should be used to match the various naturals. The polycelon, which Orvis call Fly Foam, is a highly buoyant material useful for a range of fly-tying situations. Polycelon is a Traun River product and available in 13 colours. The polycelon is tied in first over the eye. The body and wing are then tied in and the polycelon doubled back over itself and tied off over the wing roots.

DRESSING

Hook: 10–16 Code CS20 or E6A.
Thread: Yellow.
Body: Coloured polypropylene dubbing.
Wing: Brown deer hair.
Head: Yellow polycelon or Orvis Fly Foam.

4 Goddard's Poly Caddis

COMMENT

So successful are these two dressings for their creator that for an evening sedge hatch he uses them exclusively. They are virtually unsinkable and even if the hackle becomes saturated and collapses the buoyant body keeps them in the film and they become a good imitation of ovipositing adults of some species. John Goddard suggests three colour combinations: dark-green body with dark-brown wings; olive-green body with either cinnamon-coloured or dark-brown wings. The second style has a head hackle without a body hackle.

DRESSING

Hook: 10–14 wide-gape Code A.
Thread: Brown.
Body: Wound polypropylene yarn.
Hackle: Palmered grizzle or medium-red cock trimmed flat at the top.
Wing: One strand of polypropylene yarn doubled back flat over the top.

5 V-Wing Caddis

COMMENT

When two separate quill sections are used they are normally known as tent wings because of their shape when tied in. The V-wing is a single rolled quill section tied in low round the body. They are excellent in the medium and small sizes. Don't be afraid to fish a sedge pattern down to size 22. There are many very small species that hatch and attract trout attention. Too often our imitations relate to much bigger naturals. A low-floating version has the upper and lower hackle fibres cut away. This is a system fly which should be colour-matched as appropriate.

DRESSING

Hook: 14–22 lightweight Code L3A or E1A.
Thread: Brown.
Body: Very fine natural fur or poly dubbing.
Wing: A section of fairly stiff wing quill in an upturned V or U shape low over the body and extending beyond the bend.
Hackle: Cock hackle to match the natural.

6 Para-Poly Sedge

COMMENT

The parachute hackle is an excellent way of supporting a fly body on or in the film, depending on where the hackle is placed. Its position in this pattern ensures that the body remains in the film with the polypropylene wing above the surface. Although the body rests in the water, the fly does float very well due to the lightness of the poly body and wing and if lightweight hooks are used. It works equally well as an imitation of the emerging adult or ovipositing female and should be fished in a drag-free drift. This was devised by Hans van Klinken.

DRESSING

Hook: 12–18 lightweight Code L3A.
Thread: Sparton Micro or similar.
Body: Fly-Rite poly dubbing to match the natural.
Wing: Polypropylene yarn tied upright behind the head and bound in again to rest at 45 degrees.
Hackle: Cock hackle to match the natural wound round the base of the wing.

7 Squirrel Tail Sedge

COMMENT

This hairwing sedge design is popular in the States and in Europe and has become the basis for many British caddis patterns, including the popular Walker's Red Sedge. The hair wing is an excellent representation on the natural wing. It is a good pattern to tie in the smaller sizes for those difficult fish rising on slow clear water. On size 20 and smaller the wing should be tied slightly longer than the body to emphasise it.

DRESSING

Hook: 14–22 lightweight Code L3A or L4A.
Body: Cock pheasant tail fibres.
Rib: Finest gold wire.
Wing: Grey squirrel tail hair.
Hackle: Cock hackle to match the natural.

8 Microcaddis

COMMENT

Where the tiny adult sedges are being taken by trout often only an artificial of similar size will attract attention. One suitable pattern for such an occasion is this one from American fly tyer John Betts. The tying order and method need a little explanation. First dub a slim body (a tying thread body is an alternative for very small flies), then tie in the wing fibres forward-facing. Tie in and wind in parachute style 2–3 turns of cock hackle round the wing base and secure. Bring back the wing fibres and bind in about a quarter of the way along the shank, avoiding trapping the hackle fibres.

DRESSING

Hook: 16–20 lightweight Code L3A or L4A.
Thread: Sparton Micro or similar.
Body: Fine dubbing or tying thread.
Wing: Partridge, pheasant tail or cock hackle fibres tied to extend just beyond the bend.
Hackle: Cock to match the natural wound round the wing base.

TERRESTRIALS

Introduction to Terrestrials

There's no escaping the fact that although the fly fisher enjoys more than anything matching the hatch and representing an aquatic fly with a floater, a nymph or a wet fly, there are going to be times when one of an assortment of land-based bugs, flies and creepy-crawlies is what trout really want. In an earlier book, *To Rise a Trout*, I quoted from British and American surveys of surface food and of trout stomach contents. They showed the importance of terrestrials as a food source for trout. As the season progressed towards midsummer trout increased their terrestrial intake until they were *the dominating food source* in both British and American surveys. More interestingly, in the survey on the Welsh Dee, during all but one month from May to October terrestrial insects were *the single largest food source and often more than the total of all other food sources*. Other surveys also showed an increased terrestrial consumption in older trout. I'm not suggesting that these surveys would be replicated on every trout stream but they make me more aware of what trout might be feeding on. Ignore them at your peril.

As the trout season progresses and the weather warms up, terrestrial activity increases. The hotter the summer the more active and more abundant are many terrestrial species. All land-based insects end up on the water surface only by accident – by falling off bankside grasses, bushes and overhanging trees. They are most likely to be encountered on windy days, when even the slightest breeze can dislodge insects and beetles, or send some of the ungainly fliers like the cranefly reluctantly onto the water. Most terrestrial species float and with the exception of some beetles and a caterpillar pattern all the imitations I've included in this section should be fished dry or awash in the film.

I do not advocate fishing a terrestrial pattern when trout are obviously feeding on something else, but for the majority of the time when there is no hatch in progress trout would expect to feed on any terrestrials that come their way. Indeed, in summer this may be a major food source. It is also one tactic that can bring to the surface trout that won't look at aquatic fly patterns. The sight of a beetle or hawthorn might stimulate it into feeding. Terrestrial patterns are also excellent search patterns when cast over known lies or likely-looking lies on an unfamiliar water. If in the lethargic hours of a sunny summer afternoon there are no fish rising to betray their presence, the odds are that if anything will tempt them to the surface it will be a terrestrial. If a gentle presentation doesn't work try the unorthodox; let the fly land with a plop, as though the beetle had fallen from a height. This can attract a trout's attention, which on a sunny day might not be focused on the surface. Or the more aggressive presentation of a twitched cranefly struggling on the surface might stimulate or annoy a fish into rising. Of course, it may also put a wary fish down, but I prefer to at least try to rise it rather than pass by the trout or lie without trying out an alternative to the familiar dun imitation fished in a straight drift.

The obvious places to use a terrestrial pattern are in those areas where they are most likely to end up on the river – along the margins and under trees and bridges. Fish rising in these areas, when there is no obvious hatch in progress, are probably taking something falling onto the water. But remember that the insects falling onto the river in the margins will soon be fed into the main current, the principal food lane where trout will feed on them. The mysterious fly a trout is rising to midstream, yards from trees or the bank, may still be a terrestrial.

I don't rate trout intelligence too highly, but one thing they become aware of is that terrestrials on the surface rarely leave it. They learn that here is a food source that won't suddenly take flight and disappear. With the exception of an aggressively plopped or twitched fly or one that lands on the trout's nose or is on fast water, most land-based flies are taken in an unhurried and leisurely manner.

There is a body of opinion that scorns the use of terrestrial imitations except as a last resort when the imitations of aquatic flies fail. Unless trout are rising to aquatic flies I often fish with a black gnat or beetle as a search fly. In reality, many trout consume large numbers of land-based flies; a positive terrestrial strategy is well worth employing. A criticism sometimes voiced is that on a fishery like the classic chalk streams or others which experience excellent aquatic fly hatches there is no need to fish terrestrials, and that their use should be confined to streams with relatively minor fly hatches, where land-based insects are more likely to be taken by ever-hungry trout. The truth is that streams which enjoy good fly hatches are usually well fished by anglers offering aquatic fly imitations. The more sophisticated trout that are produced where angling pressure is heavy and few fish are killed are more likely to be duped by a well presented terrestrial.

Terrestrials 1

If I ever was in any doubt about trout selectivity in feeding on terrestrials it was soon dispelled by a friend, Roy Shaw, who caught a 2lb rainbow trout which had more than 1,800 black gnats in its stomach, representing 99.9 per cent of the contents. It was caught on a chalk stream where traditionally the aquatic fly life is most abundant and where trout selectivity is greater than on most freestone rivers. Where land-based insects are regularly blown onto the water trout become accustomed to their presence and will take up lies around the area where the terrestrials land. They feed on them at least as enthusiastically as on aquatic flies and sometimes with a high degree of exclusivity.

1 SuperANT

COMMENT

Whenever ants become available to trout they are eagerly accepted. Warm weather brings them above ground and, whether there is a wind or not, they can be found on the river surface. Because of the weight and spread leg support they rest in the surface film, neither floating on top nor sinking. This makes detection of them on the water very difficult. One clue to their presence is the sip rise-form that characterises the trout's effortless feeding on them. This is Randy Swanberg's dressing using Plastazote, a buoyant cellular foam which can be bought in pre-cut shapes.

DRESSING

Hook: 12–20 Code L3A or E6A.
Thread: Black.
Thorax and abdomen: Black Plastazote polyethylene foam SuperANT body.
Legs: Black polypropylene monofilament (available from Flycraft; see appendix).

2 Black or Brown Ant (Goddard)

COMMENT

Some ants possess wings. The only time they take flight is for the purpose of mating and then dispersal. This mating flight occurs only during periods of relatively high humidity and afterwards the male dies almost immediately. Frequently they are blown onto the water. Some hold their wings upright rather like a tiny dun and others have them in the spent position. The wings can be represented with small white cock hackle tips or poly yarn. This ant dressing from John Goddard floats very well to produce an unsinkable fly.

DRESSING

Hook: 14–16 Code L3A or E6A.
Thread: Black or brown.
Body: Two small painted cylindrical pieces of cork, one at each end of the shank, split and pushed over the shank and glued. The middle of the shank is wound with thread and whole body clear-varnished.
Wings: Two white cock hackle tips tied in upright or spent between the bodies and angled towards the rear.
Hackle: Small black or brown cock wound over the wing roots.

1 SuperANT **2** Black Ant **3** McMurray Ant **4** Cowdung Fly
5 Hawthorn Fly (Price) **6** Hawthorn Fly (Warrilow)
7 White Ermine Moth **8** Skittering Moth

3 McMurray Ant

COMMENT

This is the most effective ant imitation I have come across. It is a North American pattern which is highly praised on its home waters. I have caught my fair share of trout on this pattern, often where there has been no sign of a real ant on the water. One American expert fly fisher described it as 'one helluva fly . . . absolute dynamite'. It is well worth a try any time from June to August. The pre-made body can be obtained from Orvis. Is it still a fishing fly or does all this balsa wood make it more like a model?

DRESSING

Hook: 14–22 Code L3A or E6A.
Thread: Black.
Body: Two small cylinders of balsa wood affixed to a strand of nylon mono and varnished black or red.
Hackle: Black or natural red cock wound in the middle of the body and clipped top and bottom.

4 Cowdung Fly

COMMENT

These hairy yellow flies have as their principal habitat and breeding ground the common cowpat so liberally scattered in fields adjoining the waterside. A less appealing fly there could hardly be, though trout are known to take them quite freely when they are blown onto the surface. They are taken most readily from late March to early May. They are flat-winged and the imitation should be tied with a wing across the back.

DRESSING

Hook: 12–14 Code L3A or E6A.
Thread: Yellow.
Body: Mixed yellow and olive seal's fur substitute.
Wing: Cinnamon hen wing tied flat.
Hackle: Light-ginger tied as throat hackle for the wet pattern, as a collar for the floating fly.

5 Hawthorn Fly (Price)

COMMENT

In late April and May hawthorn flies are regularly found on rivers and stillwaters. Any even slightly windy day in the vicinity of hawthorn bushes will mean that these large black hairy flies end up on the water. One distinctive characteristic is the pair of long black legs which trail behind in flight. This is Taff Price's dressing.

DRESSING

Hook: 12 wide-gape Code A.
Thread: Black.
Body: Shiny black rayon floss.
Rib: Fine silver wire.
Legs: Two knotted black pheasant tail fibres.
Thorax: Black seal's fur substitute.
Wing: Grey duck tied flat over the back.
Hackle: Black cock.

6 Hawthorn Fly (Warrilow)

COMMENT

My most satisfying use of a hawthorn was on Leighton Reservoir in North Yorkshire. There are very few trees and bushes around this windswept water but on one breezy May day the trout were rising continually along the upwind shore near a solitary hawthorn bush. Throughout most of the day a fish would rise every few minutes when there was barely any other surface activity on the whole reservoir. Over the course of the day eight trout fell to an imitation drifting in the ripple just below the surface. This is Ian Warrilow's dressing.

DRESSING

Hook: 12 Code L3A or E6A.
Thread: Black.
Body and head: Black-dyed pheasant tail fibres.
Legs: Two knotted black-dyed pheasant tail fibres tied each side of the body.
Wing: Traun River stonefly wing.
Hackle: Black cock.

7 White Ermine Moth

COMMENT

The low light of dusk gives a false confidence to those wary, canny trout which have been reluctant risers during the day. Needless to say, some of these wary fish are the wiser, bigger trout well used to the angler and his artificial fly in daylight; dusk offers one of the few chances of hooking them. Sedges, a small floating fish or a moth give the best chance of success. This moth dressing is a well established pattern. It may pay to experiment with fluorescent materials for fishing in low light.

DRESSING

Hook: 12–14 Code L2A or A.
Thread: Black.
Tail: Orange wood divided into a V shape.
Body: Dubbed white wool or fur.
Rib: Black thread.
Hackle: Grey partridge with an optional additional white cock tied behind the partridge to aid floating.

8 Skittering Moth

COMMENT

Trout are much better equipped than man to see in low light conditions and they continue to feed long after we lose sight of a fly on the water. One of the best ways of enticing a fish to surface-feed is to give some animation to the imitation. It may even be that movement of the fly is the key to any success at all. A fly conforming to the current's drift may go unnoticed but the twitched or skittered moth often produces a savage take. On so many occasions my last cast of the evening with a moth has risen trout. This is my dressing based on Gary LaFontaine's Dancing Caddis.

DRESSING

Hook: 14–18 Swedish Dry Fly hook Code K3A.
Thread: White.
Body: Dubbed natural or polypropylene grey fur.
Wing: Any grey or off-white elk or deer hair.
Hackle: Cream or white cock.

Terrestrials 2

Observation is an important key to success in all trout fly fishing, whether it is the skill of spotting trout in their lies, assessing the rise forms or identifying the species being preferred during a multiple hatch. It is often possible to detect trout feeding on terrestrials by their position close to a bank or by the absence of aquatic flies. Close observation of the trout's behaviour and of the water surface should be a revealing exercise. Some small terrestrials are hard to see on the surface except at close range and the tiny insects such as ants and aphis are taken with small sip rises that barely break the surface. The close observer will see the rises or know where to look for fish. Be aware of the likely food sources and offer a suitable imitation. Observation and the application of appropriate skills make the complete fly fisher.

1 Deerhair Beetle (Warrilow)

COMMENT

With more than 4,000 species of beetle in Britain it is not surprising that some of them end up on the river surface. When they land on the water trout find them as acceptable as any aquatic fly species. Thankfully, the differences between species are minimal apart from the coloration variation of their undersides between brown, orange and black. The only other considerations in imitation are size and whether the fly should float or sink. This is an unsinkable buoyant pattern from Ian Warrilow, an excellent professional dresser from Birmingham.

DRESSING

Hook: 10–12 Code E1A or L2A.
Thread: Black Monocord.
Legs: Three strands of girdle bug elastic.
Detached Body: Black or natural deer hair encircling a needle shank secured in the vice. Bind the thread to flare the fibres. Pull the flared hair back towards the vice and secure and whip finish in two places to produce a two part body. Trim the hair and varnish. Remove the needle and bind onto the shank.

2 Eric's Beetle

COMMENT

Eric Horsfall Turner devised this pattern for the River Derwent and the other streams flowing off the North Yorkshire moors. It is now very widely used, on stillwaters as well. It is my favourite beetle dressing and, although I cannot claim that it has accounted for the hundreds of trout it did for its creator, it serves me well whenever I use it. I prefer to fish a beetle just a few inches below the surface on a greased leader. Fished in this way along a tree-lined bank in midsummer it is an effective way of motivating lethargic trout into feeding.

DRESSING

Hook: 10–14 Code A or G3A.
Thread: Black.
Body: An underbody of yellow wool with bronze peacock herl wound over, leaving the wool exposed as a butt at the rear. The body should be quite fat.
Hackle: Two turns of black cock or hen.

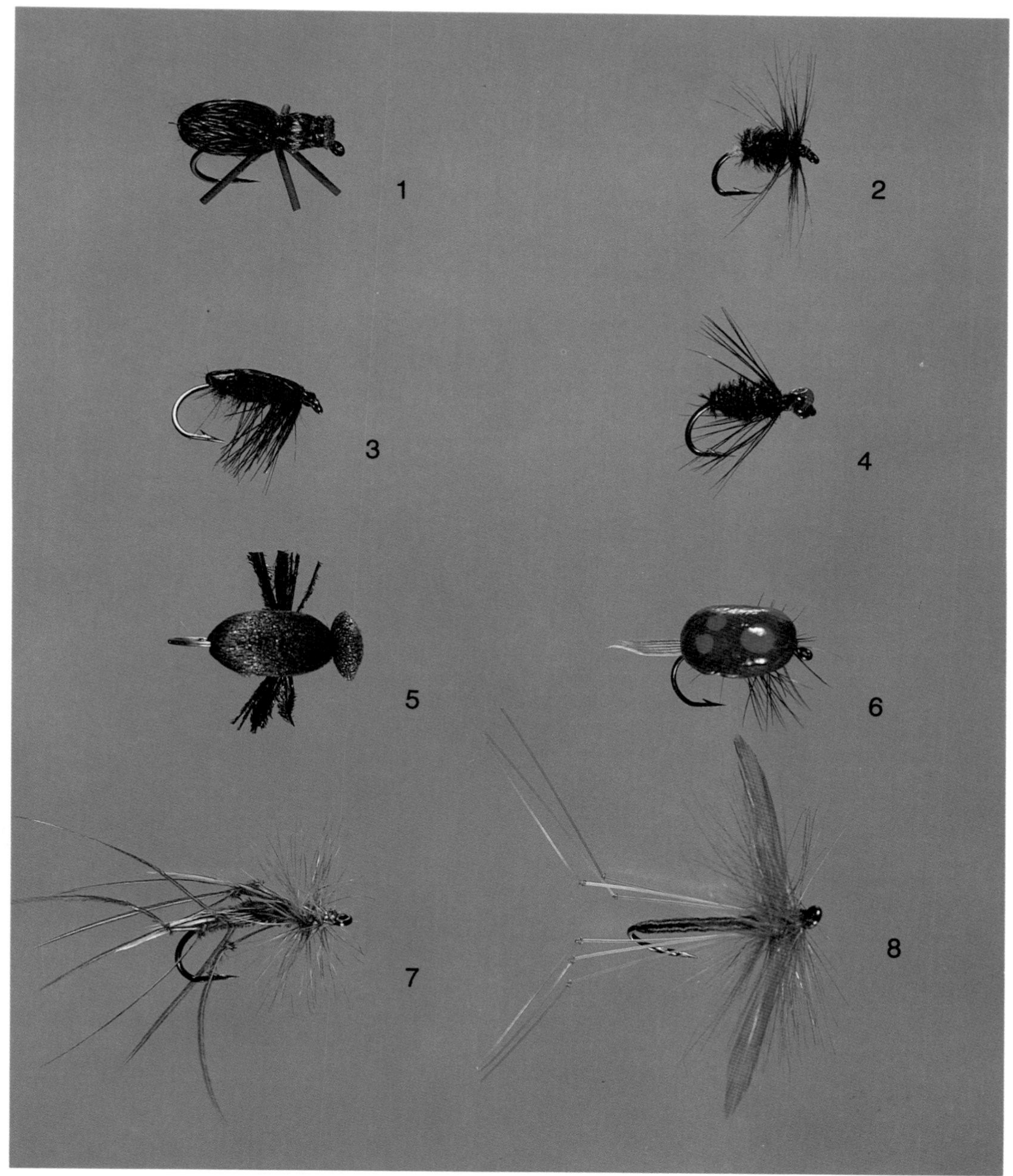

1 Deerhair Beetle (Warrilow) **2** Eric's Beetle **3** Black Beetle (Price)
4 Red-Eyed Derbyshire Beetle **5** Jansen Beetle **6** Coffee Beetle
7 Cranefly **8** Daddy-Long-Legs

3 Black Beetle (Price)

COMMENT

Angling opinion has varied as to the effectiveness of a beetle imitation. No lesser figures than John Goddard and C. F. Walker doubt their usefulness but I would not fish during high summer without one in my fly box. Very many times I have caught fish when there had been no surface activity for hours and nymphs brought no response. A plopped beetle cast upstream and allowed to drift naturally, slowling sinking, catches more trout for me between 2 and 4 p.m. in late June and July than any other fly. I am a believer. The following is a Taff Price dressing.

DRESSING

Hook: 12–16 Code L3A or E6A.
Thread: Black.
Body: Black seal's fur substitute or polypropylene dubbing.
Hackle: Palmered black cock or hen trimmed top and sides.
Back: Varnished black Raffene.

4 Red-Eyed Derbyshire Beetle

COMMENT

This unusual pattern was tied by Allyen Hardy in 1907 to match a terrestrial beetle with large red eyes that was falling on the water. In just one day in its first season it caught 79 trout for its creator. It can be fished wet or dry. Although I have not used the fly because Eric's Beetle usually works so well I was once shown how it should be done by an angler using this pattern. When I could catch nothing he succeeded four times. How important the red eyes are I wouldn't like to say. I do know that there was nothing falling off the trees with eyes like these.

DRESSING

Hook: 12–14 Code A.
Thread: Black.
Body: Bronze peacock herl.
Hackle: Long-fibred black cock or hen.
Eyes: Two small red beads.

5 Jansen Beetle

COMMENT

Frans Jansen ties this floating beetle imitation with very buoyant materials. This fly really is unsinkable as its principal material is probably the most buoyant material a fly dresser can use. The polycelon, which is also marketed by Orvis as Fly Foam, is impregnated with tiny air bubbles and comes in a wide range of colours. The back and legs of this dressing suggest a very clear beetle silhouette.

DRESSING

Hook: 10–18 L2A, L3A, A or E1A.
Thread: Grey or black.
Body: Grey or brown polypropylene dubbing.
Legs: Peacock herl fibres tied in the middle of the shank and clipped to length.
Back and head: Black, grey or brown polycelon or Fly Foam.

6 Coffee Beetle (Ruane)

COMMENT

I haven't been able to trace who was responsible for discovering that the humble coffee bean makes a useful body for a floating beetle imitation, but I suspect that it began in North America. This pattern also looks as though it might pass for a trout food pellet – a thought worth remembering for any newly released hatchery fish! This example is tied by Terry Ruane.

DRESSING

Hook: 12 Code L2A or A.
Thread: Black.
Tail (optional): Slip of grey duck quill or similar.
Underbody: Palmered black hackle.
Body: Coffe bean, glued over the hackle and then varnished. Decorate as required.

7 Cranefly (Walker)

COMMENT

I am much keener on this as a stillwater fly, where it has provided some fascinating fish and produced some good trout. However, it does have its uses as a river fly, and, indeed, it was on a river that I first had any success with it. Its potential was graphically brought home one hot sunny afternoon when the river I was fishing was very low. I was standing at the head of a pool when I knocked from my face a daddy-long-legs which fell onto the water. It drifted on the slow current until a trout seemed to bolt out from nowhere to devour it. This is Richard Walker's dressing.

DRESSING

Hook: 8–14 long-shank Code E1A or D5B.
Thread: Brown.
Body: Pale-cinnamon turkey fibres.
Wings: Two badger cock hackle points tied slanting over the body and divided.
Legs: Eight knotted cock pheasant tail fibres trailing to the rear.
Hackle: Pale-ginger or ginger grizzle.

8 Daddy-Long-Legs (Bucknall)

COMMENT

Craneflies are ungainly fliers and seemingly only an experimental model when the Creator was bringing flying creatures into being. Even in a slight wind they have little control over their direction and are often blown onto the surface. Geoffrey Bucknall's dressing is one of the most durable, with the monofilament legs being almost indestructible compared with pheasant tail fibres.

DRESSING

Hook: Long shank 10 Code E1A or D5B.
Thread: Brown.
Body: Brown floss.
Legs: Strong knotted black or grey nylon mono.
Wing: Ginger cock hackle tips tied spent.
Hackle: Ginger cock.

Terrestrials 3

If I had to be restricted to a single fly pattern for my dry-fly fishing I would be hard pressed to make my mind up between all the good general patterns that seem to suggest so many things to a hungry trout, or the excellent sedge patterns that can be used as a search fly when nothing is rising. A terrestrial pattern would certainly feature in the final short list and I would probably opt for a black gnat with a couple of variations such as winged and wingless versions and fore-and-aft style as well. A very wide range of black insects and flies fall onto trout streams throughout the world. I bet nondescript black flies figure daily somewhere in the diet of the majority of most summer trout. It is also a good search fly when nothing is rising.

1 Black Gnat (Roberts)

COMMENT

Many members of the flat-winged Diptera order bear the common name of black gnat. Their differences are insignificant for the fly fisher and a general black fly of the correct size is usually adequate. The males are all black but the females generally have a dark brownish-olive body and legs. A representation of the mating pair is a useful fly and the inclusion of an additional rear hackle makes it a better floater. This is a simple pattern of my own. It is very easy to tie and very effective. The version with a poly yarn body is almost unsinkable.

DRESSING

Hook: 14–18 Code L3A or E6A.
Thread: Black.
Body: Black thread, floss silk or wound polypropylene yarn.
Wing: Light-grey poly yarn flat across the back.
Hackle: Black cock.

2 Black Gnat

COMMENT

Wherever trout of all species are fished for with a dry fly the ubiquitous black gnat is found both on the river and in the fly box. Because of the widespread distribution of black Diptera the imitation is a truly international fly. This dressing is one which, with minor variations, is fished the world over. One mystery is why almost all the dressings have upright wings when all members of this order have wings which at rest lie flat across the back. The natural also has no tail. So much for being a close imitation.

DRESSING

Hook: 12–16 Code L3A or E6A.
Thread: Black.
Tail: Black cock fibres.
Body: Dubbed black natural of synthetic fur.
Wing: Grey starling or duck wing tied upright.
Hackle: Black cock.

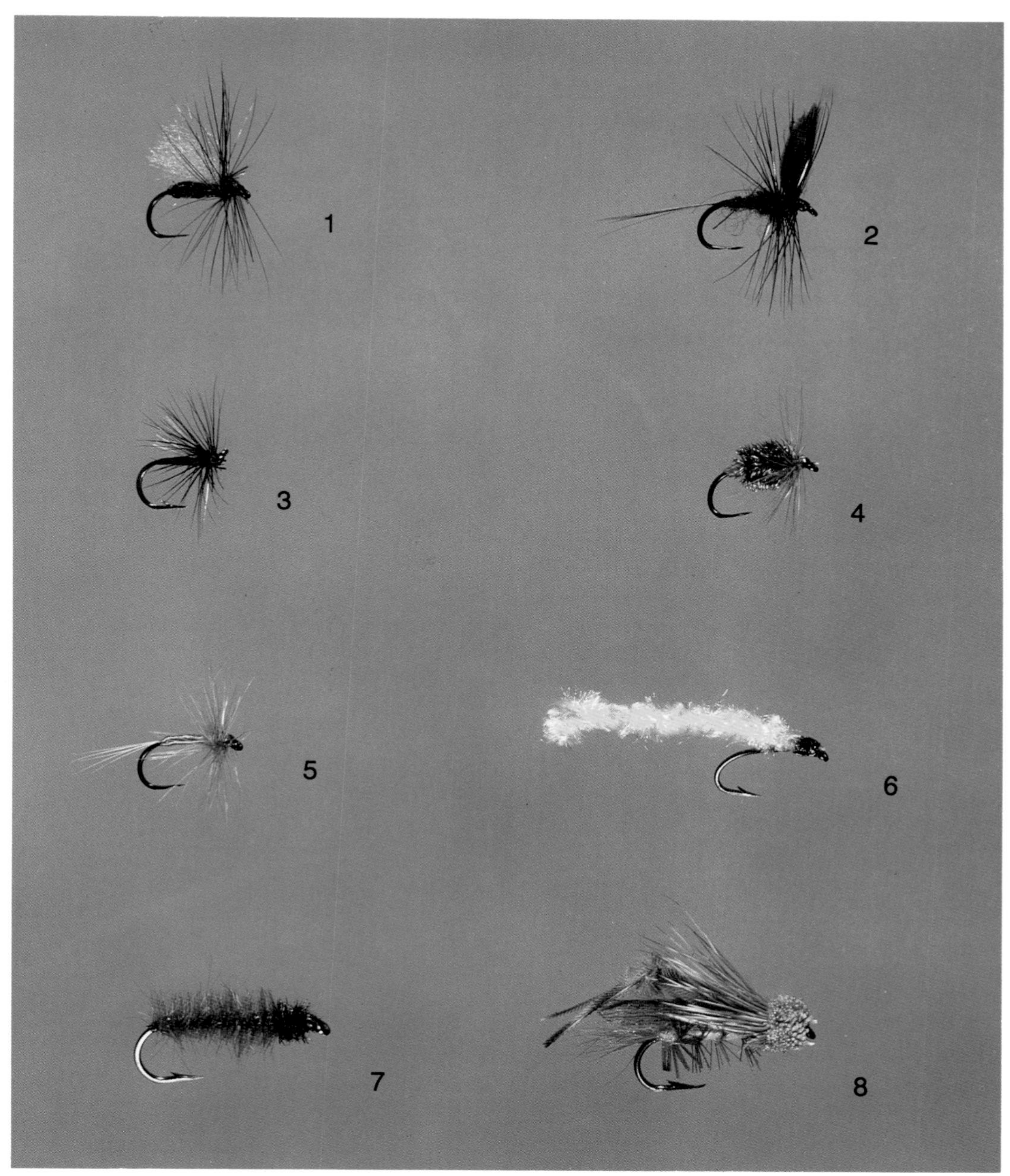

1 Black Gnat (Roberts) **2** Black Gnat **3** Black Gnat (Rice)
4 Green Insect **5** Aphis **6** Chenille Grub **7** Caterpillar **8** Grasshopper

3 Black Gnat (Rice)

COMMENT

When more than 1,800 black gnats turn up in the autopsy of a single trout it leaves no doubt about the pattern to use. That particular chalk stream trout had no doubt at all about the value of feeding on terrestrial food items. This Freddie Rice pattern can be adapted to represent the mating pair by omitting the wing and adding a slightly smaller black hackle at the rear.

DRESSING

Hook: 14–16 Code L3A or E6A.
Thread: Black.
Body: Black thread.
Rib (optional): Silver wire.
Wing: About 12 light-blue-dun hackle fibres bunched at 35 degrees over the body.
Hackle: Black cock or starling breast feather.

4 Green Insect

COMMENT

There are scores of green insects of various shades and sizes which from time to time fall onto the water. This is a general imitation. It is also a good grayling fly when the red tag proves an additional attraction, but it is primarily a very useful high summer pattern for trout. It can be fished as a floater with a cock hackle or upstream below the surface tied with a hen hackle.

DRESSING

Hook: 14–16 Code L3A or E6A.
Thread: Green.
Tag (optional): Red wool or silk.
Body: Green peacock herl.
Hackle: Small grey or blue-dun cock or hen.

5 Aphis

COMMENT

This tiny winged fly sometimes appears on the surface in June and July. One modern dressing is Roger Fogg's green latex pupa fished just below the surface. Alternatively, a floating imitation such as a very small Green Insect will work well, or the dressing below, which has a body colour closer to the natural's.

DRESSING

Hook: 14–16 Code L3A or E6A.
Thread: Pale-green.
Tail: Short-fibred blue-dun cock.
Body: Light-green floss.
Hackle: Blue-dun cock.

6 Chenille Grub

COMMENT

Roger Fogg devised this general grub or small caterpillar imitation primarily for stillwater use. The leaded version lands with an attractive plop; the unleaded one floats or sinks very slowly. Takes will come on the drop and the end of the leader must be watched carefully for a sudden dip or acceleration in the sinking rate.

DRESSING

Hook: 12–14 Code A.
Thread: Black.
Body: White, green, yellow or brown chenille attached to the shank behind the eye, with the remainder left free to move in the water.
Head: Black tying silk.

7 Caterpillar

COMMENT

Although I don't think trout eat too many caterpillars in the course of a season there are times when the artificial dropped in front of a lethargic fish will produce an automatic reaction. It is simply too big and tasty a mouthful to let pass by. The choice is one of colour and whether to use a floating or sinking pattern. My own preference is for a slow sinker. An additional feature to include is to bend the hook in the vice, which gives a better impression of the wriggling natural.

DRESSING

Hook: 10–16 Code H1A or 8–14 Code K4A.
Thread: To match the body colour.
Body: Black, brown, white or green ostrich herl over a layer of floss silk of the same colour.
Head: Peacock herl.

8 Grasshopper

COMMENT

Generally speaking the British summer is too wet for the grasshopper population to reach the near-plague proportions of parts of North America where the summers can be semi-arid. Whenever we do have good hot long summers the number of grasshoppers significantly increases and so does the likelihood of them falling onto the river surface. This dressing is a hybrid of some of the best American dressings.

DRESSING

Hook: 12–14 long shank Code D5B.
Tail (optional): Red deer hair.
Body: Yellow wool or poly yarn with a clippec palmered brown or grizzle hackle.
Wing: Mottled turkey wing quill segments treated with artist's fixative.
Overwing: Yellow deer hair.
Hackle (optional): Rear-sloping natural deer hair.
Legs: Two knotted brown grizzle saddle hackles tied in before the head is tied.
Head: Deer hair spun and clipped.

GRAYLING FLIES

Grayling Flies 1

What makes grayling flies any different from trout flies? Of course there is often no difference since grayling feed on the same aquatic fly life and other fauna as trout do. However, it could be argued that there are probably three principal differences in fly patterns or their presentation.

Grayling take much more of their food from closer to the riverbed and imitations of shrimps and small caddis larvae as well as weighted general grub patterns are often required to take deep-lying winter grayling. Second, grayling are much easier to dupe with a fancy pattern than are wild brown trout of a similar age. Third, there are more times when only small patterns – size 16 and 18 – will succeed in rising surface-feeding fish.

1 Imp

COMMENT

H. A. Rolt devised this fly for the southern chalk streams. It is fished wet or dry but it is as a floater that I have found it the most useful. I've never used it on the streams for which it was intended but I've caught many grayling and trout on it on freestone rivers. Although the gold tip might be a distraction for trout it is also probably a passable iron blue imitation.

DRESSING

Hook: 14–18 Code L3A or E6A.
Thread: Black.
Tail: Red ibis substitute.
Tip: Flat gold tinsel.
Body: Heron herl.
Hackle: Black cock or hen.

2 Orange Otter

COMMENT

I'm not sure whether this pattern's reputation as a killer has been exaggerated over the years as the dressing has been reprinted in different books. Courtney Williams gave it high praise in his dictionary and reported that its creator the Revd Edward Powell, claimed that it was the only fly he knew to bring up grayling from the bottom when they were not surface-feeding. It still catches grayling, but I know of no contemporary grayling fisher who would quote Courtney Williams' words 'phenomenal . . . devastating' for its use today. I'd love to be proved wrong.

DRESSING

Hook: 12–16 Code L3A or E6A.
Thread: Orange.
Tail: Natural red cock fibres.
Body: Mixed orange and claret seal's fur substitute (3:1) (as a substitute for the original orange otter) or polypropylene dubbing, in two halves.
Hackle: Natural red cock in the middle of the body.

1 Imp **2** Orange Otter **3** John Titmouse **4** Red Tag
5 Grayling Coachman **6** Sturdy's Fancy **7** Priest **8** Grayling Fiddler

3 John Titmouse

COMMENT

Eric Horsfall Turner devised this variant of the John Storey for grayling that were merely 'titching' at the fly. Anyone who has experienced grayling in this sort of mood will know how frustrating trying to hook a fish can be. Sometimes this pattern works well on these occasions but no fly is foolproof for the capricious grayling. It is, however, a good general floater. It caught over 200 grayling in its first season for its creator.

DRESSING

Hook: 16–18 Code L3A or E6A.
Thread: Black.
Tail: White hackle fibres.
Body: Peacock herl.
Wing: A very small mallard breast feather about 8mm long sloping over the eye.
Hackle: Short-fibred black cock.

4 Red Tag

COMMENT

Ask any angler to name a grayling fly and this is the one that comes most quickly to mind. Its origins are obscure but it seems to have been used for at least 140 years. It was popularised by Walbran, who took twenty-five grayling with his first use of the pattern. It can be fished wet or dry. Many variations have evolved, the best of which is the Treacle Parkin, also an excellent trout fly. Others are the White Tag, the Green Tag and the Gold Tag, which has a tip of gold tinsel, and the Badger Red Tag, which has a badger hackle and a silver tip.

DRESSING

Hook: 14–18 Code L3A or E6A (dry); A, G3A or CS7 (wet).
Thread: Purple.
Tag: Scarlet or bright-red wool or dyed feather fibres.
Body: Peacock herl.
Hackle: Natural red cock or hen.

5 Grayling Coachman

COMMENT

The dressing for the Coachman has been much abused to create many variants. This grayling dry fly works very well as a general imitative pattern when fish are rising, and also as a search fly when there is no surface activity. Because of the white wings it is quite visible in difficult conditions. White polypropylene yarn might be an alternative winging material.

DRESSING

Hook: 14–16 Code L3A or E6A.
Thread: Black.
Tag: A small tuft of red wool.
Body: Peacock herl.
Wing: Bunched white cock hackle fibres set upright or at 45 degrees over the body.
Hackle: Natural light-red cock.

6 Sturdy's Fancy

COMMENT

This is a fly held in great esteem by Yorkshire anglers on whose waters it originated. Tom Sturdy, who lived on the banks of the superb trout and grayling waters of the Ure at Masham, created the fly, which could be described as a Red Tag with a different hackle. Like many grayling patterns it can be fished both below and on the surface. I use a superb floating variant for which I claim no credit as I found it in an inherited fly box. It has a double tag of red and yellow alongside each other and a parachute hackle, and is very successful for both trout and grayling.

DRESSING

Hook: 14–18 L3A or E6A (dry); A, CS7 or G3A (wet).
Thread: Purple.
Tag: A small stub or red wool (or poly yarn on the floater).
Body: Peacock herl.
Hackle: Off-white cock or hen.

7 Priest

COMMENT

One of the disappointments of grayling fishing is that more often than in the trout season the water is slightly coloured and fly fishing might not be too successful. One highly visible attractor pattern which has done quite well for me, mainly as a wet fly in slightly coloured water, is the Priest. The silver body is very suggestive of a small fish. When I wrote *The Grayling Angler* I dismissed too easily any thoughts of grayling taking small fish. They certainly don't eat them in any quantity, but sometimes grayling are caught on fry patterns and I've subsequently caught them when spinning.

DRESSING

Hook: 14–16 Code A, G3A or CS7.
Thread: Black.
Tail: Red ibis substitute or a red wool tag.
Body: Flat silver tinsel.
Rib: Fine silver wire.
Hackle: Badger hen.

8 Grayling Fiddler

COMMENT

Eric Horsfall Turner fished for grayling a great deal, mainly on the streams of North Yorkshire. He tied up this small fly for selective surface-feeding fish. Eric used it on size 18 hooks but tying the fly short on size 16s is easier and usually the difference doesn't affect the grayling. Quite what grayling take the fly to be I don't know; the fluorescent red body is a mystery. The rear of the body inevitably sinks into the film and it probably represents some emerging insect.

DRESSING

Hook: 18 Code L3A, E6A or K4A.
Thread: Brown.
Body: Tying thread taken well round the bend with a small butt of thread exposed and the remainder dubbed with red wool (optionally fluorescent).
Hackle: Small grizzle cock.

Grayling Flies 2

River trout flies are fairly traditional; it used to take a long time for a new pattern to achieve national recognition. Grayling flies are ultra-traditional; many are the patterns which are used for trout. Most specialist grayling flies in regular use on freestone rivers have been used for generations; a few will have been devised in the last fifty years, but only a handful have been produced in the last twenty years. Frank Sawyer's Grayling Bug has had the biggest impact on chalkstream fishing but no other new pattern has really been adopted nationally, as yet. I still use many of these traditional grayling patterns but where appropriate I have enjoyed considerable success with heavier bug patterns fished deep where the big fish tend to stay. Some of these are found in the sections on nymphs and bugs.

1 Bradshaw's Fancy

COMMENT

The Yorkshire Dales angler, Henry Bradshaw devised this late-season trout fly in the 1880s. It is a credit to its attraction that it is in widespread use today, principally as a grayling fly. He fished in the company of T. E. Pritt and Francis Walbran, and the latter described this pattern as 'a nailer for grayling wherever it is used'. It is fished wet or dry but usually as the point on a three-fly cast.

DRESSING

Hook: 14–16 Code L3A or E6A (dry); CS7, A or G3A (wet).
Thread: Purple.
Tag: Crimson wool or floss.
Body: Peacock herl.
Hackle: Pale-blue-dun hen as a substitute for Norwegian or hooded crow.
Head: Two turns of crimson wool or floss or a small tag like that at the tail at 45 degrees.

2 Double Badger

COMMENT

There are six flies in the Badger series: Double Badger, Red, Green, Blue, and Silver Badger, and Badger Red Tag. All use a badger hackle and can be fished as both floaters or wet flies. With the exception of the Double Badger and Badger Red Tag, they differ only in their body colour. Each has a red tag, silver wire rib, floss silk body and a palmered badger hackle. The Badger Red Tag (a Roger Woolley variant) is like the Red Tag but has a badger hackle at the shoulder and a small tip of silver tinsel. The Double Badger is my favourite and is used as a dry fly only.

DRESSING

Hook: 14–16 Code L3A or E6A (dry); A, CS7 or G3A (wet).
Thread: Black.
Body: Peacock herl.
Hackles: Badger cock at each end of the body. The front hackle should be slightly longer-fibred than the rear.

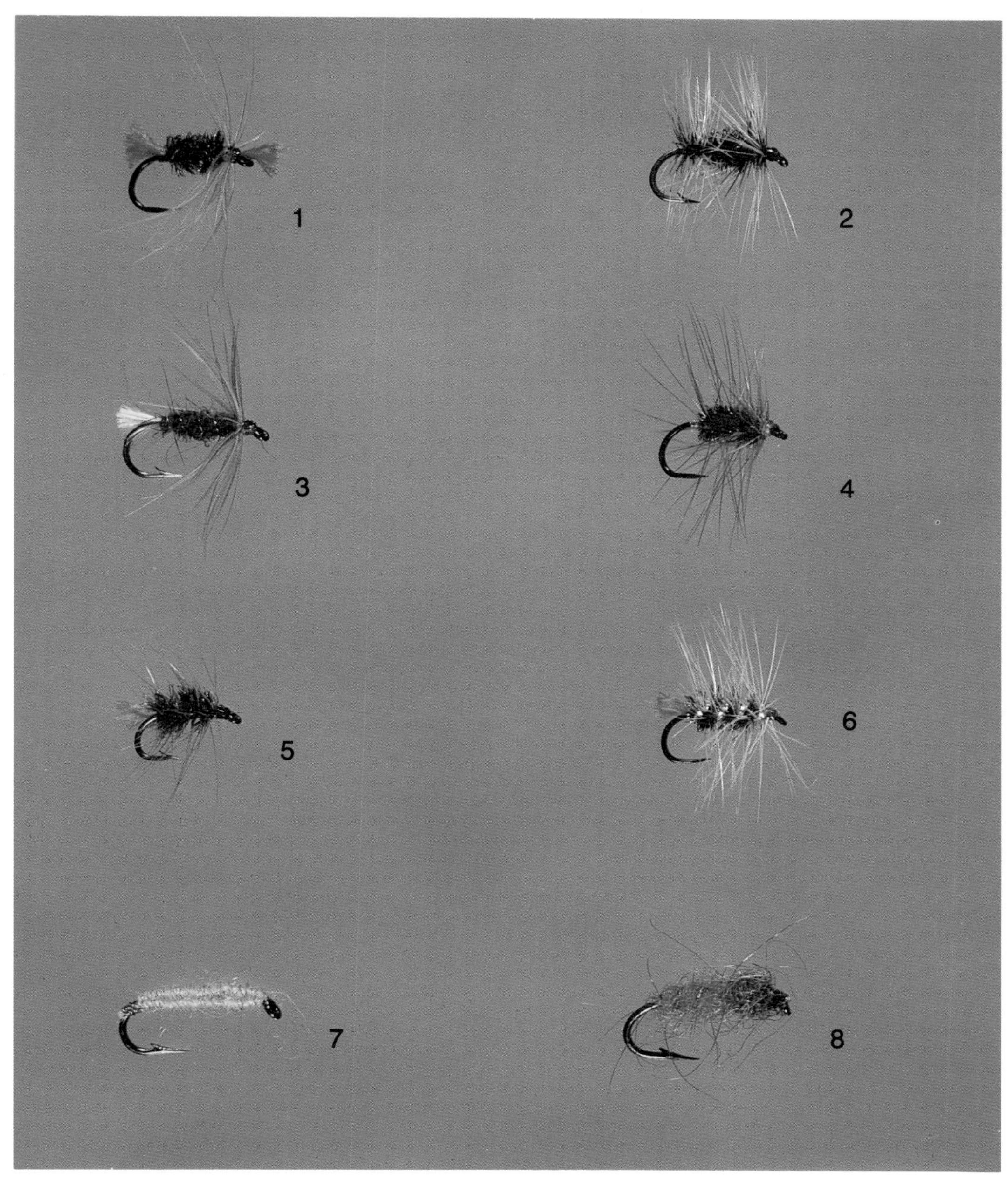

1 Bradshaw's Fancy **2** Double Badger **3** Sage **4** Grayling Steel-Blue
5 Rolt's Witch **6** Grayling Witch **7** Killer Bug **8** Dove Bug

3 Sage

COMMENT

I doubt whether there has been a grayling fisher in the last fifty years who can match the experience of the late Reg Righyni. He was not a great inventor of grayling flies but shortly before his death he introduced this pattern combining some of the successful elements he saw in other flies. He hoped the fly would pass for a spinner with the tag representing the eggs. It should be fished wet. The fly has also caught salmon, by accident, and hence its name, the Salmon Approved Grayling Enticer.

DRESSING

Hook: 14–16 Code L3A or E6A.
Thread: Crimson.
Tag: Orangy-yellow floss.
Body: Mixed claret rabbit's fur and claret polar bear fur.
Rib: Fine gold tinsel.
Hackle: Hooded crow or pale-blue-dun hen as a substitute.

4 Grayling Steel-Blue

COMMENT

This is originally a Derbyshire pattern created by Roger Woolley and is effective on all grayling streams, fished wet or dry. I don't know what it is taken for except that the palmered hackle produces a 'buzz' effect which is often so much more effective than the shoulder-hackled fly. The blue grizzle hackle originally called for is impossible to obtain and a blue dun substitute works well. The blue dun can also be wound with a grizzle.

DRESSING

Hook: 14–16 Code L3A or E6A (dry); A, CS7 or G3A (wet).
Thread: Orange.
Tip: Three turns of tying thread and a tiny tip of silver tinsel.
Body: Thinly wound peacock herl.
Rib: Fine gold wire rib.
Hackle: Palmered bright-blue grizzle or blue dun (*see* text).

5 Rolt's Witch

COMMENT

H. A. Rolt, author of *Grayling Fishing in South Country Streams* (1901), was the first fly dresser to weight the hook shank before tying in materials. He obviously had experience of those big deep-lying chalkstream grayling which won't budge an inch to take a fly. They have to be offered something on their own level. Although he couldn't have wound much lead wire on the smaller sizes, it did sink them further than normal. It can also be used, unleaded, as a floater. This original dressing has produced a number of variants.

DRESSING

Hook: 14–18 Code L3A or E6A (dry); A, CS7 or G3A (wet).
Thread: Black.
Tag: Red floss, wool or ibis substitute.
Body: Green peacock herl.
Rib: Fine flat gold tinsel.
Hackle: Palmered light-honey-dun.

6 Grayling Witch

COMMENT

Roger Woolley produced this Witch variant. Additionally there is a White Witch, which varies from this dressing by its palmered white cock hackle and silver rib. Some sources also change the tag to white floss. There is also an old German pattern, the Grey Witch, which I doubt shares the same ancestry. This has the same body, a pheasant tail herl tail and a grizzle hackle.

DRESSING

Hook: 14–18 Code L3A or E6A (dry); A, CS or G3A (wet).
Tag: Red floss.
Body: Green peacock herl.
Rib: Flat silver tinsel.
Hackle: Palmered pale-blue-dun.

7 Grayling or Killer Bug

COMMENT

Few patterns have been more aptly named than this bug of Frank Sawyer's. It is primarily a chalkstream fly, where it is unmatched in my experience for its grayling-catching abilities. The dressing is so nondescript as to be scorned by some, but the fact is that this weighted bit of wool is an extremely efficient trout and grayling catcher. The overall impression of the bug suggests that it is taken for a freshwater shrimp and it is on waters where these abound that the fly excels.

DRESSING

Hook: 10–16 Code G3A or CS7SHW.
Thread: None.
Body: An underbody of fine lead wire is overlaid with beige darning wool in a cigar shape. Fine copper wire is used to tie in and finish off the materials.

8 Dove Bug

COMMENT

I first tied this pattern in 1980 as a general food-like bug to be fished along the bottom for deep-lying grayling. It is used on freestone and chalk streams and has caught a great many trout as well as specimen grayling. I'm not too sure what it is mistaken for – perhaps a shrimp or a sedge pupae drifting along the bottom prior to swimming to the surface. I omit the small red tag I used to include as it seems to attract rainbow trout. The exact body colouring doesn't matter too much. I've also caught trout and grayling on the Continent and trout in North America on it.

DRESSING

Hook: 10–12 Code G3A or CS7.
Thread: Brown.
Body: An underbody of copper or lead wire covered with mixed seal's fur substitute; rear half, orange and pink; front half, orange and brown.
Rib: Fine gold tinsel, gold or copper wire.

Appendix

Some of the materials mentioned in the text are available only through a limited number of sources. Each of the companies and individuals below has given an efficient and reliable service.

Farlow's of Pall Mall
5 Pall Mall
London SW1
Telephone 01 839 2423

Flycraft
Box 582
Greendale Station
Worcester
Mass 01606
USA
Telephone 508 853 3676

Rudi Heger
Traun River Products
Haupstrasse 6
D-8227
Siegsdorf
West Germany
Telephone 08662 7079

Hooks & Tackle
40 Huntingdon Road
York YO3 7RE
Telephone 0904 610357

Lance Nicholson
High Street
Dulverton
Somerset
Telephone 0398 23409

Orvis
The Mill
Nether Wallop
Stockbridge
Hants SO20 8ES
Telephone 0264 781212

Piscatoria
3a Hebden Court
Bakewell
Derbyshire
Telephone 0629 814770

Terry Ruane
187 Comberton Road
Kidderminster DY10 1UE
Telephone 0562 742143

Tom C. Saville Ltd
Unit 7
Salisbury Square
Middleton Street
Off Ilkeston Road
Nottingham NG7 2AB
Telephone 0602 784248

Sparton
Unit 1
Albion Road
Sileby
Loughborough
Leics LE12 7RA.
Telephone 050 981 2186

Ian Warrilow
53 Aylesford Drive
Marston Green
Birmingham B37 7BX
Telephone 021 779 6444

Ultimate Fisherman
Chopwell Centre
Chopwell
Tyne & Wear NE17 7HD
Telephone 0207 560931

Index to Natural and Artificial Flies